EXISTENTIALISM AND CREATIVITY

EXISTENTIALISM AND CREATIVITY

by

MITCHELL BEDFORD

PHILOSOPHICAL LIBRARY

Copyright, 1972, by Philosophical Library, Inc.,
15 East 40 Street, New York, N. Y. 10016

Library of Congress Catalog Card No. 71-175204
SBN 8022-2074-6

Printed in the United States of America

CONTENTS

CHAPTER I

INTRODUCTION TO THE PROBLEM

In a most provocative book concerned with *Nuclear Weapons and Foreign Policy*, H. A. Kissinger reminds his readers that in Greek mythology the Gods often punished man by fulfilling his every wish in every detail. Kissinger asserts that it has remained for the nuclear age to experience the full irony of this penalty.[1]

Historically, man has longed for power. Great cities have disintegrated and been covered by the dust of time because their civilization collapsed for the lack of power. In the twentieth century, practically overnight, man has been given so much power that he does not know what to do with it.

Nuclear technology has brought an age in which man can rise to a level of civilization hitherto unheard of, even undreamed of. Nuclear technology has also brought man to an age in which civilization may be completely obliterated from the face of the earth.

Although man should feel that he is the master of his invention, of that which he has created, like Dr. Frankenstein he too often feels helpless in his endeavor to assume control of, and responsibility for, the tremendous power he has placed before modern civilization. To be certain, the individual may feel that collectively man does have responsibility for that which has been created, but as an individual, man feels helpless in his confrontation with his peer group, with his civic group, with his government, and even with the world.

Dr. Joseph Schlom, author of the book *Vortuka*, expresses this feeling of helplessness while isolated in a Soviet concentration camp. Not only did he feel helpless personally, the entire colony

1

felt impotent to awaken civilization to the plight of freedom in the world. One does not need to study the biography of a prisoner in a Soviet concentration camp to gain an impression of man's feeling of helplessness and ignorance in the twentieth century.[2] Gordon Allport, an American psychologist, has created a literary portrait of this type of man. "Citizen Sam" is a characterization of a man whose life is primarily one of sleeping, working so as to assure his basic needs, and seeking some diversion such as a movie or a cocktail which provides him with an escape mechanism so that he will not have to contemplate life's problems or feel responsible for what is happening in his environment.[3]

It is this widespread feeling of "escapism" from responsibility which has challenged some of the world's deep thinkers to attempt to prevent man from confusing himself, and indeed to force man to be more courageous in his living. This is the essential theme of Paul Tillich's book, *Courage To Be*.[4]

As man has courage to scan the horizon of his nuclear age, to attempt to find out what can be done to enhance his civilization, he suddenly learns that there is *No Place To Hide* should he fail in his task.[5]

The possibility of man's impotence in the nuclear age has given rise to his awareness of his own feelings of anxiety, and in turn he comes to realize that he is living in an age of anxiety and that he must come to grips with *The Meaning of Anxiety*.[6] However, to escape his feelings of anxiety, man has sought to lose himself in the security of the group; but alas, he discovers that his group is little more than a *Lonely Crowd*.[7] Rollo May has captured the quest of man in the title of his book, *Man's Search for Himself*.[8]

According to May, individual men feel themselves to be hollow, to be void of meaning. The question of giving meaning to man's life has been exceptionally difficult in the twentieth century, for even the meaning of meaning has been debated. Semantics has arisen in an endeavor to define words precisely so that any given group of people, by using properly defined words, would know exactly what the other people were talking about. The philosophy of logical positivism has arisen with one of its goals the reduction of problems which individuals should discuss to those which everyone can understand.

Religion, especially the Protestant faith, has found itself practically bankrupt in its endeavors to meet the crisis of the Second World War or to interpret the tragedies which ensued. The rise of the scientific method, the twentieth-century emphasis on open-mindedness, the rise of literary criticism and the historical method have combined to question severely dogmatic religious pronouncements. Even the concept of God has been so severely shaken that agnosticism and atheism do not share quite the same stigma which was attached to them some fifty years ago. The rapid rise of the atheistic communistic philosophy has indeed been startling in the modern world.

The scientific-religious conflicts and the conflicts between orthodoxy and liberalism in religion have placed a tremendous strain on the moral integrity of man and on the integration of man's personality.

The lack of an adequate moral and social philosophy is suggested in the discussion plan of the fifty-fourth Year-book of the National Society for the Study of Education entitled *Modern Philosophies and Education*. The editor asked the representatives of several schools of philosophy to comment on six statements. The two statements which are pertinent to this study are as follows: 1) "There is a current anxiety that modern education is adrift without rudder, compass, or chart." 2) "There is a current anxiety that, of the educational aims we have, too many are vague or conflicting, and too few generate strong loyalty."[9]

While the picture may be painted black, though man may be described as hollow, anxiety ridden, lonely and full of doubts about the period in which he lives and the role in life he must fulfill, philosophers and educators still believe that man can bring about a reunification of his total personality, and bring some order out of the potential chaos inherent in the nuclear age.

William O. Stanley, in 1953, published a book entitled *Edu-*

cation and Social Integration. In this text Stanley seeks to identify the forces and conditions which are responsible for the confusion and conflict which are evident in and about American education. He then discusses the question of how the education profession could deal with the forces and conditions which he had previously isolated. Stanley argues that the paramount problem facing education is the need for a clarification of the foundations of order and coherence in American public education. To arrive at this foundation, Stanley feels, it will be necessary for the schools to first develop a methodological character among their scholars. To do this, it will be necessary to introduce to students a disciplined study of the salient conflicts and confusions of our age.[10]

Stanley avers that there is no longer available to education an integrating and authoritative social philosophy upon which the school curriculum can be based. Thus, we must educate a whole generation in the techniques for critical thinking so that they may rebuild a sound social philosophy. To Stanley, therefore, an integrating and authoritative philosophy must be the goal of education, rather than the basis for contemporary education.[11]

Stanley does not touch upon the even more crucial problem that the confusion of the modern era extends to the basic concept of the individual himself. What type of individual do we want to develop in our society? Do we really want our schools to develop a methodological character in the personality of our children?

The conflict of different types of individuals which culture develops is discussed with some keen insight by David Riesman in his book, *The Lonely Crowd.* Riesman propounds the thesis that the steering mechanisms given to children, by which they are to guide their lives, are different according to the cultural trends in the population. According to the author, the child is guided by a reverence for tradition, by a feeling of inner oughtness, or by a striving to do what others want him to do before the others know what they want him to do. The tradition-bound child comes from a highly static environment in which there is no mobility, and in which he realizes that he must conform or

4

face ostracism from the community. The inner-directed child comes from a highly dynamic environment, one which is especially mobile. This culture places a gyroscope in the child's personality so as to guarantee that the child will want to do what he ought to do. If the child fails to do what he ought to do, he will feel the sharp pangs of guilt. This child is raised on a keen sense of competition and is encouraged to have a considerably well developed desire to perform, to succeed and to get ahead in the cultural environment. The third type of child is one who lives in an other-directed culture. This child soon finds out that his advancement in life is not dependent on how well he performs, but rather on how well he can cooperate with other people. A "radar system" is to be placed into this child's personality so that he may perceive what is expected of him by each group to which he is exposed. If the child fails to interpret the signals of the group correctly, then he will develop an intense feeling of anxiety.[12]

Education has at its disposal ways of creating different types of individuals. The question which haunts the contemporary era is what type of individual do we want to develop? Should the educator seek to develop a happy conformist, a rugged individualist, a person filled with the sense of sin, a person raised as though he has never been other than a Christian, a personality who has ingrained in him a disciplined methodology, a person who is to be left alone to be himself; or does society want the formulation of a scholar?

The Statement of the Problem

The essential problem of this study was to discern whether existentialism as a philosophical system contains within it the seed of an educational philosophy which might contribute something of value to the great educational debate of the twentieth century.

To attack this problem it was necessary to do four things. First, outstanding existential thinkers who represent different points of view within existentialism were selected. Second, the writings of these authors were examined in an attempt to identify their concepts of the authentic individual. Third, from these writings suggestions were gathered about the type of educational system which would be conducive to the encouragement of authenticity. Finally, it was necessary to compare the varying concepts of the individual and educational thought in order to discern whether there is, in fact, a common existential position on education.

The Hypotheses of the Study

The following hypotheses were evaluated in this study.

1. Each existential writer being considered has a concept of the individual — of the nature of his existence and of the purpose of his existence. This concept is expressed with some consistency in his basic writings.

2. In potential agreement with the challenging statement of John Dewey, "... if a theory makes no difference in educational endeavor, it must be artificial," the second hypothesis is that the concept of the individual has definite implications for developing an educational philosophy which could make a difference in the educational endeavor.

3. As each of the concepts of the individual is developed from the viewpoint of the men under study, it will be found that the main motifs of their concepts of the individual, and the educational implications derivable from them, are in essential agreement. This essential agreement provides a framework for the development of an existential philosophy of education.

The Scope of the Study

This study is primarily concerned with the existential thinking of Søren Kierkegaard, Martin Buber, Karl Jaspers and Jean-Paul Sartre. Three prominent existentialists who are not to be discussed extensively are Gabriel Marcel, Martin Heidegger and Paul Tillich.

Although the following rationale may be offered for selecting these four men as the most representative existentialists of the modern period, the basic reason for not discussing the other existentialists is due to a basic delimitation of the study.

Søren Kierkegaard represents the Protestant religious existentialists. Furthermore, he is credited with being the catalyst of twentieth-century existential thought.

Jean-Paul Sartre represents the atheistic wing of existentialism, and is one of the first existentialists who attempted to systematize his concepts into a philosophical framework. Sartre has also based much of his existential appraisal of the current century on the philosophical work of Martin Heidegger. Thus by sampling Sartre, one will sample a portion of the position of Heidegger.

Martin Buber represents the religious motif of existentialism which has arisen from contemporary Judaism. Buber's postulation of the "I-Thou" bears considerable similarity to the social concern expressed by the French existentialist, Gabriel Marcel.

Karl Jaspers represents the German movement in existentialism. In examining the writings of Jaspers one finds a cultural-religious existentialist. While Jaspers may be thought of as a Deist who insists on the importance of transcendence, he is not a Christian. It will be emphasized that Jaspers, in many ways, represents a Hellenistic form of existentialism.

Both Gabriel Marcel and Martin Heidegger have chosen to reject the term existentialist as applying to them. The Catholic church has officially placed a ban on existential books and frowns on existentialism to such an extent that the layman Marcel, refuses the delineation. Nevertheless, the content in Marcel's books is sufficiently orientated towards existentialism that most of the modern expositors of the movement include him in their lists.[13]

Martin Heidegger also has chosen to reject the term as applying to his philosophical concerns. But again the secondary sources usually stress that his work forms an important cornerstone in existential literature. The work which is most existentially orientated is *Being and Time*. After writing this book, Heidegger became involved in the Nazi movement. With the debacle of Hitler's Germany, Heidegger was rejected in the university circles of Germany. He has rejected his philosophical friends and is currently writing in a vein which is not characteristically existential. In order, therefore, to discuss Heidegger, it would be necessary to clearly delineate his past and present writings. To make a sharp distinction would undoubtedly prove to be a major obstacle in any attempt to interpret his writings, for even in *Being and Time* one might find some concepts which are more in accord with his later mysticism.[14]

Paul Tillich provides an opposite case to Heidegger. While his early emphasis has always shown a friendly disposition towards existentialism, only recently has he begun writing in an existential vein. Most noticeable of his contemporary existential interpretations is his small book *Courage To Be*. To review Tillich's work, with a view to separate his early philosophy and theology from his later tendencies, would provide another major obstacle for an interpretation and discussion of this existentialist.

One will find several other individuals referred to as existentialists, but the above individuals are mentioned throughout existential literature. To deal with the many philosophers who are occasionally identified with existentialism would be a prohibitive undertaking, for indeed one might first have to prove that they are talking about a true existential representative.

A Short Definition of Existentialism

Many people ask the question, "What is existentialism?" One important reason why this question is asked so often is that existentialists seldom take time to define their own philosophy in a concise manner. The best development of existentialism would probably be the following statement:

1. Existentialists believe that man is nothing else but what he makes of himself.[15]

2. Existentialism's first move is to make every man aware of

what he is and to make the full responsibility of his existence rest on him. Man must realize that he is free to shape his existence and that he is responsible for every act in which he is involved.[16]

3. The existentialists believe that man seeks to evade this responsibility by living marginally and not in accord with his full potentialities.[17]

4. Existentialism is a way of philosophizing which is designed to encourage men to philosophize and to actualize their full potentials.[18]

5. The existentialists are not interested in artificial problems, or in theoretical constructions. "They are interested rather in concrete data of immediate experience, and in describing these data so far as possible exactly as they are given."[19]

Actually this entire thesis is designed to offer a definition of existentialism. The second chapter summarizes the secondary sources and their interpretation of existentialism. The remaining chapters seek to summarize what each of the four most prominent existentialists believe.

In conclusion, the four existentialists were selected for this study because they represent the various traditions of existentialism, and they are, save for Søren Kierkegaard, admittedly within the existential stream of thought.

The Methodology for Undertaking the Research

This study is a philosophical study which involves extensive utilization of library resources to find the material necessary for studying the four chosen existentialists. The methodology for this study involved an assimilation of all the data relevant to the problem. For the most part primary sources were utilized and where necessary secondary sources were referred to in order to explain or enlarge the viewpoint of the existentialist in question. The secondary sources on existentialism have been examined in order to ascertain if the expositors, critics or apologists of existentialism have themselves undertaken to develop the concept of the individual in their interpretive writings. Special attention was given to any discussion of education, the problems of education or the nature of the learning process in both primary and secondary sources. Periodical literature was reviewed extensively and a search was undertaken for doctoral dissertations which pertained to the subject. Finally some correspondence was established between Dr. Buber and the author of this thesis to gain further insight into his thinking.[20] This information was then collated, analyzed and evaluated. Finally, an application of the pertinent aspects of this data was applied to the problem at hand.

Importance of the Problem

The past century has seen the development of three major philosophical systems. These three are dialectical materialism, pragmatism and existentialism.

Pragmatism, popularized by John Dewey, has enjoyed widespread popularity in American education. The launching of "progressive education" was the immediate cause of much writing and interpretive work in contemporary American educational philosophy.[21]

Dialectical materialism has also enjoyed widespread popularity in Soviet education where its principles have been put into action.[22]

Existentialism has enjoyed wide popularity among the intellectuals of the Continent, but has not been popularized into an educational system. As a matter of fact, as the review of the literature will indicate, a very few of its philosophers and subsequent interpreters have been concerned in the slightest with the educational endeavor.

Carl Michalson, editor of the book *Christianity and the Existentialists*, has observed that "existentialism is one of the magic words of our time. When the word is used it seems capable of powers all out of proportion to its size. It can enchant with curiosity and a passionate eagerness to know. Or, it can cast a spell of hostility and sometimes even a repressive anxiety to put it out of mind."[23]

The realist philosopher, John Wild, states that existentialism is at the present time the most influential movement of contemporary thought in France and in Western Germany, and is now intensively discussed in Italy and South America.[24]

Walter Cerf feels that existentialism is a way of thought which will pave the way towards dictatorship.[25] His assertion is well founded for in fact Heidegger, a foremost existentialist, did cooperate with the Nazi movement.[26] However, Karl Jaspers, also an existentialist, not only was opposed to the Nazi movement, he did not even seek to flee from the wrath of Hitler.[27] Jean-Paul Sartre fought in the French resistance movement against Germany and allies himself with the socialist party. Martin Buber had to flee Germany, for he was opposed to the Nazi movement and was a Jew as well. Buber is also a participant in socialistically inclined movements.

F. H. Heinemann, in his discussion of *Existentialism and the Modern Predicament,* asserts that the philosophies of existence are "philosophies of liberation". He stresses that the Bolshevists hate the existentialists for they realize that inherent in the souls of these men are the seeds of revolution in the future.[28]

Although existentialism has exerted a tremendous influence on the Continent, it has failed to make a very great impression on the American mind. It is not well known and is largely ignored in American colleges and departments of philosophy. In keeping with the slow inroads existentialism has been making upon Anglo-Saxon thought, it is not surprising to find a dearth of material relating it to educational philosophy and curriculum practices.

Considering the enormous influence which existentialism has had on the Continental mind, considering that it has been credited with forming a bulwark against the intellectual expansion of communism, and considering the dilemma American education is faced with, a study of the educational implications of existentialism might be fruitful, and even if it fails to offer some creative insights which might solve the dilemma contemporary education

11

is faced with, it might act as a catalyst for further thought which in turn may be educationally productive.

The Review of the Literature

A. The literature of Søren Kierkegaard, Martin Buber, Jean-Paul Sartre and Karl Jaspers

The midwife of existentialism is Søren Kierkegaard, a Danish thinker who was one of the first to realize and emphasize the dilemma of the individual as he confronted current crises. Many express the view that Kierkegaard was the father of existential thinking.[29] 'Father' implies creator, and Kierkegaard, who often acknowledged his intellectual debts to Jesus, Socrates and other philosophers, would hardly have accepted such an appellation. He considered himself a spy reporting objectively what was happening in the souls of men. At other times, he referred to himself as the prosecuting attorney challenging the 'leveling' effect of his age.[30]

Kierkegaard wrote in Copenhagen in the Danish language. He was overshadowed by the last days of Hegel's systematizing and by Nietzsche. The fact that Kierkegaard wrote in a rather obscure language and in the days of such great philosophical minds meant that his voice was but a whisper in the dark, and indeed he was largely ignored until Henri Delacroix discovered the significance of his work in France around 1900 and coincidentally to that, Chrisopl Schremf came under the Kierkegaardian influence in Germany. By 1920 several of the creative philosophers on the Continent had studied and were influenced by the writings of Kierkegaard. Among others, these men are Kafka, Buber, Jaspers, Heidegger, Sartre, Brunner, Tillich, and Barth.

Only faint glimmerings of Kierkegaard reached the Anglo-Saxon world until the English translations of his work began appearing in England in the decade of 1930 as a result of the biographical introduction to him written by A. E. Allen.[31] A steady translation of Kierkegaard's works in the Forties introduced his life and his philosophy to the American scholar. The primary people who sought to introduce Kierkegaard to the United States were Robert Bretall, David Swenson, Alexander Dru and Walter Lowrie. Most of this Kierkegaardian literature was picked up in the theological schools and a growing number of articles appeared about his philosophy in journals dedicated to religion and philosophy.

In the educational endeavor the works of Kierkegaard have hardly dented the surface. In the first place, Kierkegaard did not concern himself with the problems of education, not even theological education. However, Kierkegaard was not unaware of the importance of education, for in 1847, in one of his private Journals, he wrote that "everything really depends upon a religious upbringing... that God is love, an impression which has been part of one's whole being from childhood up: that is the most important thing."[32] In the same year he also noted that "the thing is this, what our age needs is education...."[33]

In a way, Kierkegaard was not a systematic writer, for in no one volume can one find his philosophy spelt out. In another sense, however, he was very systematic, for his entire literary effort was conceived according to a set plan. Kierkegaard sought to discuss first the aesthetic man, then the ethical man, and finally the religious man. For the first two phases of his literary endeavor he used pseudonyms. In his Journals he explicitly states that he must not be held accountable for any statement he made when he wrote under a false name. He felt that in his pseudonym he could project himself into the role of the person who was creating that part of the discussion. It is for this reason that much of Kierkegaard's writing appears to have contradictions. He never intended that there should be agreement unless the literary work was written under his own name.[34]

In the development of Kierkegaard's concept of the individual the following books were found to be very important:

1. *The Point of View for My Work as An Author*

2. *The Present Age*

3. *Thoughts on Crucial Situations in Human Life*

4. *Purify Your Hearts*

5. *Works of Love*

Of lesser importance in terms of the frequency referred to, but still lending important insights into the formation of the Kierkegaardian "individual," were the following books:

1. *For Self Examination and Judge For Yourself*

2. *The Concept of Dread*

3. *Attack Upon Christendom*

4. *Fear and Trembling*

5. *The Journals*

Finally the following is a list of other important Kierkegaardian works which have been referred to occasionally:

1. *Repetition — An Essay in Experimental Psychology*

2. *Stages on Life's Way*

3. *Training in Christianity*

4. *Either-Or*

The secondary sources which proved helpful were Bretall's *Kierkegaard Anthology;* Hubben's *Four Prophets of Our Destiny;* Allen's *Existentialism from Within;* and Michalson's *Christianity and the Existentialists.*

Karl Jaspers, like Kierkegaard, is another writer who is not known for his systematic approach to philosophy. Ronald Grimsley suggests that Jaspers' *Way to Wisdom* and his *Perennial Scope of Philosophy* will give the reader a firm introduction to Jaspers' work.[35] A. E. Allen, whose work on Søren Kierkegaard has previously been cited, also bases his interpretation of Jaspers on *The Way to Wisdom.*[36] The critic of existentialism, D. J. B.

Hawkins, states that the *Perennial Scope of Philosophy* is sufficient for capturing Jaspers' thinking.[37] These were found to be very important works in this study as Jaspers' concept of the individual was developed.

The most valuable work concerning Jaspers for this study is entitled *Man in the Modern Age* and it was translated into English in 1933 after being written in German in 1931.[38]

As in the case of Kierkegaard, one does not find a systematic discussion of the educational implications of Jaspers' findings in either his writings or in the secondary sources. Nevertheless, Jaspers has been more vitally concerned with education than Kierkegaard, for he has written a book concerned with German education at the university level. This was entitled, *The Idea of the University*. Furthermore, this author has been more interested in the role of reason in the twentieth century than Kierkegaard was in the nineteenth. Jaspers has produced two books on this subject. One of these books deals with the relationship of reason and anti-reason, the other discusses reason against the meaning of existence. Both texts contributed to an understanding of Jaspers' stress on the importance of reason in the individual.

Jaspers does not only deal with wisdom, reason and philosophy, he is also concerned with the deeper moods of man as is expressed in his small book, *Tragedy is Not Enough*. This book provided interesting insights into the emotional make-up of the individual.

The secondary sources which deal exclusively with Jaspers did not prove profitable in relating his interpretations of the individual or in enhancing his potential educational philosophy. Roberts, Allen, Blackham and Grimsley provide excellent introductory material to Jaspers, while Wild makes a significant contribution by relating Jaspers to the existential movement in an integrative interpretation of existentialism.

Jean-Paul Sartre is the French representative of existentialism who has attempted to spell out in great detail his philosophy of existence. The key work of Sartre, upon which the section which seeks to present Sartre's concept of the individual is based, is his *Being and Nothingness*. While this book is especially concerned with the nature of being and is germane to a discussion of the individual, Sartre is not concerned with education and seldom mentions it in his critical work.

Sartre is well known for his literary creations, and some of the most important presentations are mentioned in this study. To understand how Sartre applies some of his existential insights, it is necessary to be acquainted with his plays, especially *The Flies, No Exit* and *The Victors*. A discussion of these three plays is most adequately presented by Herbert Muller in his discussion of *The Spirit of Tragedy*.[39]

In terminology which is direct and very provocative, Sartre has actually given his talent to defining what existentialism means to him in his small book, *Existentialism*. This book proved to be very helpful in relating the 600 page opus *Being and Nothingness*, which has been previously mentioned and which is an intricate expression of his philosophy in highly technical language, to the study at hand.

Alfred Stern provides a systematic interpretation of Sartre's work in his book *Sartre: His Philosophy and Psychoanalysis*. Stern is not necessarily a friendly interpreter of Sartre, for in several places he raises some very keen questions about Sartre's conclusions. In other places he shows a slight lack of understanding of the point with which he is dealing. While one would probably profit by reading this book as an introduction to Sartre's philosophy, it did not prove to be exceptionally useful to this study as most of the interpretations followed out Sartre's discussion, which this study takes from primary sources.

Perhaps the most inadequate analysis of Sartre's work by Stern is in his discussion of Sartre's psychoanalysis. Existential psychoanalysis may be understood much more adequately if one were to examine Rollo May's conclusions as found in his book, *Existenz*.[40]

Like Sartre, Martin Buber has written one book which gives a definitive statement of his philosophy as it relates to the individual. Unlike Sartre's work, Buber's book hardly contains one hundred pages. This work is entitled *I-Thou*, and it is relied on in this study to present Buber's goals for the individual. *I-Thou* is not a good introductory book, however, for one not acquainted with his writings. One would more profitably begin to study the writings of Buber by reading his *Prophetic Faith* and then proceeding to his small book, *The Eclipse of God*. With these two books providing a background understanding of his thought, one might then read *I-Thou* and then turn to Buber's applied thinking in his book *Between Man and Man*.

Between Man and Man contains a chapter which discusses education and another chapter which analyzes the education of character. Both of these chapters were invaluable for completing this study of Martin Buber.

In his *Eclipse of God*, Buber raises several questions about Kierkegaard's concept of the individual which help to contrast their two points of view.

Buber is the only representative of the four men to be studied who deals extensively with ethical concepts. His ethical considerations are scattered throughout his books previously mentioned, but find direct expression in his interpretations of the Psalms in *Right and Wrong* and *At the Turning*.

Buber's analysis of the role of faith in the individual's life is delineated in his recent book, *Two Types of Faith*, which contrasts Pauline faith with Hebraic faith.

No study of Martin Buber's educational thought would be complete without some consideration of his interpretation of the Hasidic movement, which is a Hebraic movement which profoundly influenced Buber's philosophical-theological development. Although Buber has published two volumes dealing with the *Tales of the Hasidim*, the source material for understanding this movement is his book entitled *Hasidim*.

In a letter to the author of this study, Martin Buber identified Maurice S. Friedman as an excellent secondary source for the clarification of his work. Friedman did his doctoral dissertation on Buber and eventually published a book, *Martin Buber*.[41] Although Friedman discusses Buber's educational thought in his book, he does not offer very much more insight into the subject than does Buber himself in the previously referred to work, *Between Man and Man*.

B. *The secondary source material interpreting the educational implications of existentialism*

The secondary source material proved to be of no appreciable help in seeking to relate the concepts of the men under discussion to the educational endeavor. For the most part, secondary sources were strictly introductory expositions of existential thinking, or of the author under consideration. Nevertheless, considerable use was made of the secondary works concerned with existentialism in the second chapter of this study in the endeavor to bring into focus the main concerns of existentialism and to develop a frame of reference for the purpose of easing the task of understanding the existential authors.

The major exception to the foregoing assertion is the 54th Yearbook of the National Society for the Study of Education, entitled *Modern Philosophies and Education*. In this book there is one chapter which seeks to present the educational implications of existentialism. The chapter was written by Ralph Harper. Its location in the book was hardly a tribute to the author, for the positioning in the text was on the basis of how well the author related his topic to the statements they were asked to respond to by the editorial committee.[42] Harper fell into the trap of merely introducing existentialist thought once more to the reader, rather than translating its philosophy into its educational implications. Harper interprets the educational implications of existentialism as involving a stress on educating the total man. This means that the educational process must help to unfold in the individual a growing awareness of himself in the situation in which he finds himself. As the individual becomes aware of himself, he will realize that he is unique and that he must face the challenge of existence in the best way possible. To help the individual face his particular situation, it will be necessary for educational curriculum to be up-to-date, and it must be flexible, dynamic and modernized. The educational system must free the individual from a feeling of dependency and encourage the development of the total person.

The end of education, to Harper, "is making the individual aware of the meaning of homelessness, of being-at-home, and of ways of returning."[43] This means that existentialism is concerned primarily with liberal education, which frees man from his own anonymity, and seeks to clarify in his mind the confusions which may prevent man from making authentic choices. While this education may be liberal, the author nevertheless stresses that the existentialists insist that there are certain things, certain truths, which every man ought to know, and that foremost among these is a knowledge of himself. For man to know himself, he ought to know what it is to be an existent, a man, and he should know the limits and the powers of man and of himself.

Harper feels that the educative process involves three elements: "the teacher, the pupil and that which they have in common, the curriculum."[44] The existential emphasis in this trinity would be its point of view that the role of the teacher and the student are often interchangeable. The existentialists, to the author, would be vitally concerned with the type of person the teacher should be. They would denounce the presence of a pale, passionless teacher influencing children. The good teacher "aims to produce, not replicas, but men and women who stand apart from him even more dictinctly than when he first met them. The good teacher does not want imitators ... but men and women who through their education have experienced the shock of discovering the infinite depths of the world...."[45] The best teacher, in an existential perspective, "is the one who maintains that precarious balance" between him and his students, the subject matter, "and at the same time is so responsive to his students that he can switch his method and approach without warning even to himself."[46]

The danger existentialists find in American education is that its curriculum often implies an emphasis on this world, and a trend away from emphasizing the role of faith in personal decision making.

Although Harper is discussing existential educational implications, his discussion of the school and community seldom refers

19

to which existentialist he is talking about, and thus it is difficult to decipher what his convictions are and what is implied by the movement as a whole.

The educational consultant to Harper's interpretation was Robert Ulich. Ulich stresses that there could be nothing worse for education than a wave of pseudoexistentialism infiltrating into its area. Pseudoexistentialism involves a blind hatred of technology, a flirting with despair, a cynicism about the idea of human progress, and a profoundly reactionary antirationalism. Through the positive ideas of existentialism, Ulich underscores his belief that the movement will be a new motive power of civilization.[47]

In 1955, Robert Ulich published his book, *The Human Career*. Although Ulich does not indicate in any *way* that he was writing from an existential vantage point, the themes that the new philosophy deals with are similar to those which Ulich develops in his discussion. Ulich does state in this book that existentialism conceals more than it reveals. He also identifies Kierkegaard, Marcel, Tillich, Jaspers, Heidegger and Sartre as being existential thinkers.

In his descriptive statement of man, Ulich lists the following traits as being characteristic of man. It will be shown in the elaboration of this thesis that points one, two, three, five and fourteen are highly charged with an existential emphasis. Points four, seven, ten and twelve reflect existential thinking. Points six, eight, nine, eleven and thirteen are not antagonistic to existentialism. The following list summarizes Ulich's characterization of man:

1. Man... lives in the continual state of self-transcendence.

2. Because of this openness to the world and its impressions, man is restless.

3. Man... must make his way by intentional planning.

4. Man is political.... He needs systematic and collective organization.... He needs the fact and sense of belonging.

5. ... but man is also the creature of anxiety and loneliness....

20

6. Man is... the systematic tool maker.

7. Man is also the symbol maker.... (He) builds an order and a system, a world, beside and above the natural cosmos.

8. ... man acquires perspective ... he can choose and decide from a point of view; he can compare.

9. Man can ask questions, think, reflect and build theories which help him to assemble his thoughts and impressions in logical sequence.

10. ... man is the witness of, and at least in degree, the director of his own development.

11. Only because he is at the same time witness and director, man can have history...

12. Man is dependent and free at the same time.

13. We have the right to assume that these principles point towards certain laws which would constitute the third, highest and universal order, of the ground and end of all that is.

14. Only through the sense of participation in the three orders of nature, mind and wholeness can man fully understand his ethical responsibility.[48]

To Ulich, when philosophy is true to itself, it attempts to help man to understand himself and to master his life, and in so doing it must encounter education.[49]

Ulich repeats the challenging statement which was dealt with in the 54th yearbook. "Modern education suffers from a frightful loss of inner substance."[50] Furthermore, education has become "the handmaid of power rather than the conscience of humanity."[51] Education must not merely help man to adjust to his environment, but to transcend the existing conditions by a vision of things as they should be. To do this education must first lay its foundations deeply in metaphysical interests so as to enable individuals to find the rock of true inspiration. Education must reject superficial analysis of problems in favor of analyzing the events which may overwhelm man. Finally, Ulich stresses that education must deal with the ethical impulse of man.

Another author whose writings in the education field may be found to be fruitful for discovering existential implications in his educational philosophy is Giovanni Gentile. Dr. Merritt Thompson, in his analysis of the *Educational Philosophy of Giovanni Gentile,* identifies the thought of Gentile with the philosophy of idealism.[52] Nevertheless, there is a certain similarity between the thought of Gentile and the thought of Martin Buber. Helmut Kuhn, in his expository discussion of existentialism, pointed out in 1949 that there are marked existential emphases in Gentile's writings.[53]

Gentile stresses that all truth is found within man.[54] The aim of education is the development of consciousness in the student. The awareness of consciousness is to be identified with an emphasis on the essential unity of the psychic life of the student and that it must not be compartmentalized into separate factors such as pure reason.[55] Instruction itself must not be thought of as a process of communicating knowledge but rather that the teacher and the students are creating minute by minute their knowledge together.[56]

To the Italian philosopher, there is no pure mind, subconscious or unconscious mind, waiting for sensations to take place, since apart from the act and before the process the mind is absolutely nothing. "To act is to know, and to know is to act."[57] Instruction should begin with the concrete, that is, the stage of development at which the pupil is found. The teaching process must be a state of rapport between the teacher and pupil. "Although the teacher may leave the classroom, he cannot separate himself from their mentality, from their spiritual dispositions as these have been formed during the school period of contact."[58] During the ideal lesson both the teacher and the pupil are so completely absorbed in a single spiritual process that neither is sensible of the presence of the other.[59] The similarity between this and the preceding emphasis of Gentile will be related to

Buber's concept of the *I-Thou* during the discussion of the latter's philosophy.

The first major work to interpret the importance of existentialism for education was written by George Kneller and is entitled *Existentialism and Education*. Kneller contends that existentialists are tempted to ignore educational problems because of their suspicion that socially inculcated educational ideas and practices are spurious.[60] He states explicitly that "existentialism is not immediately useful as a source of answers to specific educational problems."[61] Kneller excuses the impotence of existentialism as "the logical consequence of a doctrine so young and free."[62] The author does credit the position with the possibility that it might be advising man to not worry about the everyday aspects of human existence, but rather to face the fundamental questions of his being. He states that existentialists share certain educational ideals prevailing in the United States; that is that the purpose of education is to enable the student to fulfill his highest potential.[63] Furthermore, he states that one of the useful aspects of existentialism is that it suggests what the educator should be looking for if twentieth-century educational problems are to be solved.[64]

Kneller asserts that existentialists believe that objective knowledge can only be hypothetical and never decisive. The individual is responsible for his own knowledge, and the knowledge that he achieves must be based on his intuitive grasp of the situation.[65] Concerning the curriculum, Kneller believes that existentialists would shy away from merely rational and empirical methods of teaching, because these can serve only to inhibit the growth of independent thought and behavior. The subject matter must be structured so as to become a tool in the realization of the student's subjective awareness of himself and his environment.[66] Basically, the student ought not exclusively learn about the subject at hand, but rather should learn to live with the content. Education for happiness is dangerous for it does not take into account the other side of life, and Kneller insists that existentialists would include cognizance of death and anxiety in the curriculum.[67] The primary goal would not be to secure the stu-

23

dent's memory of the material; each course would be structured so that he would become enthusiastic, involved, and even committed to the material at hand. In that existentialists lay stress on what the individual is becoming, the curriculum would point towards the future along the lines suggested by social reconstructionists.[68] Kneller believes that existentialists would evaluate the teacher's role very carefully. The teacher must stress a close personal relationship with the student, yet not dominate him or discourage his independent thought.[69]

Although side-stepping many educational problems, Kneller's book is an excellent introduction to existentialism. His evaluation of existentialism will be discussed in the next chapter.

A Review of the Periodical Literature

Articles pertaining to existentialism in the periodical literature begin to appear in 1934 as listed in the International Index to Periodicals, in 1945 in the Readers Guide to Periodical Literature, and in 1947 in the Educational Index to Periodical Literature. In the Educational Index to Periodical Literature there were no articles concerned with existentialism from June 1950 to May 1953. For the purposes of this study, the periodical literature does not provide a rich field of material in relating existentialism to the educational process.

A group of graduate students under the direction of Theodore Brameld cooperated in studying the educational implications of existentialism and published their conclusions in the April 1952 issue of Educational Theory.[70] The article identifies existentialism as being on the intellectual frontier of the twentieth century and carries on to observe that it has not been amply discussed in the literature.[71] The first section of the article seeks to define existentialism, the second section presents a criticism of the philosophy, and the third section discusses the constructive values of existentialism. The last section is concerned with the educational implications of the philosophy.

Brameld's students point out that, in existentialism, the partic-

24

ular situation is important. It is the subjective present which must be presented to the student. The teacher who accepts such a theory will encourage his students to emphasize their present experience. The emphasis would be on the fact that, in each day, history is being made. Furthermore, the teacher would encourage the student to be self-reliant with the present situation. He must have his own convictions and be able to understand that which he believes. Eventually such a student will deny complacency and demand to know "What can I do?".[72]

The second implication of existentialism which was pinpointed by the seminar is that the responsibility for knowledge rests with the individual. Existential knowledge, of necessity, results from what exists in the individual's consciousness and feelings as a result of his acts. The teacher will encourage students to take an attitude that all particular situations are different and must be analyzed in terms of both rational and unrational factors.[73]

The group pointed out that existentialists believe that individual continuity comes as a result of self-initiated acts of self-creation; this might enrich the conception of interest and effort emphasized in the writings of John Dewey. The core curriculum would be one methodological approach to developing continuity in the existential movement.[74]

In terms of responsible group action the existential student is not a puppet of some other authority figure. The student accepts his responsibility for action, he refuses complacency, and he attempts to avoid any panaceas which will only give symptomatic relief to the problems at hand.[75]

The seminar emphasized that, to the existentialist, values do not precede action. Values are determined in action and are based on the free decisions of the individual in question. Man must choose according to a pattern of what he, himself, would choose for all mankind. To develop values the educator must provide as much opportunity as possible for the individual to realize himself. The movement would be impatient with parents or educators who would shield the child from making responsible decisions.[76]

J. B. Coates discusses "Existential Ethics" in *Fortnightly* in

1954. To Coates, the existential ethic is founded on a primary ethical choice (a basic assumption) in the individual to be an authentic person. It is exceedingly difficult to define exactly what is meant by the term authentic person because personality is a continuing revelation, and a person continually makes and remakes himself through his decisions in his developing relationships to God, to himself, to others, and to his life situation. Authenticity does involve the individual's acceptance of responsibility for the fact that he is giving meaning to life by his every act.[77] Furthermore, authenticity depends on the individual's critical self-assessment which he is continually undertaking. Thus one finds that existential ethics may be reduced to the individual committing himself to a way of life of which he is aware, and in which he realizes that he is creating something new, and that he is responsible for that creation.[78]

An English writer L. I. Stowe, expressed some concern about the influence of existentialism in an article published in the *Journal of Education* which is printed in London. Stowe identifies existentialism with Sartrean atheism and he fears that there is an unfortunate tendency for it to dominate the intelligence of the English parents.[79] Stowe concludes that there is a mental shrinking from religious thought in England and specifically in English education which is directly traceable to the atheism emphasized by existentialism, to its defeatism about life, and to its incorrigible revolt against thinking. He believes that the school system must combat this trend by re-editing the religious syllabus so as to eliminate undue repetition of Old and New Testament stories. The content of the syllabus should not approach religion from the moralistic point of view, but rather it should create philosophical problems for students to analyze and wrestle with. Such an increase in philosophical speculation about religious matters will require more time to be spent dealing with this type of religious instruction. Most important in Stowe's approach to religion, however, will be the teachers, who must not only be informed, but they must be enthusiastic about their subject.

The article is important to this study for it shows that even though existentialism might not itself have an impact on the educational endeavor, it may force its adversaries to rethink and to enliven the curriculum for which they are responsible.

Another author antagonistic to existentialism is Charles Glicksberg, who published an article entitled "The Lost Generation of College Youth" in the *Journal of Higher Education*. Like Stowe, Glicksberg identifies existentialism with the atheistic school of Sartre, and expresses his concern about how influential the movement has become in the United States. Paradoxically, he concludes the article by praising the religious insights of Reinhold Neibuhr and Paul Tillich. The latter has often been identified as an existential theologian.[80]

Glicksberg thinks that our colleges are producing a beat generation which is weary, dispirited, disillusioned and generally lost. It is infected with Sartre who denies life. He goes on to describe Sartre as believing that God is dead, that man must make his own decisions and shape his own destiny, that he must stand alone and, because everything is relative, needs no remorse or penance.[81] The greatest crime of Sartre's influence on the college student is that he offers no vision of hope or redemption for man, but rather involves man in a quasi-neurotic pessimism, for man must be confronted prematurely with anxiety about death.[82]

To Glicksberg, the major need of the contemporary college generation is to discern some meaning in life, for without it life is hardly worth carrying on. To find meaning, the author suggests a study of men like Neibuhr, Tillich and Erich Fromm.

A more general article which has pertinence to this study but which does not discuss existentialism directly, is one written by John White for the *Harvard Educational Review* entitled "Anxiety, the Activity Program, and Individual Initiative." White observes that there is very little exact evidence about the role played by anxiety as a motivational factor in human learning, and that we are ignorant as to whether anxiety is, or is not, basic to all learning.[83] It will be shown in the development of this thesis that existentialists feel that anxiety is a vital motivational force in the learning enterprise.

White is aware that modern educational pedagogy tends to

reduce the individual anxiety threshold to the minimum. Yet White feels that it is probably undesirable to eliminate anxiety altogether, if indeed it is possible. The author answers his own question by emphasizing that a little anxiety ought to be injected into the curriculum and that schools which arouse student anxiety by entrusting them with the responsibility of making decisions and initiating activity are not in error.[84]

James Magmer, author of "Why Protestant Theologians Use Existentialism", published by *Catholic World,* states that few people are willing to realize how widespread existentialism is in the United States, if not as a formal philosophy, then as an aesthetic attitude. To Magmer, existentialism will not make many inroads into Catholic education because it is a movement of protest which attacks the infallibility of the Church, makes the church's sacraments empty formalisms and tends to pry man away from the spiritual values of life.[85]

Articles have appeared in the periodical literature which have been written by some of the men under discussion in this study. The works listed below are definitely relevant and germane to this study, but will be discussed in detail in the sections reserved for analyzing the primary source material for each man respectively.

Jaspers has published two articles of note. A most important one for this study was published in the *American Scholar*[86] and is concerned with the "Re-dedication of German Scholarship". The second article is not crucial to this study because its ideas have been forcefully presented in his books, especially in *Man in the Modern World.* However, the idea which this article develops is essential to an understanding of how Jaspers would re-direct the curriculum attention of the secondary schools and certainly the curriculum of higher education. It is concerned with "The Axial Age of Human History" which Jaspers feels took place between 800-200 B.C. To understand the twentieth century, man must understand the forces of thought which were initiated during this era. The article was published by *Commentary* in 1948.[87]

In three 1948 issues of *Commentary* one may find Sartre's discussions of anti-Semitism. These articles are important to this study for they offer Sartre's concept of the formation of prejudice and what authentic people ought to do about it. The articles provide insight into existential theory as applied to a real live issue facing the twentieth century, they are also studies in existential ethics. Furthermore, one can discern from these articles part of his concept of the individual with which this study is directly concerned.[88]

In speaking of the ethics of Sartre, one may bear in mind the previously mentioned articles by Stowe and Glicksberg, who felt that existentialism left one without an ethical orientation. In an article written by Robert Champigny entitled "Translations from the Writings of Contemporary French Philosophers" for the *Journal of Philosophy,* the author stresses that Sartre's existentialism is a philosophy of consciousness and conscience. To Champigny, the main perspective in Sartre's philosophy is moral because the latter's concept of freedom is indissolubly linked to personal responsibility.[89]

An article revelant to Martin Buber's concept of the individual was published by him in *Commentary* under the caption, "The Man of Today and the Jewish Bible." Its general concern is that each generation must struggle with the Bible and come to terms with it. Buber seeks to point the way by which man ought to approach the Bible.[90]

Paul Tillich's article, "Martin Buber and Christian Thought," is a sequel to the above article by Buber. Tillich finds that Buber's existential interpretation of prophetic religion, his rediscovery of mysticism within the prophetic religion, and his understanding of the relationship between religion and culture are vital concerns to the Christian movement.[91] To Tillich, Buber's work is existential, for an interpreter is existentially orientated if he emphasizes the two-way character of every genuine religious experience, the involvement of the whole man in religion and the impossibility of God standing outside the situation.[92]

The great existential problem for Tillich is how the individual can become an 'I' instead of an 'it' in the contemporary world. Existentialism, whether atheistic or religious, is intent on re-discovering life under 'things', freedom under 'mechanisms', meaning under 'means', the 'Thou' under the 'it'.[93]

Maurice Friedman attempts to pinpoint the educational concepts of Martin Buber in an article published in *Christian Scholar*. To Friedman, Buber would differentiate between propaganda and education, both of which are influential on modern man. Propaganda seeks to impose its subject matter on the mind of man; education seeks to discover and nourish in the soul of the other that which one (the teacher) has recognized in oneself as right.[94] The existential communication is formed, not through instruction, but through "meeting." The nature of this meeting forms the subject matter for the discussion of Buber's educational theory, and is to be analyzed during the discussion of Martin Buber's theories.

According to Friedman, Buber would emphasize that too much intellectualism cuts man off from the totality of life. It is this that would separate Buber from the thinking of either Hutchins or Dewey.[95] Friedman feels that Dewey and Buber both stress the continuity of mind and nature and indeed that Dewey stresses the whole man, but that nevertheless Dewey fails to understand the 'spirit of man.'[96]

To Buber, according to Friedman, the education of character is attained only when the cruel, hard demands of the hour are stressed in their importance. There can be no universal education because each hour presents important demands which must be understood and in which the student must become involved.

Buber and Dewey also would differ, in Friedman's estimation, over their methods of verification. Verification to Dewey involves objectification; whereas, to Buber verification involves authentication of one's truth in the whole of one's personal life. In that one's whole life must be involved, it is vital that students not be asked to study unreal questions about life and that the classroom be allowed to become an experimental laboratory which provides the opportunity for testing concept reality.[97]

A Review of Doctoral Dissertations

Titles of recent doctoral dissertations were examined in the

Index to American Doctoral Dissertations and in *Doctoral Dissertations Accepted by American Universities* for studies which have a bearing on this study. No dissertations were found which duplicated the general theme of this study.

Most relevant to one portion of the current study is a doctoral dissertation submitted to the University of Southern California by William Frank O'Neill. He sought to analyze Jean-Paul Sartre's concept of Freedom and its implications for American public education.[98] O'Neill concludes that to Sartre, man is that being through whom all values come into the world. The character of the educational process is ultimately reducible to the character of those individuals who have conceived the process and who are by definition free to conceive any program imaginable.[99] He furthermore states that existentialism is "categorically devoid of educational implications" because of the emphasis on the priority of existence, whereas education deals more with 'essence'.[100] Thus, educational implications which he derives from Sartre are based on the "study of the something more" than the existentialism which is to be found in Sartre's writings. According to O'Neill, the educational implications of Sartre's writings may be reduced to five main categories which are as follows: 1. The development and propagation of existential insight among all individuals. This involves the encouragement of existential conversion where possible, and an endorsement of the existential concept of man. 2. The encouragement of an attitude of positive affirmation towards existence. 3. The development of personal autonomy through the creation of an allegiance to a system of personal values. 4. The encouragement of a program of active engagement on the part of each individual. 5. Aiding the individual to become dedicated to the ideal of social liberty.[101] An ingredient which is essential to all of the five goals is the necessity of the individual to come to know himself in the Socratic method. To facilitate the development of these goals the educational curriculum must be designed to offer the ontological rules which govern man's existence and have established programs to help the students become the arbiters of their own personal destinies with only a minimum of institutional guidance.[102]

O'Neill states that Sartre was not an educational philosopher and that he seldom utilizes the word education.[103] He cautions that any attempt to develop the educational implications of Sartre must be done with considerable reservation. Nevertheless, O'Neill develops the following immediate aims of education as being implied by the Sartrean viewpoint: 1. The fostering of the fundamental skills which are involved in basic communication and self-expression. 2. The discovery of aptitudes and the exploration of interests and abilities which lie within the student. 3. An active participation in some activity which is of vital concern to the student. 4. The development of an understanding of the existential emphasis on authenticity. 5. A maximum amount of guidance. 6. A maximum exploration of the vocational possibilities of the individual. 7. Finally, stress on an adequate state of physical fitness.[104] In regard to the latter point, O'Neill points out that Sartre would not be in favor of the emphasis on physical fitness currently in vogue in public education in the United States.[105]

O'Neill realizes that most of the above goals would be more suitably carried to fulfillment at the secondary level rather than in the elementary school. He concludes that there would be a minimal emphasis on existential insight in the elementary schools because the child of that age would lack insight into the existential challenge. O'Neill avers that the child, while existing in bad faith, is not aggressively so, but really so by default. This is to say, his bad faith is dormant. Children are too deeply threatened by reality and they also lack the 'tools' of handling reality concepts. Furthermore, they abide in too much bad faith at home to be existentially awakened.[106]

Finally, in terms of curriculum organization, O'Neill believes that the existentialist would align himself with the educational reconstructionists.[107]

A second dissertation, also presented to the University of Southern California, which has a direct relation to this study and was written by Richard Stanley Ford, compares the experimental approach with some aspects of existentialism. Ford, who is primarily concerned with the field of religious education, asserts that educational procedures should not be contrary to theological assumptions about the nature of man.[108]

Ford's study seeks to relate seven aspects of existentialism to the experimental approach. These aspects are listed as follows: 1. existence is prior to essence; 2. existence transcends the rational; 3. man is condemned to be free; 4. the basic characteristic of man is existential anxiety in the face of nothingness; 5. the realization of existence means estrangement; 6. the existential individual endures crisis; and 7. existence means a return to immediacy.[109]

Ford concludes that there is no adequate basis upon which existentialism and experimental religious education may be synthesized. Experimental religious education insists upon concepts of continuity, progress, growth, reason and a relevant world view. To Ford, existentialism rejects these basic assumptions. The only points of similarity between the two viewpoints are the worth of man, the epistemology of the two movements, and the placement of the locus of educational authority. Ford states that existentialism contains no basis whatsoever upon which one might establish a concept of learning and educative process. The characteristic of anxiety, which is basic to anxiety, is a solitary experience, and in itself has little to do with the goals of education. There are no external criteria existing within existentialism for the establishment of an interactive process by which the individual can move towards his goal.[110]

Existentialism, to Ford, may contribute to education indirectly by its emphasis on the dire predicament of man and man's threatened loss of identity in the twentieth century. The tragic element in man's life has been soft-pedaled by the dominant pragmatic philosophies.[111]

Ford stresses that educational philosophers will have to examine the existential assertion that the world is meaningless to determine whether the statement is true, or whether it is merely the expression of a frustrated soul.[112]

Another study which should be noted, but which is not extensively used in the development of this thesis, is one by Paul Pfeutze which is concerned with "The Concept of the Asocial

Self in the Thought of George Mead and Martin Buber." This study was presented to Yale in 1951. Pfeutze concludes that Mead and Buber have several similar emphases. Some of these are listed below:

1. The individual and the community are equally primordial and correlative entities.

2. Speech, dialogue, is the chief mechanism which is constructive of selfhood.

3. Reality itself has a social structure.

4. The integrity of the social individual is greater than that of the atomistic individual.

5. Both men support democratic or slightly socialistic movements politically.

6. Both reject Hegelian absolutism and rationalism.

7. Both stress the primacy of acting over pure thought.

8. Finally, there is a transcendent element in both writers, although it is stronger in Buber.[113]

Pfeutze states that Mead writes from a "pragmatic-naturalistic-behavioristic framework," whereas Buber "writes out of an attitude of faith."[114] The result of the writing orientation of each man leads Pfeutze to conclude that Mead provides the "scientific floor" for the concept of the social self, whereas Buber provides the "metaphysical ceiling" for the same concept.[115] To understand Buber, Pfeutze states, one must be capable of encountering God, for Buber does not write about religion, his writings are religious per se.

To Buber, as with Mead, the fundamental reality is not single man, but man with man. The essence of human life is that which happens between man and man. Educational processes must involve the influencing of the lives of others with the teacher's own life.[116]

The Organization of the Remainder of the Study

This chapter has been concerned with establishing the nature and importance of the problem to be considered. It has established the basic hypotheses which are to be tested in the study and has delimited the scope of the study. The methodology for undertaking the study as well as a review of the basic literature concerned with the men being studied was undertaken.

Chapter II presents a survey of the secondary sources which contain discussions of existentialism so as to highlight the main concerns of the existentialists as discerned by their critics and apologists. This chapter seeks to answer partially the question: "What is existentialism?" The chapter also serves the purpose of building an existential frame of reference which will make the existentialists a little more understandable to one who has had no previous acquaintance with their writings, and more particularly their choices of words. The second part of the chapter seeks to answer the question, "Who are the existentialists?" This section gives substance to the claim of this study that the men being discussed are existential writers.

Chapter III is divided into four parts which present in succession each of the existentialists. The organization of each part depends on how the man in question develops his concept of the individual. No stereotyped discussion of the men was developed because their interests vary so widely that a convenient organization of their viewpoints would not do each man justice. This organization was reserved for the fifth and sixth chapters. As much material as possible was presented in each part to delineate clearly the concept each man has, not only about man in general, but more to the point, about the authentic man. To gain a clearer impression of the authentic man, the man who exists in bad faith was developed in each section.

Chapter IV analyzes the concept of education which is implicit and explicit in the point of view of each of the existentialists. As with the previous chapter, so this chapter was divided into four parts and a fifth part which accepted the hypothesis pertaining to the chapter. To gain clearly an insight into the educational philosophy of each man, his concept of childhood was developed if he discussed the subject at all. This chapter concludes with the interpretation that existentialists do not demand that children be treated as adults, but rather that their happy juvenile ways ought to be encouraged.

Chapter V is the first summarization of the material of the thesis. It particularly addresses itself to the third hypothesis. The chapter is divided into two parts. One seeks to present a comparison of existential concepts of authentic individuals and the other part compares the existential educational thought. Thirteen charts are presented in part one to facilitate the comparison of existential concepts of the individual, the traits of authenticity and of bad faith as well as how the individual is involved in his culture, how he relates to God, and the importance of reason to him. The final chart seeks to compare the optimistic outlook of each man. Too often existentialism has been thought of as dreadful. In the educational section eight charts were devised to present a comparison of existential viewpoints pertaining to education. These charts include a comparison of the nature of the child, the purposes of education, the problems of education, the type of teachers one ought to select to instruct children, the methods these teachers ought to use as well as an analysis of the curriculum which existentialists would recommend.

Chapter VI presents the summary and conclusions of the study. It is also divided into two parts. One develops the existential concept of the authentic person based on the agreements attained in the previous chapter. The second part develops the educational implications which the four men, or possibly three of the four, would agree with. This section is broken down so that an analysis is presented of the education of children, of youth, of adolescents and of adults. The final section analyzes the type of teacher who should be teaching in the public schools.

CHAPTER II

A SURVEY OF THE DEVELOPING AWARENESS
OF EXISTENTIALISM IN THE UNITED STATES

The purpose of this chapter is to establish evidence for the fact that the men being discussed in this paper are considered representatives of the existentialist tradition. It is also the purpose of this chapter to present the interpretations of existentialism which one currently finds in vogue among the secondary source writers who attempt to interpret the philosophy to the American reader. By approaching the material in this manner the reader of this study will be able more readily to ascertain whether the four men being discussed are accepted as existentialists by critical thinkers and whether the critiques of existentialism adequately present a well-rounded interpretation of existentialism.

Although existentialism has proved itself to be influential on many of the scholars of Europe, its real impact did not involve the American mind until 1948. In that year three books were published in English designed to introduce the existential movement to the American reader. Two of these essays tended to be positive towards the movement; the third was hostile.

Recurrent in the literary discussions of existentialism is the book *Dreadful Freedom* by Marjorie Grene. Miss Grene states that in the main her book was designed to be a prefatory essay written in order to introduce existentialism and to dispel the notion that "every treatise that dooms man to destruction, every novel whose characters are mad or bad, every play that depresses without elevating ..." is an existential masterpiece.[1] Grene states that the first principle of existentialism is simply that existence is prior to essence. The existentialists that she chooses to discuss are Kierkegaard, Heidegger, Sartre, Jaspers and Marcel.

Another book often referred to by the later discussants of existentialism is Helmut Kuhn's book, *Encounter With Nothingness*. Kuhn is aware that the term 'existentialism' was being used to cover a great diversity of ideas and tendencies. Nevertheless he feels that one can discern a uniform pattern of thought in their writings.[2] To him, the existentialists as a group share the emphasis that it is necessary for man to die in order to live. He feels that the existentialists are insisting that the walls that enclose and narrow man's existence must be torn down, and that man must be exposed to the realities of factual existence. To tear down the walls one must bring man first into an awareness of personal crisis. Up to this point the existentialists do not differ much from several great philosophers of the ages, but when the existentialist finally arrives at the crisis, at Calvary, he finds the place empty, save for the two thieves who are dying there. This is to say, the existentialists do not promise man 'victory' in life or even after life; there is no primrose pattern waiting for man at the end of his struggles. In existential crisis, one encounters nothingness.[3] Basically, Kuhn argues, existentialism is designed to do something to us (not for us); its intent is to seize upon the whole mind, to challenge the individual. Once more, in this intention, it does not vary from authentic philosophies, but this movement seeks to arrest the normal function of the processes of thought and will, to challenge them, and then to precipitate them into fresh activity.

Kuhn stresses that the existentialists ask one basic question of their fellow man: "What do you will with unwavering devotion, so that everything is willed and loved only for the sake of this first objective and greatest good?" The reply to this rhetorical question must involve a series of negations which will eventually obliterate man's complex standards by which he so comfortably abides. As the dialectic destroys man's artificial standards, he is revealed as naked and in an abyss, or a vacuum of experience, or in nothingness. From this vacuum man realizes that he is free, all are free. Man must make a deal with this feeling of nothingness in order to be able to assert himself.[4] Because man must step from the experience of nothingness in which he finds himself engulfed, he realizes that his decisions are acts for which no rational account can be given. This fact produces considerable anxiety in individuals who have been used to living by some authoritarian standard.[5]

The unique dilemma with which existentialists are confronted is that the theoretical position attained through the concept of crisis will either be able to integrate, that is, explain the crisis, or it will not be able to do so. If explained, the crisis would cease to be a crisis, and this would involve a new certitude which existentialists object to. If it does not explain the crisis, then the position would tend to be worthless. To avoid this dilemma, Kuhn feels that existentialists shift towards the direction of historic-theology, idealism, or Christian theology.[6]

Kuhn identifies Jaspers, Heidegger, Sartre, Simon de Beauvoir, Albert Camus, Unamuno, Ortega y Gasset, Berdyaev, Chestov, Marcel, Tillich and Buber as being existentially oriented.

A writer hostile towards existentialism is Guido de Ruggiero, whose book is entitled *Existentialism: Disintegration of Man's Soul*. Ruggiero labels Kierkegaard, Heidegger, Jaspers and Marcel as being the masters of existentialism.

Ruggiero falls into the trap of treating Kierkegaard in terms of one of his pseudonyms. Thus, many of the criticisms he makes of Kierkegaard would have been agreed to by the 'master' himself. Ruggiero feels that Heidegger empties Kierkegaard's philosophy of its religious content and generally has depersonalized the philosophy. Jaspers, he writes, is an even more diluted writer than Heidegger, but is one who is trying to enrich and extend the existential sphere.[7]

Ruggiero suggests that existentialism lacks continuity and that it denies reason. He finds it tied in to the Nazi movement in Germany and feels that it took decadent roots in France. Its popularity in Italy is due only to the Italian predilection for copying Northern thinking, and in the Anglo-Saxon world it is toyed with as an item of curiosity.[8] Ruggiero feels that the irrationality that

39

existentialists stress is not as irreducible as they make it out to be, for he feels that birth, death, 'here' and 'now' are subject to rationality. He charges that existentialism has banished all intrinsic differentiations of existence, and this has resulted in eliminating the concept of ideal ends that man may achieve. In doing this existentialism has made life appear to be a mere vain race with death.[9]

Ruggiero was one of the first to declare that existentialism was made popular only as a result of the war. He labeled it as metaphysical pornography and dismissed it by quoting the Italian idealist, Croce, who denounced existentialism as being overstimulated, poisonous and perverse.[10]

In 1949 the translated work of Emmanuel Mounier, an existential apologist, appeared on the English market. The book was entitled, *Existential Philosophies: An Introduction*. Mounier explains that existentialists emphasize the transcendence of existence over nothingness, the transcendence of the existent in respect to the world, the transcendence of the world in relation to the existent, and the transcendence of the existent in relation to himself by means of the movement in which he is projected in advance of himself towards the future.[11]

Mounier denies the contention of Ruggiero that existentialism is a form of irrationalism, but goes on to stress that it asserts that reason is not the sole basis of becoming aware of existence.[12]

The apologist deeply regrets the popularity of existentialism on the continent. He feels that it was indeed bad luck for the movement that in France it tended to degenerate into idle daily gossiping, an especially ironic fate for a philosophy whose whole purpose is to drag man away from his idle gossiping. Mounier suggests that the existentialists in France ended their understanding of the movement following their stimulating discussion of it when it was time to go home from their cafes. He also objects to the fact that Sartre has tended to turn the focus of existential attention away from the 'normal' real to the perverse.[13] The emphasis on the perverse was the result, according to Mounier, of Sartre's interest in existential psycho-

40

analysis. As far as Sartre is concerned, Mounier feels that he is a philosophical sadist according to the former's own definition of the term. He objects to Sartre's attempt to reduce existence, which cannot be appropriated by any individual, to a philosophical meaninglessness.[14] Mounier summarizes the recurring themes of existentialism as follows:

1. The contingency of the human being.

2. The impotence of reason alone.

3. The use of the dialectic.

4. The boundless leap of the individual as typified in the idea that man is always a 'being-in-advance-of-himself' must be dealt with in terms of being a power that is becoming. This may be summarized by stating that man does not fully coincide with himself.

5. There is a basic instability characteristic of the human being who must continually be reassuming 'being'.

6. Man's estrangement from himself and his continual living at the lower stages of existence (Kierkegaard) or in inauthentic existence. (Sartre, Heidegger)

7. Most existentialists treat the conclusive-finality man continuously faces, the knowledge that he must die, that he must become an object for others pessimistically. Most emphasize that man's empirical existence is always threatened.

8. There is a solitude which is characteristic of man, there is an inner state in which man must orientate himself. This is best expressed in the idea that man must be an individual.

9. Finally man is constantly plagued by the 'nothingness' of existence. This includes the nothingness from which he came, and it is the nothingness he experiences in the present and it is the realization of the nothingness of the future.[15]

Practically all of the existentialists insist that everything about man is ambiguous, that he is an extremely complex mixture which must not be analyzed but only understood as a whole. Furthermore, because of the complexity of man, one finds that most of the existentialists emphasize the Socratic dictum — Know Thyself. Most existentialists are introspective, and often their writings are an expression of their own intense spiritual wrestling match with the meaning of their existence.[16]

Mounier also prepared the ground work for the reply to the critics of existentialism who accuse it of dealing with meaninglessness. This negative appraisal of existentialism is expressed by D. J. B. Hawkins, in a paper read to the Aquinas Society of London in 1954 dealing with the "Meaning of Existentialism." Hawkins states that it is the business of philosophy to deal with problems (problems that are solvable, and thus meaningful to work with), not mysteries. The only homage one "can pay to the mysterious is silence" writes Hawkins.[17] To Mounier, the first concern of existentialists is to keep the mysterious from becoming identified with the problem. A mystery is a problem which intrudes upon its own ideas, a problem which attacks its own ideas but which never overreaches itself (in terms of the solvable) in the same way as an ordinary problem does. This is to say, the mysterious interacts with the person who projects himself into the mysterious. This process is a creative one which is treasured by existentialists.[18]

Mounier identifies Sartre, Kierkegaard (the existential titular father), Jaspers, Buber, Marcel, Scheler and Heidegger as existentially oriented.

Concurrently with the publication of Mounier's apology for existentialism there appeared Jean Wahl's translated work, *A Short History of Existentialism*. Wahl discusses the philosophies of Kierkegaard, Jaspers, Heidegger and Sartre in the first half of the text. The second half is concerned with a discussion of existentialism by several European philosophers, among whom were Berdyaev and Marcel.

Wahl feels that existentialism is making man witness and participant in a new mode of philosophizing, for existentialism has dislodged previous philosophical concepts and has tended, paradoxically, to make more acute philosophical concepts.[19] Classical philosophy was concerned with essence; it tried to rise above the realm of becoming and find a universal truth, the eternal. Existentialism has reintroduced the question of being — "to be or not to be" — as the central problem of this philosophical endeavor.[20] To Wahl the challenge of 'being' could not be confined to Europe, but must become a world problem.[21]

The dilemma confronting the new philosophy is that of existentialism versus the philosophy of existence. There is the danger of the emphasis on the existent, on his problem of being, becoming an organized "ism".[22]

In 1950, the previously cited Helmut Kuhn was invited by Vergilius Ferm to write a chapter on existentialism for his book *A History of Philosophical Systems*. By this time Kuhn stresses that contemporary existentialism was underway before 1914, and that it therefore could not be tied in directly to the aftermath of the world wars and the resultant disillusionment.[23] Essentially, existentialism is encountered rather than something which is thought. The problems with which existentialists deal must be real. If the age involves destruction, sorrow and death, then existentialism would deal with destruction, sorrow and death. The essence of philosophical truth makes little difference unless there are immediate and practical implications for that truth.[24]

By 1950, Kuhn delineated two forms of existentialism. One form is critical existentialism which, to the author, is more emphatically existential, more uncompromising in subordinating essence to the existing, and more violently anti-traditional and anti-rational. Critical existentialism is the basis of Kierkegaard's writing and the Heidegger-Sartre position. The other form of existentialism emphasizes man's contact with being and with 'otherness'. It is a social existentialism, and the position is most forcefully put forth by Martin Buber.[25]

In 1952 James Collins undertook a critical study of existentialism. He feels that there is no common ground between the

43

existential emphasis and the scientific-semantic-pragmatic triumvirate characteristic of American philosophy. For this reason, the
real meaning of existentialism was still misunderstood on the
American scene at the time of his writing. Collins became interested in his subject as a result of reading the writings of Søren
Kierkegaard. His text contains discussions of the work of Sartre,
Jaspers and Marcel. To Collins, the strength of the movement
is that it has refused to become "abstracted on scientific methodology," and has retreated from the realm of "eternal verities" in
favor of staying close to the terrain of ordinary living and life
problems.[26]

The author ties in the nightmare of the European situation
with existentialism to the degree that the existentialist writers
were in fact Europeans who lived through the holocaust and
who, in terms of their philosophical approach, dealt with that
which they saw and experienced.[27] Collins picks up another note
which ought to be emphasized, namely, that all the existential
authors have tended to treat their thought against the background of their own life situation. To a degree this philosophy
reflects an autobiographical testimony. These existential philosophers have written out of their need for redemption.[28] The
common ground of existential writers, according to Collins, is
to be found first in the fact that these men feel that philosophizing
is a personal venture, if not an adventure.[29] The second emphasis
shared by existentialists is their tendency towards "descriptive
metaphysics". To begin to philosophize one must begin with an
analysis of the questioning self in its situation.[30] As a third point
Collins explains that their concern is for 'man in the world'.[31]
Existence means having one's being as a human individual in
the world and ought not concern some mystical world of ideals.
Finally, Collins points out that whether the existentialist is
religiously oriented or not, all of them feel, and tend to emphasize, that there is a widespread separation between man and
God in the contemporary world.[32]

H. J. Blackham's *Six Existential Thinkers* was also written in
1952. The six men who were chosen for discussion are Kierke-

gaard, Nietzsche, Jaspers, Marcel, Heidegger and Sartre. To Blackham, existential authors are concerned with the maneuvers of existing individuals whose being is ambiguous in a total existence which is ambiguous. In this ambiguity is found no universality — no universal principles — because man is constantly in question. Man is continuously an open possibility. The existential writers are trying to make man aware of his essential separation from himself and from his world. They are challenging man to become aware of who he is, and to choose himself as being who he is.

William Holden published in the same year, 1952, his text concerned with the forerunners of the existential movement — Kierkegaard, Dostoyevsky, Nietzsche and Kafka. The work was definitively entitled *Four Prophets of Our Age*. Like Collins, Holden stresses through the words of Otto Weininger that "great men speak and write only about themselves."[33] One must know that the lives of these men were characterized by unhappy families, broken love affairs, poor health, the need for personal confession, feelings of being ignored, rejection of logical careers which were open to them, and that they were all city men in order to fathom their emphasis on anxiety, dread and gloom.[34] These men were also destined to die young. What these men held in common was that they were suspicious of man's pretenses before themselves and others. They vehemently accused their contemporaries, especially those of the middle class, of not living up to any, or very few, of their publicly proclaimed moral standards. To their contemporaries, these men were a contradiction, and an offense, but they were still a sign.[35] The prophets of Holden realized that they were the end product of a dying civilization and in some respects they were clairvoyant as to the coming chaos of the twentieth century.[36]

To Holden the existential predicament was one of being in "an infinite universe of indefinite limits" which "has no place for finite man."[37] Holden emphasizes that the existentialists agree on man's separation from God and thus agrees with Collins. As for the anti-rational charges against existentialism, Holden defends the movement by insisting that they are merely being realistic. The author believes himself that it is a truism that pure thinking is a phantom. Man's intelligence can never remain outside the totality of life, and therefore it must be involved in subjectivity. Man's thinking, upon the very act of thinking, must be an integral part of his becoming, of his experience.[38]

E. L. Allen published his study of existentialism, *Existentialism from Within,* in 1953, because he felt that most books in English concerned with the subject appeared to be based on inadequate knowledge, or were mistaken in judgment. He, also, believes that there is a need for a sympathetic presentation of the subject.[39] His book contains chapters on Kierkegaard, Heidegger, Sartre, Jaspers and Marcel. First of all, Allen stresses that existentialism cannot be presented in the same way as other philosophies because it puts the "how of truth as important as the what".[40] This is to say that existentialism is an attempt to philosophize from the standpoint of the actor, instead of, as has been customary, from that of the spectator. To think in an existential manner is to come to grips with the human situation as one in which we are actively involved. The existential thinker is thus the actual, living, striving person whose thought is embedded in his life and, perhaps better said, in the process of living.[41]

To Allen, the existentialist is acutely aware that the human situation is an intensely precarious one in which man must be continually concerned about himself; there must be no pretense towards disinterested knowledge (such as dealing with the immortality of the soul), for man must be preoccupied with the fateful possibility and certainty of his own death. This preoccupation gives life an urgency, a coloring, for man can not afford to postpone his problems; he must round off his life in each here and now and give meaning to it while he still has the opportunity. To be certain, Allen points out, existentialism is rooted in the post-war situation, but existentialism insists that the war-like conditions be transcended.[42] One thing this author rejects is the concept that existentialism is a philosophy of despair. He is in agreement with Simone de Beauvoir who emphasizes that existentialism is not based on despair, but is a philosophy of hope. Existentialists do not deny the more pleasant emotions of love, friendship and brotherhood, but instead of assuming them, point out that they must be won by the actions and choices of the individual in each moment of existence.[43] In agreement with Grene, Allen believes that existentialism is an ethic of integrity, for it forces one to run away from hypocrisy towards reality.

In 1953 David Freeman translated the work of the Dutch philosopher, J. M. Spier, whose critical study of existentialism is entitled *Christianity and Existentialism*. To Spier, the rise of existentialism is the direct result of the misery created by the world wars and the disillusionment which accompanied them. The crisis produced by the wars and their aftermath could not be met by Christianity because the Christian faith had been weakened by the scientific emphasis of the twentieth century.[44] Spier adds a new name to the existential roster — the Dutchman Loen, director of the Rijks Hoogere Burgerschool in the Netherlands. Otherwise, Kierkegaard and Nietzsche are the prophets of the movement, Heidegger and Jaspers are the German representatives, Marcel, Lavelle and Sartre speak for the French school and are familiar names.

The first section of the book discusses the philosophies of the above mentioned individuals. The second portion of the work is concerned with a critical analysis of existentialism. Basically, this latter part of the book spells out the characteristics of the movement, the truth of existentialism and then the reason why it must be rejected.

To Spier, existentialism is a philosophy of reaction. It is reacting against rationalism in favor of irrationalism because it defies the subject of existence.[45] Existentialism is a philosophy of crisis, and it is responsible for increasing the pessimism, defeatism and general feeling of despair characteristic of the age. The movement became popular on the continent solely because it dealt with the above themes, and these themes were close to the heart of the people.[46] The author feels that this movement is a form of

47

reduction-philosophy which is guilty of tremendous oversimplifications concerning the problems of living and being. Spier insists that the movement has minimized and at times overlooked the richness of life which "God has placed in created reality".[47] He feels that existentialism rejects the revelation of God in the holy Bible. The author states that existentialist philosophy is a limited one because it views the world only "as a pragmatic object, an object of our human action."[48] As recorded in the introduction, Spier insists that there is a theistic meaning behind the universe which existentialism rejects.

Spier summarizes the following points of emphasis as recurrent themes in existential literature:

1. there is a stress on the humanistic ideal of personality.

2. there is a stress on irrationalism.

3. there is a stress on radical subjectivism as the approach to philosophizing.

4. there is an underlying anthropologic concern that is basic.

5. existence is self-transcendence because man is not what he is.

6. there is a pessimistic view of life.

7. there is an aristocratic individualism for only a few individuals ever realize their authentic selfhood.

8. there is a basic split in man's personality between his authentic and unauthentic possibilities.

9. there is a super-scientific character about existentialism.

10. there is a stress on being-in-the-world; and the world is defined as the sphere of our actions.

11. there is a cleft between existence and the world, the two are mysteriously divided and do not share a common root.

12. there is an existential time which is man's time and is not scientific time.

13. to exist is to make responsible decisions.[49]

Spier is quite aware of the existential position that man is his own law giver, and is the sole individual required to live in confrontation with his own self. This requires an emphasis on intuitive self-knowledge which is also found in most of the existential literature.

The moments of truth in existentialism are its warning against the magic of rationality and, on the other hand, about the pitfalls of complete irrationality. Existentialism also contributes something positive when it takes its stand against neutralism in philosophy.[50] Existential by-products have proved valuable, for it has emphasized ontology and has forced some revitalized thinking in this area. Furthermore, existentialists have brought squarely into focus the burning question of what man's place in the universe really is. Finally, it has proven beneficial for it has again challenged the legalism rampant in contemporary Christianity.[51]

The movement must be rejected, according to Spier, because it defies the historical function of human nature. It exaggerates the function of philosophy in the life of man, and it rejects as unauthentic everything which does not fit into its frame of reference. Existentialism must be rejected because it lacks a unified vision of the entire created reality, and the writers in this field are much too narrow.[52]

Unlike the work of Spier or Allen, Ronald Grimsley attempted a straightforward exposition of existentialism in his book, *Existential Thought* written in 1955. By his own admission his work is not a critical evaluation or discussion of existentialism as a whole.[53] To the existentialists, according to Grimsley's interpretation, the problem of 'what' man is cannot be separated from that of 'how' he is, and the 'how' can better be approached through the individual man than man 'in general'. He quotes Lalande's statement, "Existence must be understood in the strong, concrete sense of living or lived reality, in opposition to abstractions and theories."[54] The emphasis on the 'how' explains the generous descriptive tendency in existential thought. Because the descriptive technique aims at covering all the basic human attitudes it necessarily includes more than the merely intellectual aspects of life. The emotional life of man must be understood. This in turn precipitates the existential stress on the affective nature of man, and also precipitates the condemnation of it as being irrational and nihilistic. In answer to the charge that existentialism is irrational, Grimsley emphasizes that one needs only to examine the work of Sartre or Heidegger to experience how clearly these writers use reason in presenting their position, and in trying to bring about a commitment on the part of their readers.[55]

Grimsley writes that all the existentialists are in agreement that man has freedom of choice; that there are no preconceived patterns to fit the future into; and that to exist means, for man, that he must act, that he must be involved in personal decision.[56]

The question about the degree to which one can talk meaningfully about existence divides the existentialists into two groups. Heidegger and Sartre, Grimsley interprets, feel that their philosophy can be expressed logically. Jaspers and Marcel feel that one can not systematize their philosophy of existence. Jaspers believes that such an attempt will eventually end in "shipwreck", and that the intellectual endeavor must finally give way to the experience of existence itself.[57]

Referred to previously is the D. J. B. Hawkins paper read to the Aquinas Society in 1954 and subsequently published as a book entitled — *The Meaning of Existentialism*. Like Spier, Hawkins is antagonistic towards existentialism because, among other things, he feels that its ideas have rashly restricted the use of the intellect, and indeed have come perilously close to throwing out the human intellect altogether. He states that all would be clarified if existentialists would stop and think calmly and dispassionately.[58] As stated before, he objects to existentialists delving into the mysterious, and he feels that the problem solving method will produce more fruit and is a more meaningful way to spend one's abilities. He furthermore objects to the fact that the existentialists complicate the world picture by refusing to accept the world with simplicity and gratitude, and he points out that there are no cheerful existentialists. Because of this pessimism, Hawkins writes that existentialists foster a decadent philosophy. He goes so far as to raise rhetorically the question as to whether the existentialists are trying to resolve the modern crisis or whether they are rejoicing in an unresolved crisis.[59]

Hawkins identifies Kierkegaard, Heidegger, Jaspers and Marcel as being existential thinkers. He feels that these men have reacted to the crisis of their time and that as the crisis becomes less acute, their thought will consequently become obscure, and definitely will appear overstrained. One real unique comment the author makes is that those philosophers who emphasize anxiety about nothingness confronting man must themselves be neurotic.[60]

One of the best integrated discussions of existentialism was undertaken by the realist philosopher, John Wild. Wild's book, *The Challenge of Existentialism*, is divided into two parts. The first part presents a systematic discussion of the main themes which one finds in the existential works. The second part seeks to integrate existentialism into the philosophy of realism. This portion could be discussed under the heading — existential realism. Existentialism, to Wild, is thus reduced to proper perspective, namely that of a supportive adjective, which in itself lends direction to a very old philosophical approach. According to Wild, the more important existentialists are Jaspers, Sartre, Marcel and Heidegger. Kierkegaard is discussed in an early chapter as the forebearer of the existential tide.

As stated in the introductory chapter of this thesis, Wild believes that existentialism is at present the most influential movement of contemporary thought in France and Western Germany. Wild concludes that existentialism is "little known and is largely ignored in our colleges and departments of philosophy" (in the United States) and it is his aim "to present a critical exposition of the phenomenological philosophy of existence."[61]

For Wild, the existentialists are not interested in "artificial

51

problems, nor in theoretical constructs. They are interested rather in the concrete data of immediate experience, and in describing these data so far as possible exactly as they are given. This is the phenomenological method."[62] One finds in existentialism a new empiricism and a new ontology. Their primary concern is to describe the constant conditions of existence which are the same for all men everywhere, and then to analyze these against authentic and inauthentic criteria.[63] In this way the existentialists have emphasized that all men 'exist,' but that they exist in different ways. Each one interacts with others and communicates his awareness of them. He not only comes to an end like other animals, he also knows that he must die.[64] These are important conditions under which all men must live and all men must react to.

Wild interprets the existentialists as emphasizing the importance of human awareness and action. Action is possible because of man's freedom to choose, and freedom to choose is valid only in ratio to one's ability to be aware, if indeed the two are not identical, as Sartre emphasizes. Under the topic 'human awareness', the existentialists have sought to respond to the deep moods of man — his grief, his dread, his anxiety. The inauthentic mode of living is most strikingly actualized when men try to evade the idea of possibility by misunderstanding themselves as things which are here and now, and whose possibilities, as far as they have them, are fixed and inflexible.[65]

In another chapter, Wild presents the existential ethic as a combination of integrity and decision. Man must be radically true to himself, and man must make decisions. The inauthentic person is undecided and unsure of himself, he is not only unsure of himself but he doubts the world in which he lives. The authentic person, in contrast, is sure of the whole of himself as revealed in the light of his past possibilities. He knows that his being is not circumscribed, but rather is stretched out ahead of him, is awaiting his decisive choice. He knows the risks that are involved in choice and he knows that in choice he becomes responsible for the whole of mankind, and he indeed dreads this burden.[66]

Wild believes that the following are weaknesses in existentialism:

The method:

...they have applied this method to human existence alone, and have paid relatively little attention to other levels and manifestations of being. They have given us no philosophy of nature, but only an anthropological fragment...

Brute facts, of course, must be described as they are given. This is a necessary first step, but it does not complete the work of understanding. Causes and reasons must also be given. The data must be explained in the light of these. Here the existentialists are very weak.

...There are many data which show that things depend on one another. The denial of any causal principle is an extremely dubious metaphysical assumption lacking empirical support, and implying the ultimate unintelligibility of the universe.[67]

Metaphysics:

As Jaspers says, for this existence to be achieved, is to cease to be.

Such a view as this, as is well known, is not only self-contradictory in being asserted; it is also false to the empirical data. ...Essence is coordinate with existence; one is never given without the other. To ignore either is to commit a grievous metaphysical mistake. ...the existentialists in various ways and to various degrees have fallen into it.[68]

Epistemology:

...But here again their intense reaction to a detached intellectualism has led them to an indefensible opposite extreme of antiintellectualism which unfortunately began with Kierkegaard himself.[69]

In discussing the epistemology of existentialism Wild states that both Sartre and Berdyaev, the Russian existentialist, reflect positions containing some truth, "but also dangerous exagger ation."

Ethics:

> But sometimes they (the existentialists) press
> their assertion of freedom to such lengths that
> it becomes fantastic and unbelievable. ... For
> any critical mind, such exaggerated statements
> tend rather to discredit the notion than to con
> firm it.
> ... No adequate or even noteworthy 'social
> philosophy has as yet come from existentialis
> sources. This is a striking weakness.[70]

As previously implied, Wild's text does not mention Martin Buber who is the most outstanding social philosopher of the existential movement.

The antithesis of Spier's discussion about the relationship be tween existentialism and Christianity is the edited work of Carl Michalson, published in 1956, and entitled simply *Christianity and the Existentialists*. This book presents the existentialists who have written from within the Christian tradition. The avowed atheists like Nietzsche, Sartre, Camus and Simon de Beauvoir are not included. Furthermore, the text excludes Buber and Jaspers for while they are theists they are not within the Christian church. Due to limitations in terms of structural organization, Dosto yevsky, Scheler, and Mounier, although they professed Christian ity and wrote as Christian existentialists, were not included. Søren Kierkegaard is discussed by H. Richard Neibuhr; Miguel Una muno is presented by John McKay; Nicolas Berdyaev is discussed by Matthew Spinka; Gabriel Marcel and Martin Heidegger are discussed by J. V. Casserly and Erich Dinkler respectively. Paul Tillich analyzes existential aspects of modern art. Stanley Hopper examines some of the existential aspects to be found in the writngs of the poets Hölderlin and Rilke. Each of the contributing authors are themselves influenced by existentialism or are noted existentialist proponents.

The first chapter is written by the editor in an attempt to define precisely what existentialism means. To Michalson a fair preliminary definition would simply be as follows:

Existentialism is a way of life which involves one's total self in an attitude of complete seriousness about himself.[71]

One is existing when one is self-consciously immersed in living, not merely thinking about living. The concept of the total self means that the individual is reacting with his mind, his glands, his neural system, as against a straight exercising of the prefrontal lobes, or whatever part of the mind is responsible solely for thinking.[72]

Existentialism, according to Michalson, is the first serious philosophy in the entire history of philosophy to place considerable trust in the subjective moods of the individual. The existing man must immerse himself in his moods to find within them a trustworthy index to reality.

To exist is to take seriously these messages from deep within oneself.[73]

To know and experience trustfulness in one's moods by necessity leads towards an emphasis on the individual, for the person would find it difficult to apply to his life the universally valid truths which come from mathematical and syllogistic reasoning.[74]

There is no pattern to which man can, must, or ought to conform or by which to judge himself.

A man may know himself by living his own life seriously and reflecting on it. To exist is to be unique.[75]

Michalson emphasizes that one would be mistaken to believe that this stressing of individualism necessarily precludes community participation or social relationships. When individuals come together, they would not, or should not, lose their individuality in a collective identity which has some mystical authority in its own right.[76]

To be certain, existentialism has flowered in the tragedy of the twentieth century. Michalson writes that the movement has stepped in to nurse an aching void, and to keep the wounds of man open until they can heal properly. The existentialists are trying to detour man from a "soma pill" vacation; rather they demand that man can be an authentic individual.[77]

Another writer who sought favorably to relate existentialism to the formation of a religious belief was David Roberts. Before Roberts could complete his book he died, and his work was finished by Roger Hazelton and published in 1957.

To the question of what existentialism is, Hazelton states that there is no definitive single answer, and that one should study each man who has been identified with existentialism.[78] Generally speaking, however, one may state that existentialism protests against intellectual and social forces that are destroying man's freedom. It calls men away from stifling abstractions and automatic conformity. The existential concern is to drive man back to his more basic inner, problems — what it means to be a self, how man ought to use his freedom, how man can find and keep the courage to face death. The existential concern is that each individual wrestle with these problems until he has grown (chosen himself) into personal authenticity, instead of simply conforming to the dictates of others.[79] To summarize, existentialists are interested in arousing in the reader a spiritual struggle, not in aiding him to purvey a set of findings. In order to do this, the existential writer attempts to offer the reader a drastic, realistic introduction to the problems of human existence.

Hazelton emphasizes that in spite of the challenging message contained in the existential literature, it is still not a self-sufficient philosophy, but is merely a corrective. It will clear away philosophical underbrush and make each basic philosophy come face to face with the urgent questions of life. It, in itself, does not answer the problems, but it seeks merely to bring man to the point where he sees the momentousness of a decision, and that he must make it and be responsible for it, even if he abides in indecision.[80]

The key existentialists discussed by the Roberts-Hazelton combine are Pascal, Kierkegaard, Heidegger, Sartre, Jaspers and Marcel.

In 1958 two books appeared which present existentialism anew to the English-reading public. The first is a reader, *Four Existential Theologians* by Will Herberg. Sampling of the writings of Jacques Maritain (normally considered a Thomist), Nicolas Berdyaev, Martin Buber and Paul Tillich are discussed. It might be mentioned that these men represent the following traditions respectively: Roman Catholicism, Eastern Orthodoxy; Judaism and Christianity. The four hold in common their ontological approach to philosophy, for each basically attempts to analyze true being.[81] The writings of these authors are characterized by emphasis on experimental concreteness, personal concern and commitment, the uniqueness of the existing individual, the primacy of enacted being over the mere concept of being, and a subjective approach to the problems under discussion. These traits, Herberg feels, are characteristics of existentialism.[82] Furthermore, each of the four men referred to his own thinking as being existential in terms of his emphasis on human existence and personal involvement.

One finds a personalistic emphasis in existential writings, for all insist on the primacy of the person over all subject matter. In dealing with the person, these four are one in insisting that true personal being is fulfilled not in isolation, but in community. To them, the term community involves mutual relationships of man with man, rather than something which is institutionalized.[83] Each of the authors whose works are sampled in this book has an active social concern. All are opposed to the depersonalization and dehumanization tendencies of modern mass society. Maritain writes of a Christian democracy, Berdyaev of a "personalist socialism", Buber of a "true community", and Tillich of a "religious socialism". Finally, each of these men is caught up in a "apologetic-cultural interest", for each has an ardent desire to establish the relevance of their faith to the intellectual and cultural life of the time.[84]

In a different direction from the previous books discussed in this chapter is one undertaken by Rollo May, Ernest Angel and Henri Ellenberger. It is entitled, *Existence: A New Dimension in Psychiatry and Psychology*. This text is an introductory survey of the existential influence in the field of psychology and psychiatry, part of which is written by men who consider themselves existential psychoanalysts. Existential psychoanalysis takes into account the entire existence of the individual. It is aware that one individual may live in two or more different worlds, and that sometimes these worlds are even conflicting with each other. The analysis attempts to reconstruct the development and transformations of the patient's worlds.[85]

Binswanger (a contributor to the book who considers himself an existential analyst) states that the method does not seem different on the surface from the usual psychoanalytical situation. However, in this form of therapy, the reconstruction of experience is much more than the academic exercise that it often is in the Freudian approach. Furthermore, the analyst never seeks to consider a symptom in terms of understanding its bizarre nature but rather to understand the particular world of experience which it is cast against.[86]

The existential analysts give attention to five types of being characteristic of man's existence. The first is the existential mode which is basically the feeling of the individual that he is related to his fellow man, and is actively concerned in building a meaningful community. The dual existential mode is the stage in which the individual comes into an experience of intimacy with another individual. This stage may be characterized by the I-Thou concept of Martin Buber to be discussed later. The plural mode is the existence of the individual characterized by struggle and competition. The singular mode is found mostly in the person's feeling of narcissism, feelings in which he stresses his uniqueness and in which he relates solely to himself. The final mode is the anonymous mode in which man loses himself in collectivity by conforming to that which is in his environment. An existential neurosis may be classified as the individual's inability to see meaning in life as he abides in the inauthentic existential modality.[87]

The danger of existential analysis is that it might become generalized, as the Freudians tend to err in the direction of, rather than dealing with the particular being of the person in his own situation. This is basically the major contribution of the movement, that is, "it understands the patient as an individual who is really 'being'. It does not deny the validity of dynamisms and the study of specific behavior patterns ... but these must be understood only in the context of the structure of the existence of the person."[88]

This work considers Buber, Marcel, Kierkegaard, Sartre, Heidegger, Berdyaev, and Tillich in the stream of existentialism. Ellenberg, Binswanger and Jaspers are identified as existential psychoanalysts.

The existential therapy may be summarized as follows:

1. The existential analysts are not generally concerned with technical matters, nor will they specifically develop a stereotyped method. They use variable techniques all of which are aimed at illuminating the patient's being-in-the-world.

2. Psychological dynamisms always take their meaning from the existential situation of the patient's own intimate life.

3. There is an emphasis on the present in the analysis. The therapeutic relationship is a real one, it is not a shadowy sparring characteristic of the Freudian analyst who sits behind the patient. Jaspers insists that in the relationship the analyst's full human presence must be felt.

4. Important to receive careful analysis are those ways in which the patient destroys his presence to himself.

5. A vital aim is then to aid the patient to experience hi existence as real.

6. Finally, there is a stress on personal commitment. "Trutl exists only when the individual produces it in action", state Kierkegaard. Decision precedes knowledge. The patien must take a decisive attitude towards existence.[89]

The therapy is designed to aid the patient in choosing some thing that will come from within himself, which will be challeng ing enough to him so that he can commit himself to it in a cours of definite action.[90]

The text concludes with several case studies which illumine th existential concern.

One of the most recent discussions of existentialism is one whicl attempts to derive educational implications from the philosophy In the first chapter of this thesis the educational implications o George Kneller's book, *Existentialism and Education*, were ex amined. Kneller's book, however, is more of an introduction t existentialism as a whole, and thus merits some consideration i this chapter. The author states that his book is written primaril for teachers and laymen who are interested in educational prob lems. The treatment is not meant to be deeply philosophica but approaches the subject matter in the style the expectec audience is able to comprehend.[91] Like Wild, Kneller rejects th thesis that existentialism is a systematic philosophy, but contend that it permeates philosophies and encourages one to philos ophize. He observes that no existentialist has written about th problems of education, but this does not disconcert him as h accepts the idea that it is the educational philosopher's res ponsibility to establish the relation between existentialism anc education.[92]

Kneller believes that existentialism has several inherent weak nesses. These are as follows:

1. Existentialist criticism is leveled at fundamentally stag-

nant or repressive societies. . . . In a freedom-loving society its preachments are less poignant.

2. A second weakness lies in existentialism's attitude towards scientific inquiry. . . . It is not the discoveries of science that are malignant but the uses to which they are put by human beings.

3. Existentialism's third weakness lies in its peculiar understanding of sound values and community relations.

4. A fourth weakness, closely related to the above, derives from existentialism's very inwardness and subjectivity. . . . But introspection and self-analysis cannot take place in a vacuum. . . .

   To claim that no value system or structure exists is to declare a state of chaos.[93]

Kneller does not believe that existentialism is all evil or misleading to those who are influenced by it. There are some benefits derived from existential thinking. These are:

1. But existentialists have many gifts to offer, among them their cry against individual complacency and their demand for intensive personal commitment.

2. A second contribution . . . originates in its protest against sterile abstractions, pure logic, and objective absolutes, substituting instead an emphasis upon the concrete and the individual.

3. The third contribution is that no doctrine exists that more greatly exalts the value of the individual human personality.

4. A fourth contribution . . . is existentialism's stress on the emotional life of man, which is considered to be far more valuable than the so-called intellectual aspects of human behavior.[94]

It becomes obvious from surveying the attributes of existentialism

61

as presented by Kneller that any vital philosophy might also enrich its position in these directions. Thus Kneller is able to conclude that "if existentialism has done no more, it has loosened the rigidity and petrifying effect of many forms of intellectualism and impelled us to examine more critically our devotion to traditional subject matter structure, systematic types of logical thinking, and neat hierarchies of absolutes."[95]

Kneller chooses to discuss Kierkegaard, Heidegger, Jaspers, Sartre and Marcel as the main existentialists of the day. He has difficulty in including Nietzsche, but does discuss his philosophy extensively. He also associates Tillich, Buber, Niebuhr, portions of the Hindu Upanishads, the Buddhist emphasis (probably Mayahana) and St. Augustine with the existential outlook.

Whom do the authorities in existentialism consider to be existentialists? Chart I presents graphic evidence that most authorities accept Kierkegaard, Heidegger, Sartre, Jaspers, Marcel and Buber as the most prominent existentialists. Usually Nietzsche, Dostoyevsky and Kierkegaard are included among the prophets of the movement. Although Buber has been associated with the movement since 1948 among authorities writing for the English market, only recently has his name systematically been associated with existentialism along with Paul Tillich and Nicolas Berdyaev.

CHART I

	Kierkegaard	Heidegger	Sartre	Jaspers	Marcel	Beauvoir	Camus	Buber	Unamuno	Berdyaev	Tillich	Ortega y Gasset	Nietzsche	Dostoevsky
1. Grene	x	x	x	x	x									
2. Kuhn		x	x	x	x	x	x	x	x	x	x	x		
3. Ruggiero	x	x		x	x									
4. Mounier	x	x	x	x	x			x						
5. Wahl	x	x	x	x										
6. Kuhn	x	x	x		x			x						
7. Collins	x		x	x	x									
8. Blackham	x	x	x	x	x								x	
9. Holden	x												x	x
10. Allen	x	x	x	x	x									
11. Spier	x	x	x	x									x	
12. Grimsly		x	x	x	x									
13. Hawkins	x	x		x	x									
14. Wild	x	x		x	x									
15. Michalson	x	x	x	x	x	x	x	x	x	x				x
16. Roberts	x	x	x	x	x									
17. Herberg								x		x	x			
18. May	x	x	x	x	x			x		x	x			
19. Kneller	x	x	x	x	x			x			x	x		

1. Scheler is mentioned by Mounier and Michalson.
2. Kafka is mentioned by Holden.
3. Pascal is named by Roberts.
4. Maritain is discussed by Herberg.
5. Michalson identifies Mounier as an existentialist.
6. Ellenber and Biswanger are identified as existential analysts.
7. Spier discusses the Dutchman Loen and mentions Lavelle.

CHAPTER III

THE EXISTENTIALIST'S CONCEPT OF THE INDIVIDUAL

Part I: Søren Kierkegaard

One hundred years ago, in a rather remote corner of Europe a Danish thinker challenged the "System" of Europe's dominant philosopher, Wilhelm Hegel. Søren Kierkegaard's voice was a cry in the wilderness, for save in his own homeland, his utterances were ignored. Even in Denmark, although he enjoyed some notoriety for his wit, and was a sought-after speaker for "folk-school" commencements,[1] he was ridiculed and made a laughing stock by the popular scandal sheet, The Corsair.[2]

Almost one hundred years elapsed before the impact of Kierkegaard's thought began to inspire philosophers and theologians on the Continent and to influence divinity school students throughout the United States.[3] Scholars who have dealt with the theology, the philosophy, or the thinking of Kierkegaard have found it necessary to tie in his life with his writings in order to grasp the meaning of his philosophy more thoroughly. Søren Kierkegaard believed that he wrote in order to save his life in the sense that Scheherazade had to tell stories to save her life.[4]

Many students have been confused by the apparent contradictions which are to be found in Kierkegaard's writings. The Danish author's main thought is to be found in writings to which he affixed his name. He disclaims responsibility for the content of any of his writings that are signed with one of his many pseudonyms.[5] In his pseudonymous works, Kierkegaard tried to present the intellectual climate as it was in his era. Wishing to hold himself aloof from his generation, he preferred to portray it from the viewpoint of one of its members who, being in every sense a part of it, believed in it. For this purpose he projected himself into the role of such a person, gave him a name, and permitted him to describe the conditions which were evident around him. Kierkegaard's serious works, which reflect his own beliefs and which are pertinent to this study, are his *Journals* and his book, *Point of View as an Author.*

The Stages Along Man's Way

According to Kierkegaard's analysis there are three primary stages through which man evolves in order to become "the individual." The Dane divided his writings into three main categories paralleling the stages along life's way. The aesthetic and ethical stages are best described in Kierkegaard's *Either-Or,* written under the pseudonym Victor Eremita and in *Stages Along Life's Way,* signed by the name Hilarius Bookbinder.

Either-Or was the work which made Kierkegaard well known in Copenhagen. He himself was not a little distressed by the fact that his aesthetic works made him more famous and had more of an impact upon the populace of Denmark than his later religious works which summarize the third stage along life's way. The particular section of *Either-Or* which caught the public's fancy was the Diary of a Seducer. This work created considerable antagonism towards him on the part of respectable society because it paralleled too closely his own engagement, which was broken off very tragically by the author.[6]

The seducer, to Kierkegaard, perfectly portrays a man who exists in the aesthetic stage. He seeks only his personal pleasure. Kierkegaard did not permit his villain to actually seduce his victim, but rather to bring the woman to the point that she wanted him to seduce her, and to volunteer herself for such a relationship. At this point the seducer took great delight in breaking off the relationship, for indeed he had seduced already the woman's soul.

Perhaps the best characterization of the aesthetic stage is to say that life is lived only on the surface of the 'now', of the present, with little or no regard for the past or for the future. Basically this stage is similar to the popular conception of the Epicurean philosophy as being one of solely "eating, drinking and being merry for tomorrow we die." The primary difference between the two philosophies is that in the aesthetic stage the prospect of death is necessarily hidden from the person's awareness. Although the asthetic stage may take several forms it is basically the striving to satisfy one's own pleasure immediately and to secure imminent happiness. This stage does not permit man to realize his full potentialities, for here he is limited to vanity and to the search for pleasure. The stage is necessarily divorced from any moral or ethical struggle which life might involve. The person, in this first immediacy, does not seek to expose himself, and therefore keeps his interests unrevealed for fear he might be seduced into responsible living. Even his laugh is a mask, and thus, the aesthetic personality is almost entirely a 'persona', for he cannot open himself up spontaneously in order to be a real person.[7]

The aesthetic personality has no ability to cope with time because he is always forcing himself to live in the present moment. He has no true understanding of his past or of his future. The aesthetic is like a 'traveling scholastic' who is running through life but who is failing to grasp its true meaning.[8] When this person achieves the pleasures which he is seeking, he finds that they do not satisfy him, and he is disappointed. The disappointment which the individual in this stage experiences will often reduce his buoyant personality to a generally unhappy state, which often precipitates melancholy. The person in this mode of life finds himself, more often than not, in a state of boredom. This emotional condition, boredom, cannot be escaped by one who is living in the first immediacy, no matter how diversified his activities become. Too often he will find himself to be hollow, and only a shell of a man, and this too will distress the aesthetic.[9]

The recurrent dissatisfaction with life which is characteristic of the aesthetic will cause him to question the meaning of his life. With the rude beginnings of this philosophical questioning there awakens in him an interest in other men, and thus in society in general. With his becoming aware that he has a relationship to his fellowman and to his society there develops a consciousness in himself that he has a self. To Kierkegaard, to be aware of oneself means also to be aware that one is responsible for one's selfness.[10] The feeling of responsibility leads the person into the second stage along life's way, which is the ethical stage.

The aesthetic stage, strictly speaking, is not abandoned, but is relegated to a relative or inferior position.[11] Man's existence in the 'now' is abandoned as man finds that he has a history, and indeed that he is historically conditioned. He becomes aware of the influence upon his life of the past, and of the present historical moment upon his future activities, and indeed, happiness. Furthermore he realizes that he can be a director of the historical moment in which he is caught up.[12] As matter of fact, he realizes that whether he wants to be or not, he is free to influence the historical situation and that the flow of history is influenced by him no matter what he does. The self therefore becomes responsible for its behavior, and is no longer detached in momentary existence.

In answering the question for whom tolls the bell, the person in the ethical stage decides that it tolls for him, for he is a part of the larger whole which is humanity. As a part of humanity, he begins to create for himself a 'universal man.' The ethical person becomes subjected to what is universally valid rather than what is advantageous for him as a single being.[13] The ethical person thinks not in terms of his own welfare alone, but instead in terms of that which is good for universal man. He believes that there must be a universal ethic, based on universal laws which make certain behavior right or wrong, good or bad. The man of ethics believes that it is his responsibility to discern right from wrong, the good from the bad, the godly from the sinful before he acts, so that his actions will always be rooted in that which is right and therefore noble. He does not believe that his ethical inquiry will be in vain, but rather that an ethical judgement can be rendered which will, in a pure sense, be appropriate in every situation.

The ethical man is not unaware that at times there will appear to be conflicting interests in the ethical sphere, but he does believe that it is possible to untangle the conflict according to a hierarchy of moral evaluation. When in doubt, the ethical man will rely on what man today thinks about the problem, and he will accept the majority opinion.

Instead of wrestling with ethical problems most people lazily abide in the dawning of the ethical stage waiting for others to tell them what to do, and only a few individuals will travel as far as the religious stage along life's way. No individual maintains himself in the religious stage very long; he continually slips back into an advanced ethical stage. To exist permanently in the religious stage would be as impossible as to exist on a diet of Holy Sacrament. It is in the fleeting moment of man's ascendancy into the religious stage that one will discern Kierkegaard's ideal man, 'the individual.'[14]

To be in the religious stage, 'the individual' must rise above the universally valid and subordinate himself to the absolute, which is God.[15] The religious stage was first demonstrated by Abraham's willingness to sacrifice Isaac. To Kierkegaard, there could be no ethical justification for this potential act of horror. The act would involve the teleological suspension of ethics.[16] As a result of the conflict between the absolute particularization and the universal generalization, between the ethical and the religious modes of life, fear and trembling arises in the being of 'the individual.'

Critics of Kierkegaard have challenged him to explain how 'the individual' knows the voice of God, how he knows the will of God. Kierkegaard's answer is that 'the individual' chooses to recognize that which he believes to be the command of God to be the command of God.[17] It is an act of free choice on the part of the person. His decisions, in the religious stage, are entirely his own. This act of free choice is an unknown experience to the aesthetic person who does not know what choice means because he is unaware of his own existence as a self. The experience is unknown to the ethical man because he has subordinated himself to what he believes is a universally valid system. The religious man, however, takes a leap of faith into an encounter with God; he chooses to confront God, he chooses to be an identity, he chooses to be an individual before God. To be certain, the religious individual is immersed in dread because he knows that he might choose irresponsibly and according to the dictates of his own self-love.[18] The religious stage does not offer man the security of the universal. Many men aspire to an encounter with God, but few are willing to leave the security of the universal.

Each act of choice taken from the religious point of view is valid only in one situation, thus the religious person must be continuously choosing himself as a self before God in order to sustain such a relationship. It would not be enough for the prophet to once and for all say, "Here am I Lord, send me!" One must continually be willing to go forth, to take the next step. In a way, this helps to guard the individual against irrevocable erroneous choices. His choices are not made once and for all and then acted upon without further consideration. The individual must continually reconsider and rechoose his action, for no action acquires being except that it be continuously chosen.

The religious individual lives in the particular situation, in the particular moment. This bears a certain similarity to living in the aesthetic stage in which the person lives only in a particular moment. The essential difference is that the religious individual brings into the present the past and the future in proper proportion. Even his experiences on the aesthetic level and the ethical level are included in the religious act. The religious personality is not without ethical insight as he chooses, he has merely transcended his ethical understanding.[19]

The religious individual, knowing that his existence is limited by death, realizes that he is a traveler in a strange land. He knows that he is fettered in the finite, yet in his human frailty he is confronted by the absolute concept of God.[20] Like Isaiah, he knows the feeling "woe is me, for I am a man of unclean lips." He knows that his every act is inadequate because he does not possess omniscience for evaluating his every act, or even one grand act. He realizes, but accepts the fact, that before God he is always wrong.[21] Nonetheless, even though suffering under the burden of his inferiority and in great fear and trembling, he chooses to approach God. Before God he is alone, he is unclothed, the depths of his heart searched. He finds no hiding place for any undesirable aspect of his personality. In the opened relationship with God, not only does God know man's heart, but man also comes to know himself as he is. As God penetrates the innermost regions of man's being, as God illumines the dark places of man's soul, man learns facts that he has never known about himself and he comes to see himself for the first time. In the presence of God man finds that his inevitable self-love tries to close himself up. "What struggle is so protracted, so terrible, so complicated, as the battle of self-love in its own defences?"[22] However, the love of God breaks through the defenses of man's self-love and thereby is able to maintain a spontaneous relationship with man when he chooses to meet God.

Requisites for Becoming 'The Individual'

Søren Kierkegaard refused to become definite about the personality of 'the individual.' He did not want his concept of 'the individual' to be reduced to a paragraph in a system.[23] It is a difficult task to clarify the nature of 'the individual' because he escapes classification and analysis simply because he is an individual.

Yet, because the matter of being 'the individual' is the most decisive thing in life, because one fails in his earthly mission if the courageous step of becoming 'the individual' is not taken, the Danish author did seek to create an image of this person so that he could be portrayed to the Danish people. Kierkegaard believed that the importance of 'the individual' was decisive for Christianity, and that religion will stand or fall with the presence or the lack of such a personality.[24] It is not a matter of numbers, for Christianity will be preserved if one 'individual' chooses Christ. This in turn has meaning for Kierkegaard's literary endeavor. He was not interested in writing for the mass man, he was trying to stimulate the thought of the few, even the one, who might be 'goaded' into the act of choosing to be 'the individual.'

'The individual' must determine his relationship to the universal by his relationship to the absolute, and cannot approach God in reverse order as does the ethical man. If the equation (absolute to universal) should be reversed, then the universal would shape the absolute, God. In that man interprets what the universal is, according to his universal needs, this would pose the absurdity of man determining the personality of God and the nature of His being.[25]

Kierkegaard felt that 'the individual' in the modern age would be like the citizen who singlehandedly held the foot bridge against an army at the battle of Thermopylae.[26] It is the task of 'the individual' to stand firm against the collectivists of the twentieth century (nineteenth in Kierkegaard's case) who are trying to standardize conduct and for that matter, God. Kierkegaard, who aspired to be 'the individual', believed that he was that soldier, and that he was holding the bridge of Christianity against Christendom and Hegelianism.

The concept of 'the individual' is not limited to a few, although only a few attain the being. Everyone is or can be 'the individual.' Everyone has the opportunity and the ability to choose for himself eternal validity.[27] The reason why most men do not become 'individuals' is that they lack courage. They may be overcome at the bridge by the enemy, and as in Ibsen's *Brand*, not many are willing to die for a cause that they do not know will be successful in the long run. Courage, in Kierkegaard's sense, is the self-affirmation of man's essential nature; it is the will to be oneself, and this means to follow one's inner aims. To follow one's inner aims is to go against the grain of the universal and the masses, and indeed such a person risks becoming an isolate.[28]

To follow his inner aims requires 'the individual' to know himself. To know oneself requires the understanding that the human self is a self which has been created by God, yet is still a self-constituted entity.[29] It is the knowledge that one is an autonomous self created by God that makes possible the recognition of the self which otherwise is hidden. The more one feels oneself to be, the more consciousness of self he realizes, the more he realizes his real self is confronted by God.[30] Therefore self-awareness is becoming aware of one's individuality in the eternal field. Although 'the individual' feels himself inferior to God, and infinitely, absolutely under God's obligation, he feels unconditionally accepted and needed by God, which is a paradox.

Carl Rogers states that successful psychotherapy brings the individual to the point where he is capable of undertaking explorations of increasingly strange and unknown feelings in himself. These explorations are possible only because the person gradually realizes that he is accepted unconditionally. He finds himself experiencing these feelings fully and completely in the therapy relationship, so that for the moment he is his fear, or his anger, or his tendencies.[31] To Rogers this is the experience of the individual before the therapist, to Kierkegaard this is the experience of 'the individual' before God. 'The individual' is more capable of being a whole person in this relationship and is more able to translate his self-understanding into new modes of action.

The act of choosing the self, of self-knowledge or of self-acceptance is not definitively conditioned in a momentary conversion. 'The individual's' existence is an experience, or a process of sustained becoming. Man himself is continuously evolving. It is essential to choose the self in every moment, in every new situation for life is a moving dynamic experience and the self itself is evolving.

It is not enough merely to state that one must know himself for the problem is — how does one begin to know himself? The knowledge of one's self is based on the experience of love.[32] 'The individual' starts becoming an individual when he loves himself which is to say, when he accepts himself. This sounds paradoxical because it was stated that love of the self prevents or seeks to prevent the person from attaining the religious stage. The basic problem in this paradox involves a breakdown in communications for the same word is being used with two different meanings. Man exists at different stages along life's way. In the ethical stage man's true self is pushed into the background while he seeks to adapt to a universal concept of behavior. This universal concept of behavior tends to develop into a 'functional autonomy' which has little to do with the real self of the person. It is equipped with self-protective devices and cultural reenforcements so that it tends to reject any changes in its nature. To utilize the terms of Snygg and Combs, the universal personality seeks to defend itself from being hurt and to enhance itself over what it has been.[33] This universal self is similar to Karen Horney's presentation of the 'idealized self.'[34] It is a love of this idealized ethical self which hinders one from advancing into the religious stage. The love which is necessary for the development of 'the individual' is a basic feeling of love towards one's essential self. Kierkegaard accepts the idea that man cannot love at all unless he has been loved first.[35] To Kierkegaard this love could originate only from God and would act in accord with the New Testament understanding of God's love and man's relationship to it. Love of oneself is made possible only by the love of God, who accepts man for what he is. In that man is loved unconditionally by God, he can accept himself and feel that he is lovable in spite of himself and his fallibility. If one does not know himself to be in a relationship with God, then he does not conceive himself as being loved. If man knows that God loves him then he knows that his own self has value and is therefore worth affirming.

Love is an essential ingredient in the man who would be 'the individual.' This love will be expressed first as a love for oneself as a result of the realization that one is loved by God, secondly it will involve loving God and finally it will culminate in loving one's neighbor. One loves one's neighbor partly because God loves one's neighbor, but also because 'the individual' is full of love which in itself seeks an object. As stated, it is important for a person to develop love for himself in terms of his worth as an individual, this love is not something which is spontaneously there, but rather must be learned. One must learn to love himself.

When 'the individual' loves himself, he feels himself to be of value, to have an unconditional worth as a personality. He will not waste his life in frivolity. "When the busy man wastes his time and energy on vain and unimportant projects is this not because he has not rightly learned to love himself?"[36]

The love of 'the individual' is not an eros love, but rather it is an agape love. 'The individual' is not seeking to enhance or defend himself because he is unconditionally accepted in the presence of the only authority which matters. He is therefore capable of loving others without expecting a reward.

'The Individual's Relationship to His Society

In speaking of the love of 'the individual' some have sensed that there is a quality of warmth about the personality of such a person. Semantically, Kierkegaard's term 'the individual' is a cold term which is suggestive of a stone wall, an isolate, a solitary figure. T. H. Croxall suggests that Kierkegaard really meant person rather than individual. The word for person and for individual are interchangeable in Danish. Kierkegaard's 'individual' is very much related to God, to his neighbor and to himself. He is not an isolate; he is not cold; he is a figure of warmth, concern and above all he is sensitive to the way of life he has chosen. In that 'the individual' will not intentionally waste time, he will seek a vocation which has meaning, which affords him a chance to be creative and to express his abundant feelings of love.[37] Kierkegaard accepts the Lutheran dictum that man's vocation ought to be a divine vocation.[38]

'The individual' knows the rewards which society bestows on the person who belongs, who basks in the warmth of fellowship, and who accepts the universal. He knows also that higher than the universal, than social acceptance, winds a solitary path which is narrow and steep. He knows that to climb this 'high' way will mean that he will lose contact with the average and the acceptable, that he will walk alone and that he may not meet a single traveller along the way of his life. He will often find himself unable to communicate intelligently with anyone, and because of this lack of proper communication, humanly speaking, Kierkegaard believed, he will appear to be crazy.[39] Yet 'the individual' knows where he is and how he is related to man because he has chosen his route. He realizes that the more the eternal stirs within him, the mightier will be his struggle as he attempts to forge ahead, alone save for the presence of God. He knows that in the universal setting he will be considered a failure, and that a man who strives in the temporal will seemingly achieve more than he. Yet he realizes that in a spiritual sense he would experience a wasting sickness if he did not climb the higher way, if he did not experience the feeling of risking.[40] The man who makes no mistakes, and therefore suffers no punishment, is making no venture in life and therefore is actually making no progress in life. 'The individual' ventures out into life in faith, beyond the ken of reason, beyond the security of knowing what the next step is to be.

'The individual' believes that man must be willing to make every sacrifice in order to proclaim the 'truth', and to do this he must conversely be unwilling to make the least sacrifice of the 'truth'. To take this position in regard to 'truth' (as 'the individual' interprets it) will result in eventual aloneness for to participate in the group involves accommodation, a leveling process no matter how minor. Any accommodation of the 'truth' is untruth, according to Kierkegaard.[41] The major difference between 'the individual' and the group is that the former must understand himself and know how to make distinctions no matter how trivial they may appear to be, while the group tends to gloss over the trivial and make decisions only when major issues imperil the group.

The 'truth' which is mentioned above is undefined for it will be experienced by 'the individual' in a direct encounter with God, and therefore is not yet available for discussion and definition. There is also an historical truth which has been handed down through the ages from 'the individual' of one era to 'the individual' of the next generation. A record of this truth can be found in the Bible, especially in the Gospels. To Kierkegaard, when the Gospels speak, they speak to 'the individual'; they do not speak about we men or to the group; they speak to 'the individual' and they command obedience.[42] The Bible is tribulation to man for its demands are mighty. To Kierkegaard, most people interpret the Bible aesthetically in order to escape the Biblical imperatives, or else they interpret it and then reinterpret it until it is filtered into the realm of placid possibility which means that then men could live by it without having their daily lives greatly affected by it.[43]

'The individual' who chooses to stand for 'truth' must oppose all leveling processes and therefore must stand apart from any collective activity. 'The individual' who is responsible only to himself before the Absolute is not responsible to 'the geese', to the crowds which characterized living in Kierkegaard's day.[44] The group resents anyone, who will not accommodate himself to their position in democratic agreement. A survey of history offers ample proof that the group resentment can be so great that it is willing to kill 'the individual' who will not compromise. The crowd is made up of persons who do not have the courage to choose for themselves, and they resent anyone who has. 'The constant nagging reminder that they are failing to realize their individuality' reminds them of what they should be; his life is a eternal destiny or validity. To Kierkegaard, the crowd is sought after for it offers a person mutual support in his despair of not having the courage to choose for himself. This despair, Kierkegaard felt, is a sickness unto death.[45] Yet, submergence in the group fails to provides the sought after security. When 'the individual' appears he casts the failure of the group to provide real security the member seeks into bold relief.

The question occurred to Kierkegaard as to how far the 'individual' ought to go in open defiance of the group. Should he become a martyr? The problem for Kierkegaard was not so much whether he should die for what he believes, but rather whether he should make others guilty of murder. On the other hand, one who is put to death for 'truth' accomplishes four things. He remains true to himself, he has fulfilled absolutely his duty towards 'truth', he has succeeded, perhaps in awakening the people and thus helps 'truth' prevail, and finally, he stands as an awakening example for succeeding generations. Although 'the individual' is responsible for increasing the guilt of a persecuting crowd, in the noblest sense of serving 'truth,' he is innocent of increasing the guilt.[46]

In Kierkegaard's era, the problem was not one of whether a person might be put to death as a result of clinging to a position which was socially unpopular but rather of having to submit to the cross of public opinion, especially ridicule. To Kierkegaard 'the individual' does have the responsibility of not waving a red flag in the face of the crowd. He should avoid any incident which might raise the ire of the crowd unnecessarily. Nevertheless when 'truth' is at stake, it must not be compromised.

'The individual' and the true Christian dwell in truth. It is possible for the latter not to be 'the individual'.[47] If these two persons come into contact with each other, they have no right to force the martyrdom of the other. Neither 'the individual' nor the Christian should seek to force his own opinion upon the other.[48]

'The Individual' and Sin and His Need for Confession

'The individual' feels no sense of superiority over others because he is constantly aware that he is a sinner. In fact, his consciousness of sin is so great that he often feels himself to be the greatest of all sinners because he knows himself so well.[49] He does not state that he is a sinner with his tongue in his cheek, nor will he attempt to level the resultant dread by comparing himself with the multitude, and then feeling that he is better than the rest, as the pharisee might do. 'The individual' does not stand in the market place and announce that he is a sinner. He does not believe that he has the time to tell others of his condition for he knows that he must already be actively engaged in the present moment and not reflect on his past errors. It is not even a simple question of repenting for he knows that he can do nothing about his own sinfulness. 'The individual' must confess to God, not for God's enlightenment, but for the sake of his own self-validation. This confession cannot be a mere enumeration of particular sins, but should reflect an understanding of an accounting before God of the continuity of the sinful condition in which he exists.[50] In that he is aware of the constant state of sin in his being, he feels that he is nothing before God, and that he is constantly in the wrong. However, even though he might be nothing he does stand before God. He has the ability, even the right to confront God, to speak to God, even though he be the most down-trodden person on earth. Kierkegaard stressed that 'the individual' would eventually accept his unacceptableness before God because God, paradoxically, accepts him as an individual.[51]

It is interesting to note that the therapeutical approach of either Carl Rogers or Harry Stack Sullivan accepts the thesis that it is most difficult for an individual to help himself without the aid of an expert therapist. The essential purpose of the therapist, according to Rogers, is to accept the patient as being a valid person no matter what he does or says during the therapy session. It will take many hours of therapy for the patient to become convinced that the therapist will accept him and when this insight is fully understood, then the patient relaxes and tends to develop the potential in him which was smothered by his fictitious self.[52]

According to Kierkegaard, before a man is able to repent his guilt must stand out vividly.[53] This statement also is underscored by Rogers who states that before successful therapy can be undertaken, the client must feel that the pain of what he is doing is greater than the pain which he would feel after exposing those experiences he is now trying to hide from himself which are the primary cause of his personality trouble. Harry Stack Sullivan states that the self-system (a defensive set on the part of the personality of the individual to meet situations of threat or stress which has been developed since anxiety provoking situations in infancy) does not permit one to be exposed to a lessening of euphoria, and is thus opposed to the feeling of guilt. This self-system attempts to shield the personality from any realization of the personality's failures or sins. The sense of the failure of the self-system must stand out vividly before a man will evaluate it and seek to correct its manipulation of his being.[54] To Kierkegaard no sense of failure can be greater than the failure of the self-system when it faces its own extinction in death. No bowstring can be drawn so tight, and can speed the arrow so powerfully, as the thought of death. Life becomes earnest when confronted by death. Death is the teacher of earnestness, and it leaves man to search out himself and his relationship to what lies beyond, to what he has already accomplished and to extinction itself. This is so because death and procrastination are mortal enemies.[55] Procrastination is the main reason that man does not seek to know himself as an individual who participates in an eternal situation. Men characteristically put off decision and action until a more appropriate time when it will be, they feel, less inconvenient, or less painful, to act or to even decide.

Death, through earnestness, teaches man that he has no time to waste in his effort to know himself and his possible meaning in life. Death strips man of all his defenses. In death all men are equal. In death man is forced to cast off all of his persons and to be himself. He is forced to die alone and to abandon the security of his group.[56]

Kierkegaard analyzed the dread of death as being the dread of freedom.[57] Man has not been free in his self-defensive system, he has not been opened to experience. He has not chosen to be true to himself, to validate himself or to know himself and thus he faces the experience of death without personal unity or understanding.

Kierkegaard accepted his responsibility to explain how the false self-system developed. He linked it with his concept of sin. Kierkegaard did not believe that man is innately sinful, but that he acquires the sinful condition. Basically, man is born in a state of innocence.[58] Innocence is not an exacting state, however, and it becomes a state which precipitates boredom in the person. Boredom, Kierkegaard stressed, is the root of all evil. Not only is boredom associated with innocence, ignorance is also a by-product of innocence. In innocence man is not determined by spiritual or intellectual reason but is determined in the immediate unity of his natural biological condition and his external situation. In innocence there is no experience of good or evil; there is not even any striving of the organism for future goals. Because of the lack of the foregoing facts, the innocent person is, for all practical purposes, nothing; he is a non-being, or at best, his being has not come into existence. Nothingness, which is the experience of non-being, produces anxiety. It is not a guilt feeling, but a heavy burden which cannot be brought into harmony with the felicity of innocence. The boredom experienced in innocence acts as a catalyst between this anxiety and the person's non-being and sets the power of evil in motion.[59] The influence of boredom in this regard is almost magical. It is the desire to avoid this boredom which breeds sinfulness. Sinfulness precedes sin. The original sin enters the world as a result of the feeling of sinfulness, and this original sin has a snowballing effect. The sinfulness of the race acquires a history which influences man towards sin.[60] Man develops several modes of living as methods of combating anxiety and the dread which is experienced in the act of boredom.

Sullivan writes that the infant experiences a 'protaxic stage' which includes all the experiences of the very early months before the development of the self, before the 'I' becomes the center of reference. All experiences during this stage are undifferentiated and are not integrated into any schemata. In this stage of infancy one has no capacity for relieving any condition which threatens one's euphoria. Events of anxiety are produced in the infant by lowering the feeling of euphoria. These events may be the result of conscious or even unintentional acts initiated by the 'mothering one'. The infant has no insight into situations which threaten his well being. As the well being of the infant is diminished, his anxiety rises. Should the mother become upset because she perceives her infant to be upset, then the infant becomes even more distressed and his anxiety is compounded. Thus, there is a snowballing of anxiety in the infant. To reestablish euphoria the infant gradually learns techniques which tend to encourage a maintenance of his feeling of well being. As he applies these techniques successfully he slowly builds a self-system which is composed of manipulative devices which secures euphoria and in turn prevents anxiety. These techniques are not evaluated by the young child for he exists in the aesthetic stage, not the ethical stage. The self-system becomes autonomous and is itself capable of truncating experiences which appear to be threatening to the organism, but which might be very meaningful to the organism's development. This self-system, as Sullivan understands it, is essentially neurotic and is the enemy of a healthy personality.[61] Kierkegaard's analysis of the development of sin and Sullivan's analysis of the development of anxiety are not far removed from each other even though the two systems were developed in different academic situations and utilized different sets of concepts to arrive at their positions.

Kierkegaard believed that sin comes into the world everytime that a person sins and that the act of sin is a personal responsibility. Man is responsible to God for his acts. Humanity, however, does not begin with each individual; therefore the sin of an individual takes its place in a continuum of sin which influences succeeding generations. The sin acquires a history, for its influence lives on. Man is not born in sin, but he is born into a humanity which is sinful.

Kierkegaard was aware that his doctrine that man was not born in sin is similar to that of the Pelagian heresies. He felt that he avoided the heresies because in Pelagius's view man is completely free of sin, whereas Kierkegaard insisted that man is a part of humanity which is sinful, and thus shares responsibility for the sinfulness.[62] 'The individual' does not stand alone; he is not an island unto himself, but is indeed a part of the main, a member of humanity. 'The individual' realizes that he participates in the sins of humanity because he knows himself and his relationship to humanity. Persons who have not aspired to be responsible for themselves seek to repress this consciousness of sin.

'The individual', His relationship to Faith and Reason

The question of faith and reason stimulated Kierkegaard's interest. He believed that over-emphasis on either leads one

80

astray. He criticized Hegel's followers for their dependence on reason, and Luther's followers because of their emphasis on a type of faith which bordered on triviality. Most people, to Kierkegaard, have neither reason nor faith, but hurry along, always on the move, and attempting to do something on principle. It is acting on principle that precludes the vital distinction which constitutes decency; it eliminates the basic impulses and behavior resulting from the inner enthusiasm and spontaneity of the person.[63]

Reason had a place in Kierkegaard's thought, but he felt that it was so misused by Hegelian philosophy that he seldom spoke about it positively. Reason, he believed, has usurped its proper role. It was like a general who conquers a foreign country, and then rebels from the government in whose service he was, to keep the land for himself.[64] Reason's task was to understand natural existence. It succeeded in understanding partially, but in so doing it sought to set itself up as the supreme judge. In spite of this act, reason is not to be discounted, wrote Kierkegaard, but certainly one must recognize the resulting lack of proportion.

To the father of existentialism, reason produces skepticism. By its credo a person is not to make any decision unless he knows the facts objectively. Reason warns man that he cannot be too trusting or too daring, that he must be skeptical. Skepticism encourages man to place God on the same level as those with no authority, or at very best on the same level with the genius whose wisdom is judged from an aesthetic or ethical point of view. 'The individual' is not skeptical when he is in absolute relation to God. He does not seek to evaluate God's commandments, but to fulfill the task which has been assigned to him.[65]

'The individual' is not even a prudent person, for prudence itself is a by-product of reason. Prudence opposes decision; it is a form of evasion. It is the prudent mariner through life's struggles who hugs the coast; it is the prudent person who does not leap into the unknown.[66] Paradoxically, prudence is of value to 'the individual' if used in an 'inward' sense. It may forestall evasion of action, and so help 'the individual' to hold to his decision and not be enmeshed by reflection.[67] Reflection is a snare in which one is caught most of the time. It becomes a noose when present in 'the individual' who has taken the leap enthusiastically. Like the farmer who plows a crooked furrow because he looked backwards, 'the individual' may steer a crooked course when he reflects on his decision. Reflection can tempt man to go astray for it presents so many views of the problem that decision is forestalled.[68]

Kierkegaard believed that only in faith decisions ought to be made. To him, most people live by virtue of a faith, yet their lives are so heedless that it is not noticed. Some people who are aware that they have a faith, hesitate before deciding from the vantage of faith in an effort to validate their decision by reason. Few are able to live and act by faith alone.

Faith transcends the historical and permits 'the individual' to be a contemporary of Christ.[69] Reason would seek to keep Christ an historical figure and would encourage the person to evaluate his teaching rather than to live by his teaching. Faith is a paradox in that it is a particular that is higher than the universal, and it is thus more potent than reason.

The highest expression of faith is found in the personality that Kierkegaard identified as the 'knight of faith'. The 'knight of faith' is always 'the individual', but 'the individual' is not always the 'knight of faith'. The 'knight of faith' has experienced infinite resignation, which means that he has broken with the temporal existence and has accepted God's authority. Though he renounces all, he realizes that by faith all is acquired.[70]

To Kierkegaard, the 'knight of faith' becomes God's intimate acquaintance; the Lord's friend, and he is capable of saying "Thou" to God, whereas all others address Him only in the third person. The 'knight' exists in the encounter with God more steadily than 'the individual' who is not a 'knight of faith' and who may not be a Christian. 'The individual' finds that he must constantly reaffirm his decision to be 'the individual', for he constantly slips backward into the ethical sphere of existence. The 'knight of faith' does not have to meet the element of choice as desperately as 'the individual', for the I-Thou experience sustains him over a longer period of time.[71]

The true 'knight' is the Lord's witness; he is never a teacher. He cannot communicate to another his innermost experiences because they are ineffable. He is obliged to rely upon himself alone. He feels the pain of not being able to communicate to others, for he feels that he has so much to disclose; but he feels no vain desire to require others to walk in his lonesome path. The 'knight of faith' believes that all men are equal, and that no man needs his sympathy.[72] The 'knight of faith' may or may not be an apostle. The latter is always the 'knight of faith'. The apostle is called by God and he is given authority to proclaim God's message.[73]

'The Individual' and the Crowd

To be in a relationship with God is to be alone with God. Andre Gide captures the flavor of Kierkegaard when he states that "many people suffer from the fear of finding themselves alone and so they do not find themselves at all." [74] Kierkegaard emphasized that because of this fear of loneliness man attempts to conceal himself in the crowd. The crowd eclipses man's relationship with God. Kierkegaard attacked the crowd vigorously. He was very impatient with anyone who defended a cause because the majority were behind it; as a matter of fact, he believed that the crowd is a treacherous recommendation for a cause. He believed that the crowd is a noisy, audible group which evidences little respect for truth. The crowd renders the person unpenitent and irresponsible, and at the very least, it weakens man's sense of responsibility by reducing it to a fraction.[75]

Kierkegaard believed that the crowd is synonymous with the public, which to him is a seamy organized majority which is never identifiable, but which slips from position to position depending upon irrational whims. The majority itself is not an identity but it also shifts within the crowd. The public always exists at the aesthetic level; it has no reference to the ethical stage and certainly cannot approach the religious mode of life. The public has no feeling of responsibility for it is not itself a true entity with a conscience; it is more than the sum of its parts, and thus relieves its parts of responsibility. The crowd or the public is opposed to 'the individual' who must experience guilt and responsibility for his every action, or even for his lack of action. This is not to say that 'the individual' cannot participate in a group, but when he does he becomes responsible not only for his own actions, but the actions of the group.[76]

Kierkegaard felt strongly that his era supported a gigantic program of equalization. He felt that this leveling process was a great threat to man for it tended to chip away at man's greatness and his uniqueness, so that eventually the great man will not make the average man uncomfortable.[77] Current existentialists emphasize that nothing has reversed the trend which Kierkegaard sought to reverse. Kierkegaard felt that his age was an age of dissolution comparable only to the fall of the Greek city state. Everything goes on as usual, but underneath there is no one who believes in the age, there is no spiritual bond to hold it together.[78] He was suspicious of the revolutionary movement that was taking place in his age because its members defended their cause on the basis of reason. Although they gave lip service to the concept of equality, Kierkegaard believed that they could appreciate the equality of man only after they had encountered God and had become 'individuals'.[79]

'The individual' and His Neighbor

The 'equality' of all men is revealed in the relationship between 'the individual' and God. Man must love God as an 'individual' in somewhat the same way as two lovers who want to be alone. If one is to love God, then one must love himself which, as has been discussed, is predicated on God's initial love. To understand God's love man must go within himself, because God's love is not external to man but is internal. God is within man. If man is to love God he will necessarily have to love himself because God is within himself. Man must also love his neighbor because the love of God abides within him too.

Kierkegaard stressed that all men are equal before God; they share in God's love equally; and this means that there must be infinite equality between man and man. Man's love for God must be expressed in his love of his neighbor because God exists in his neighbor as much as He exists in 'the individual'. One may recognize the Christian's love for his neighbor precisely by the degree of anxiousness he expresses in terms of his feeling of responsibility for his neighbor.[80] A Christian never needs to go a single step out of his way, for the moment that he leaves his closet where he has been busy praying, the first man he meets is his neighbor whom he must love.[81] This is expressed slightly differently by the twentieth century psychologist, J. L. Moreno, who states.

... the spatial-proximity hypothesis which postulates that the nearer two individuals are to each other in space, the more they owe each other their immediate attention and acceptance, which means their first love.[82]

Moreno believes essentially what Kierkegaard expressed, namely that man should not concern himself with another until his responsibility to a nearer one has been resolved.

To Kierkegaard, one must not limit Christian love merely to one's neighbor whom one chooses to be one's neighbor, for 'the individual' is obligated to love all men unconditionally, for all men are of equal worth before God. This means that one must love one's enemy too, for no exceptions can be made.[83] This is a doctrine traditionally accepted in Christendom, but one to which only lip service is given. To Kierkegaard, the least worthy in Christendom are those people who know that they ought to love their neighbor but who then do not put their knowledge into action.

Incipient in loving one's neighbor is the possibility that one may bring the neighbor into a clearer awareness of his closeness to God, and thus enable the neighbor to become a Christian, or even to 'individualize' himself. Kierkegaard supported his idea with the concept of love previously applied to God, namely, that when the neighbor experiences the Christian's love, he will experience himself as lovable, and therefore come to know love.

Upon coming to know love, he will be in a better position to become aware of God's love and in turn be able to love God more effectively. Conversely, to not love one's neighbor would eventually result in 'the individual's' keeping the neighbor away from God, and preventing him from attaining self-understanding. It is therefore essential for 'the individual' to love his neighbor regardless of what stage along life's way the neighbor is in; nor should the moral or ethical standards of the neighbor precipitate a rejection on the part of 'the individual'.

Kierkegaard was sensitive also about the man who spends all of his time meditating about God or praying to God but who as a result has no time for his neighbor. One must never focus one's attention so exclusively on God that one's neighbor is ignored. As a matter of fact, the situation would be practically impossible in the pure sense, for, to Kierkegaard, God dwells in each man in terms of spirit, and that to ignore one's fellow man would be to ignore God. Thus at no time should 'the individual' separate himself from mankind. To Kierkegaard, an hour well spent, in a Godly sense, is spent going back and forth among the common people.[84]

In going forth to meet the common people, or one's neighbor, 'the individual' will seek to edify those with whom he comes into contact. The chief characteristic of love is that it edifies.[85] Love is not the domination of another person, rather one becomes permissive of the will of the other person. 'The individual' who loves his neighbor does not assume an unwarranted interference in another's life. 'The individual' experiences much self-constraint in his not constraining others.[86]

'The individual' does not act towards his neighbor merely on impulses or inclination. These are traits of the aesthetic person, and are at times to be found in the ethical person too. The spiritual love which 'the individual' exercises requires self-understanding and an evaluation, based on the past, present and future possibility, of each action he undertakes in the moment. He does not act on whim but from the context of an existential time which fuses past, present, and near future into the moment of existential reality.

The most important thing which 'the individual' could do for another, according to Kierkegaard, is to bring to birth in him ideas which are present in embryonic form in the soul of man.[87] 'The individual' functions as mid-wife to his neighbor for he helps him in the process of gaining new insights which are inherent in his being. Actually the greatest help which 'the individual' can be to another is to deepen his ('the individual's') own self-understanding. Before one undertakes to change the world one must first examine his own being, and take seriously the injunction of Christ not to be over-concerned with the mote that is in another's eye. Kierkegaard wrote

"Every individual in each generation has likewise every day his own troubles and enough to do in taking care of himself, and does not need to embrace all the contemporary world with sovereign and paternal concern."[88]

One might again stress that Kierkegaard emphasized that one was not converted to the role of being 'the individual' once and for all, but that it is a state which requires constant reaffirmation.

Kierkegaard's social concern for his neighbor may be sampled by examining his attitude towards the poor. To express love for one's neighbor who is poor does not mean that 'the individual' ought only to give alms. Love is expressed by 'the individual's' effort to know himself, which in turn means to know God. This fact provides him a proper frame of reference for understanding and really accepting one's fellow man.[89] Kierkegaard's disparagement of money should not be taken to mean that he would withhold charity for in fact he was very generous with the poor. He also suggested that conceivably Christianity is possible only when one is materially poor, for otherwise one has too much in life to defend ethically.

The individual As a Psychotherapist

One might equate the relationship between 'the individual' and his neighbor as that between psychotherapist and patient. The therapy in question would be similar to that of Carl Rogers. Kierkegaard, as it has been developed in this discussion, believed that all people are near to God and equally loved by God. In that all individuals are in such a close relationship with God, all are equal to each other. 'The individual' perceives this fact and thus accepts any man unconditionally. In that 'the individual' feels accepted by God he is not one who is seeking to defend or enhance his personality, and as a result of this he is able to open his emotional resources and share them with his neighbor unconditionally. It is the function of 'the individual' to understand his neighbor from an internal frame of reference, for God abides in the internal. If this internal understanding is not felt by the neighbor, then 'the individual' has failed his neighbor, for he has not established a proper communication with him. An implication of the fact previously mentioned, that all men are responsible solely to God, is that 'the individual' cannot assume responsibility for his neighbor's activities. This has the effect of freeing 'the individual' so that he can relate to his neighbor unconditionally in love. Furthermore, because 'the individual' is not the judge of another man, he will accept his neighbor for what he is, and not for what he should be, for actually 'the individual' does not know what another man should be. Therefore when 'the individual' expresses his love of, and concern for, his neighbor, he enters the relationship in a comfortable manner and without knowing cognitively where it shall lead. 'The individual' is satisfied with loving his neighbor, as an individual, unconditionally. He knows that his neighbor is in God's hands. With the knowledge that each man must find his own relationship to God, and that it is possible for every man to find his relationship to God, he does not feel that he must force the other person into such a relationship. At any rate, he realizes that his neighbor is not an object to be manipulated as either the person who exists in the aesthetic or ethical stage seeks to do.

Carl Rogers has stated "My views came entirely out of clinical experience and research, and it was only within the past year or two that I realized the significant parallels that existed in Kierkegaard's thinking."[90] Rogers avers that the client-centered therapist must feel that his client is of unconditional self-worth no matter what his condition, his behavior or his feelings are. The therapist must be able to let himself go in understanding the client; no inner barriers should keep him from sensing what it feels like to be the client at each moment of the relationship, and he must be able to convey some of this empathetic feeling to the client. The therapist must be comfortable in entering this therapeutic relationship without knowing where it will lead, satisfied with only providing a climate which will free the client to become himself.

Part II: Martin Buber

For all practical purposes the writings of Søren Kierkegaard almost died as a result of their being overshadowed by the dominant German philosophers, such as Hegel, and of their being written in an obscure language. Nevertheless, in the beginning of the twentieth century his writings were rediscovered almost simultaneously in France and in Germany. His influence on European philosophers, and especially theologians, of the twentieth century has been extensive. Pre-eminent among European theologians to have been influenced by Kierkegaard is Martin Buber. Buber discovered Kierkegaard's writings during the former's youth.[91]

As is the case with Kierkegaard, it is difficult to understand the message which Martin Buber has for his reader if one does not understand some aspects of Buber's life and his style of writing. Unlike Kierkegaard, Buber's life is not in the earliest years saturated with the tragedy of a despairing, melancholic father. Nevertheless, as an infant, Martin Buber experienced the permanent loss of significant people such as his father, his mother and his maternal grandparents. From about the age of two he was raised by his paternal grandparent who has been described as the last of the great Zaddikim.[92] A Zaddikim was a man of great personal power and prestige among the Judaic community in which young Buber grew up. Buber's childhood had stability but apparently his adolescence was a painful period of growth. He overcame the stresses and storms of adolescence, stresses which at times made him fear he was losing his mind and precipitated thoughts of suicide, following his studying of Kant's book, *Prolegomena to All Future Metaphysics*. The teachings of the hasidim also helped him to overcome the crisis of this period.[93] During his twenties Buber became very personable and drew to him a wide circle of friends and acquaintances. One day a young man came to talk with him. Buber, who did not treat the young man unkindly, but who did not concentrate his full being in the relationship, thought that the young man had come for a chat. The two talked, Buber discussed with him the problems which the young man had brought, but he did not discern the unasked questions. Later he learned that the young man had committed suicide. Buber realized that the person had not come to him "for a chat but for a decision." Buber thought of this and asked himself what he could have done. He realized that the young man sought for a presence which would convey to him the belief that there is meaning in existence.[94] From that day to this, Buber has sought to meet anyone who comes to him with the fulness of his being, so as to communicate to the other the meaningfulness which Buber believes to be in the universe.

The theme of Buber's life is captured in the title of his novel, *For the Sake of Heaven*. He believes that everything that one does must be done for the sake of heaven.[95] This is partially a reflection of the influence upon his life of the Hasidim who maintain that God is present in man's every act and therefore his every act should be done as reverently as possible, even to the tying of his shoes. Although Buber believes that every act should be a consecrated act, he disagrees with Kierkegaard's category of 'either-or', by which the Dane meant that one must entirely serve God to the exclusion of worldly affairs. Buber does not believe that one needs to divorce himself from civic and social responsibilities. To Buber, one must simply do the best he can with whatever he is doing, and he should do as much as he can for the community in which he lives, and for the God in whom he believes.

Buber is part and parcel of the prophetic faith of which he

writes. In many ways he is the leading Hebraic prophet of the twentieth century, calling man to return to God in the tradition of the prophetic fathers of the Old Testament. The prophetic faith encompasses the men who

> trust the Lord of this Kingdom, that He will protect the congregation attached to Him; but at the same time who also trust in the inner strength and the influence of the congregation that ventures to realize righteousness in itself and towards its surroundings.[96]

Yet the prophets find that man has turned from God, and that they walk in unrighteousness towards their own destruction. Yet no matter how errant the congregation has become the prophets are still able to say, even as does Buber

> Thus hath YHVH, the Holy One of Israel, spoken: In turning away and in rest you will be saved, in *keeping still* and in confidence will be your strength, but you would not.[97]

Buber repeats the earlier warning of Kierkegaard that man's pace is too fast, that he is acting without due consideration of the consequences of his action, nor is he pausing to come to an understanding of himself or of his relationship to God. The theme of Buber's writing is that man should turn from the direction he is now trodding and turn towards God in whose presence man will find salvation. The fact that Buber is trying to fashion a teaching for his age is best summarized in the introduction to his book, *Prophetic Faith*. In this introduction he wrote as follows:

> The task of this book is to describe a teaching which reached its completion in some of the writing prophets from the last decades of the Northern Kingdom to the return from the Babylonian exile. . . . This is the teaching about the relation between the God of Israel and Israel. It did not begin with the first writing prophets. Generally speaking, it is not a new teaching they advance, but they fashion its form to fit the changing historical situations and their different demands, and they perfect a teaching they have received . . .[98]

91

Buber is attempting to refashion the prophetic teaching for his own era.

Buber does not like to write, although he has written extensively for periodicals. Unlike Kierkegaard, who wrote to save his life and who organized his home around his writing chores, Buber doubts the ability of the written word to convey the meaning of his thought and of his ideas.[99] In complete agreement with the Dane, Buber feels that the person who is next to him in physical distance is the most important being for him to come to know with the fullness of his being. When one writes, one writes for a distant audience and as a result neglects one's own students, one's own neighbor, and those who have come to him for meaning. In accord with this theme, he stresses that persons must be more important than books.[100] One must know how to approach a book in order to master its contents. Buber illustrates the proper approach by a comment he has made concerning the way he reads the New Testament.

> For nearly fifty years the New Testament has been a main
> concern of my studies, and I think I am a good reader who
> listens impartially to what is said.[101]

To Buber, a book is not just an object composed of words to read; but is a creation which has being. The reader must meet this being and listen to the message which often is hidden within the book's content. Buber hopes that his reader will listen to him as he attempts to communicate to the reader through words. As a result of his concern for persons he has in fact written few books, and those which he has written tend to be very short, seldom exceeding two hundred pages. His most profound work, which has influenced men like Tillich, Brunner and Neibuhr, is pocket-sized and is composed of one hundred and twenty pages. Yet within this mighty work one finds the main substance of Buber's philosophical anthropology. The book is entitled *I-Thou*.

In at least one instance Buber felt he had been commissioned to write a book. Although the nature of this commission is not discussed in detail, one is left with the impression that Buber felt it came from God. About this work, *Two Types of Faith*, Buber wrote

> I wrote this book in Jerusalem during the days of its so-called siege, or rather in the chaos of destruction which broke out within it. I began it without a plan, purely under the feeling of a commission, and in this way chapter after chapter has come into being. The work involved has helped me to endure in faith this war.[102]

The Individual Faces an Age of Crisis

Much in agreement with the current existential analysis of man's plight, Buber finds modern man to be a rather sterile soul,[103] who has been uprooted from a universe in which he could trust by the revolutionary discoveries of Copernicus,[104] and who is becoming more and more engulfed in a deep feeling of homelessness and meaninglessness.[105] As with Gordon Allport, creator of Citizen Sam, Buber finds man swamped by a non-personal world which tends to be beyond his comprehension.[106] To Buber, the world is definitely not comprehensible, but, it is embraceable![107] In this world man has the possibility of living a full life; on the other hand, Buber finds that most people are living faintly, quite anemically. The Hebraic philosopher challenges man to live earnestly.

> You, imprisoned in the shells in which society, state, church, school, public opinion, economy, and your own pride have stuck you, indirect one among indirect ones, break through your shells, become direct; man, have contact with men![108]

Buber calls for man to develop a feeling of fraternity.[109] More than fraternity, the prophetic voice challenges us to escape from our partial experiences and to enter into a dialogue with another, be the other a beautiful sunset, a neighbor or God.[110] Men, to Buber, must come to live as though they are all brothers, for in fact they are.[111] Yet, this thinker is quite aware that men are not living with neighbors in a spirit of brotherhood, and he accounts for this with the fact that man no longer has trust in the universe in which he lives; indeed, man no longer has trust in God, and as a result of this, he finds himself unable to open himself up to his neighbor, instead he seeks to protect himself as much as possible. Thus, Buber challenges man to return to the experience of trust.[112]

The development, or redevelopment, of fraternity, of dialogue, of brotherly existence, and of trust is not just a moral imperative, but indeed, God demands this of man. The greatness of man is the fact that man has believed that he can live up to God's expectations. Buber has confidence in man, he trusts man, and he believes that no matter how far away from real existence man has wandered, no matter how long he has sojourned from God, no matter how corrupt man has permitted himself to become, man can always reform.[113] Buber is not an optimist. He knows that few people listened to the prophetic voice of old; he knows that he has no reason to expect his voice to influence man to use his ability to decide for himself any more effectively than the great prophets. Nonetheless, even against the probability that his challenges will not be listened to, Buber, with the fulness of his being, challenges man to turn from his way, and to find his way back to God, back to existence. Significantly, he records the story of a young man who went on a prophetic journey and who failed to rouse an audience. He then went to the kingdom of God, and outside the gate challenged God to listen to him, for he was tired of not being listened to by all the people. God responded, I will not listen to you here for I will only hear you through the silence of the people.[114]

As with Kierkegaard, Buber insists that the world must be educated anew to the Spirit which gives meaning to existence.[115] The basic content of this teaching is to be found in the prophetic faith, but this faith must be reinterpreted to meet the needs of the twentieth century.[116]

In his treatment of the Psalms, Buber's interpretation of the age in which the psalmist finds himself is not a far cry from the dilemmas which Buber believes his era is faced with.

. . . the psalmist confronted by a world dominated by the smooth tongue, by unscrupulous falsehood, and up to every trick which makes false appear and be accounted as true, and violence as right order. Where is there a hiding place for loyalty?[117]

Our age, to Buber, is one of great industrialization. He finds that man is not only incapable of controlling the complicated industrial mechanisms of his society, but also he is becoming a cog in the wheels of industry which are far beyond his ken. Institutions of the age are outside of man, they are neutral and indifferent to man's concerns. In that man does not feel that he can be a person when dealing with the institutions of the twentieth century, he has tended to retreat into himself, and there live and experience his own feelings. Here man can indulge in love and hate and in the pleasure of his prejudices. "Here he is at home, and stretches himself out in his rocking chair." Unfortunately, man, who is buffeted around by the industrial might of his surroundings and who attempts to plunge deeply into a life of feeling, does not have access to real living. The realization of the hollowness of man as he exists in the twentieth century is increasingly becoming the concern of psychologists and philosophers.[118] The ability to live in close personal contact with friends and loved ones, in marriage, in work and in one's community is rapidly decaying in our age, and as a result man's awareness of his solitude and loneliness is intensified with each generation.[119] Man is becoming increasingly worried that he no longer is able to master his world; he is becoming aware of his dependence upon circumstances beyond his control.[120]

As man surveys his world, everything tends to remain as it has been for several generations, but underneath the old forms there is rot and decay. As in his interpretation of the psalms, Buber avers that the age is spinning a way of thinking which for itself does not follow.[121] The relativization of the highest principles which man has heretofore believed in marks the intellectual interest of the age.[122]

More serious than the mere decay which Buber finds in the twentieth century way of life is the fact that nothing new is coming into the age which will edify man. This perpetuates anachronisms because a new spirit cannot be established which will bring harmony into the dissonant period.[123] In this age people are looking for a leader, a spell-binder, to bring meaning into their lives. They fail to realize that they must find a teacher; for they must again be taught how to achieve meaning in life.[124] The whole generation, as a matter of fact, is a lie. We exist in delusion. Oddly enough, the lie is an invention of man, and man's lie in our age has caused the eclipse of God's light, so that man now exists in darkness.[125] One of the tasks of the prophetic teacher in this age will be to break through the lie, which in many cases will shatter man's security.[126]

The Individual and the Community

Although there is marked similarity between the thought of Søren Kierkegaard and Martin Buber in relation to their era and to the crowd, Buber not only is more permissive in his belief that the individual must work with a community, he insists that it is necessary if the individual is to be a whole person. Buber stresses that a person loses none of his individuality when he chooses to associate himself with a community, although a person's individuality is swamped when he becomes identified with a crowd. The community of individuals is a necessity, for within the fellowship one is able to receive a common teaching, know the security of law and order, and is able to live at peace with his fellow man.[127] The strength of a community is founded on the fact that everything belongs to God, and that therefore the land and the property thereon should be shared in a common ownership. This theory provides Buber with the foundation of his belief in religious socialism.[128] Buber is far apart, however, from the communistic collective, or for that matter from any party discipline.

> Today host upon host of men have everywhere sunk into the slavery of the collectives, and each collective is the supreme authority for its own slaves; there is no longer, superior to the collectives, any universal sovereignty in idea, faith or spirit. Against the values, decrees, and decisions of

the collective no appeal is possible. . . . In order to enter a personal relation with the absolute, it is first necessary to be a person again, to rescue one's real personal self from the fiery jaws of collectivism which devours all selfhood.[129]

Opposed to the community is the crowd. The community is an organized group of individuals who respect one another, who try to be brothers. The crowd is unorganized and treats people as objects which are to be manipulated. God does not want a crowd, he wants a community.[130]

Paradoxically the crowd, according to Buber, is made great by those who hate it, by those who speak against it, for then "the shapeless thing has come into being" and surges against the security of the individual who has attacked it.[131] This was basically Søren Kierkegaard's experience, for the more he wrote against the crowds in Copenhagen, the more he became the object of ridicule until eventually even the children on the street would throw stones at him. Conversely, the road to worldly success is one which involves flattering the crowd. The crowd itself is not untruth as Kierkegaard labeled it, but rather it is nontruth and unfreedom. One never realizes his full freedom when he participates in a crowd.[132]

The crowd is formed as the result of the sterilization of man's life which has been precipitated by the industrial order. Even though the industrial order creates many evils, Buber doubts the wisdom of attempting to destroy the order thereby reverting to an earlier society. He disagrees with Tagore who once suggested that much of the western industrialization is unnecessary, and should be junked. Buber talks about a man who wanted to climb a high mountain with a certain symbol he wanted to place on top of the mountain. For the most part the ascent is slow and tedious and the man suffers many reversals. An observer calmly suggests that if the man wants to climb the mountain he should leave the symbol at the foot of the mountain, to which the climber would respond, "I intend either to ascend with this symbol or to fall headlong with it."[133] Western culture aspires to climb to new heights with its new technology, and it prefers to destroy itself attempting to reach a new height in living rather than accept the old form of living.

In the establishment of the community which Buber envisions the moral and divine responsibilities of man will interlock.

> The people's goal was set not by their being bidden to become a 'good' people but a 'holy' one. Thus every moral demand is set forth as one that shall raise man, the human people, to the sphere where the ethical merges into the religious, or rather where the difference between the ethical and the religious is suspended in the breathing space of the divine.[134]

According to Buber, if one studies the Biblical prophetic message one would become aware that the concern of the prophets was not the bettering of the living conditions of society, but was concerned with establishing a true people.[135] The true worshipper does not want to hasten the work of God in the universe.[136] This is because the true worshipper trusts God and knows that man exists under God's destiny and not his sport.[137]

Martin Buber's Basic Motifs, The I-Thou and the I-it Experience

Buber suggests that to man the world is twofold, in accordance with his twofold attitude. Underneath man's twofold attitude is man's need to enter into relationships. Man may enter into two types of relationships, one which is characterized by I-Thou, the other, I-it. For the most part, man exists in the attitude which precipitates the I-it relationship. As a matter of fact the growing complexity of the twentieth century industrial order apparently is forcing man from the I-Thou mode of existence to the level of the I-it experience.[138] The I-it involves man's meeting with objects which he can manipulate, whether the objects are inorganic, organic, animal or human. When one who exists in the I-it existence meets another person he seeks to analyze the person and if at all possible to manipulate him. To Buber, men in the twentieth century, tend to enter few relationships which do not involve manipulation. The I-thou experience is expressed in the attitude of meeting, which is the situation in which two people encounter each other in such a way that they do not really perceive the object reality of each other but instead blend together in such a way that there is a feeling of unity between the two. Neither is trying to accomplish some alternative motif but both find themselves lifted above the time-space sphere so that they are hardly aware of interrupting forces in their environment, or of the time which passes during their encounter. The I-thou can be an experience between a person and things, such as a book or the objects of nature, between people as mentioned before, or between the eternal Thou which for all intents and purposes is equivalent to God. In the realm of nature the I-thou experience is manifest when man views a beautiful sunset and finds himself lifted above the cares of the world or the analysis of the scientific explanations of the sunset phenomenon. In man's encounter with man in which the I-thou is experienced nothing needs to be said, in fact, one of the persons does not even need to be aware that he is the thou for the I of another person. The latter situation is sometimes experienced in a railroad station or a restaurant where another person is seen who attracts the full attention of the individual for a period of time.

The primary encounter of the I-thou can only be experienced by the person who gives his whole self to the meeting. "He who gives himself to it may withhold nothing of himself."[139] In that the whole person must be involved in the encounter man can do very little to initiate the action. Man can do nothing to manipulate himself into an I-Thou experience except for the fact that he can make himself available for the relationship.

> Concentration and fusion into the whole being can never take place through my agency, nor can it ever take place without me. . . . The Thou meets me through grace — it is not found by seeking. . . . The Thou meets me. But I step into direct relation with it.[140]

To Buber the complete I-Thou relationship is experienced before the individual becomes aware of his own I. The first I-Thou situation occurs within the womb of the mother, between her and the fetus.[141] This intimate relationship continues, psychologically, even after birth. During the youth of a person this experience is in some way terminated and the person temporarily falls from such a positive relationship. To become truly an existing adult it is necessary to again meet another within the bonds of the I-Thou relationship.[142]

It should be emphasized that when man meets God in an I-Thou situation man is not absorbed into God but stands in relation to God. God in fact is enhanced by man who stands in within such a meeting. It is for this reason that Buber can insist that God needs man.[143] In fact to guarantee the separation of man from God, the creator "gives to all His creatures his own boundary, so that each may become fully itself."[144] Buber is often labeled as a mystic, but to the degree that mystics believe that man and God blend as one, this theologian certainly does not qualify as a mystic.[145]

Man's access to the eternal Thou is in danger of being blocked, for the characteristic of time in history is the eclipse of God.[146] This is due to the fact that man is being split asunder by his technological order. In this technological age man finds it difficult if not impossible to bring his whole self together so that he might approach the eternal Thou.

> The thinking of our time is characterized by an essentially different aim. It seeks, on the one hand, to preserve the idea of the divine as the true concern of religion, and, on the other hand, to destroy the reality of God and thereby also the reality of our relation to Him.[147]

> Understandably, the thinking of the era, in its effort to make God unreal, has not contented itself with reducing Him to a moral principle.[148]

Inevitably the type of thinking about God which has been characteristic of the last three hundred years has led to Nietzsche's proclamation that "God is dead, that we have slain Him . . ."[149] In that man is finding it difficult to relate to God, Buber has turned his attention to helping man meet man, for if man can accept another man as a thou, then he is continuously ready to meet the eternal Thou.

The rise of objectification, of the 'it', is a characteristic of the age.

> The history of the individual and that of the human race, in whatever they may continually part company, agree at least in this one respect, that they indicate a progressive augmentation of the world of IT.[150]

The 'it' increases because man is constantly expanding his capacity to experience and to use the objects which he finds in his natural world. He tends not to be interested in meeting the objects, or to enter into a relationship with them, but to seek their usage.

This world of the 'it' relationship is not an evil in itself. Man, in order to exist, must know how to utilize and to manipulate his environment. He must exist in the 'it' sphere of life much of the time. He is able to enter into the fullness of his being and, in turn, of the 'thou' only upon occasion. The 'it' becomes evil when it

> presumes to have the quality of present being. If a man lets it have mastery, the continually growing world of 'it' overruns him and robs him of the reality of his own I. . . .[151]

The 'it' assumes an evil aspect when it blots out, when it eclipses man's ability to perceive the thou.

The Importance of Man

Buber, although disavowing any variation of determinism, states "I hold that each man in some measure has been called to something, which, to be sure, he in general successfully avoids."[152] Each man has a destiny which he might fulfill if he could come into a valid relationship with the central Thou, which is to say, if he could be a whole person. Man is under the influence of divine destiny, and not divine sport as Greek mythology would purport.[153] As stated previously, man is important because in the I-Thou relationship he complements God.

The earth and all that is in the earth is dependent upon man and his initiative. The earth, according to the prophetic way of thinking, is good or bad depending upon the ethical caliber of her master. Man's rebellion against his being corrupts the earth, man's working together in community blesses the earth.[154] Man is completely free to choose the way he shall treat the earth. He can manipulate it, he can destroy it or he can embrace it. The earth is truly the domain of man. Nevertheless God demands all of man's efforts to be used in his service which means the forming of His "holy community". This too is a testimony of man's importance, for God does not demand what man cannot give. Therefore it is possible for man to give all to God and thereby fulfill his destiny.[155]

Man is granted the power of decision, but God demands that man utilize his ability to decide, and not to drift through life merely buffeted by the events which involve him.

> The divine demand for human decision is shown here at the height of its seriousness. The power and ability are given to every man at any definite moment really to take his choice, and by this he shares in deciding about the fate of the moment after this, and this sharing of his occurs in a sphere of possibility which cannot be figured either in manner or scale.[156]

Not only does man have the power to decide, he can actually partially determine the character of the next moment which is to be, and thus man is a co-creator with God. This in itself is an important emphasis for those who are concerned with the nature of evil and from whence it originates. As stated previously, man is the only being, according to Buber, who can lie, and unfortunately he has turned his generation into a lie. Man has the power to bring evil into the world, as well as the ability to choose the way of God.

> The way of God is by no means to be understood as a sum of prescriptions for human conduct, but rather primarily as the way of salvation of men since it is the prototype for the imitation of God.[157]

Although man is absolutely free to decide the course of his life, God has provided him with a model which man may choose to pattern himself after.

> . . . everywhere transcendent Being has a side facing toward man which represents a shall-be; everywhere man, if he wants to exist as man, must strive after a superhuman model; everywhere, the outline of a true human society is traced in heaven.[158]

It is, of course, difficult to discuss the shall-be, the superhuman model, or the outline of the heavenly community because these must be experienced in a relationship in the fullness of one's being, and it cannot be properly discerned in the world of objectification, the world of the 'it'. "To man who can only think and not meet, he must always say that there is no God."[159]

No matter how much dominion man has over the earth, no matter what power of decisions he ultimately has, these facts by themselves do not give man a feeling of worth. Man's concept of worth comes to him by way of God. It is God who views man as being of worth thus enabling man to believe that he has worth. Man, by himself, can only evaluate and estimate the significance of individual phenomena. Man learns of his worth as he meets the eternal Thou.[160] The corollary of this is that man who does not know God faces a meaningless existence which will be filled with little but ruin. Interpreting the writings of the Habbakuk, Buber indicates that the

> . . . presumptuous man, the man who recognizes no other commandment than the never-resting impulse of his own force to become power, who refuses to know moderation and limitation, who refuses to know God has nothing in common with genuine trust and he exists in nothing else but self-deception.[161]

The Development of Man's Moral Nature

Buber is essentially challenging man to return to the wholeness of being. He insists that man's rationality cannot solve his

103

moral or ethical responsibility by itself. Yet, this age has seen the tremendous upsurge of cold logic in dealing with man's problems.

> My rationality, my rational power of thought, is merely a part, a particular function of my nature; when however I 'believe', in either sense, my entire being is engaged, the totality of my nature enters the process, indeed this becomes possible only because the relationship of faith is a relationship of my entire being.[162]

The existential theory of Buber is not anti-rational, but it does demand that rationality work together with the whole being of the person, and not usurp a calculating control. On the other hand, Buber also warns against those who, like Faust, give free rein to their feelings as the answer to finding real life.

> Feeling is by no means 'everything', as Faust thinks, but is at best only an indication of the fact that the being of the man is about to unite and become whole, and in other cases it is an illusion of becoming a whole without its actually being affected.[163]
> Man simply cannot live by the heart alone.[164]

> The way of man must be something more than merely the way of animals, which is the way of feelings. The way of man must involve his ability to enter into positive 'Thou' relationships with the fullness of his being.[165]

Man has a moral nature because human life is distinct from all other forms of life.[166] Man exists in positive morality only when he is fully engaged and all of his being is functioning in harmony.

In spite of man's need for faith, for a relationship with the spiritual nature of the world, man seems perpetually to resist the spiritual.[167] Yet, he who resists spiritually successfully, he who lives without God, is not *to be*.[168] He will never know the meaning or the fullness of existence. Without God many men, if not all men, become sterile souls.[169] Many who have not entered into a positive relationship with the thou only exist, and do not really participate in life. It is this type of person who, says Buber, characterizes our age; he permits things to happen without attempting to bring to bear his decisive ability. Indeed he permits himself to be determined by the cause-effect forces which buffet him around.[170]

This sterile soul will often feel homeless, for indeed the tapestry of a life which is not supported by God is to be torn asunder, and life will appear meaningless if not unfriendly.[171]

Man has become problematic to himself.[172] He no longer knows what he essentially is, but at the same time he also knows that he does not know. To rise above this problem man must learn to live forcefully. Buber challenges his audience to live fully rather than to live faintly. The more forcefully we permit ourselves to live the more we enjoy ourselves. In forceful living the content of living does not much matter, for joy and anger, sin and holiness, heroism and despair, all tend to be merged into a sameness.[173] However, man is not living forcefully, he is not living fully; he knows only how to skim the surface of existence, and how to guarantee his economic necessities, and to secure a few hours of pleasure from standardized daydreams such as the movies. Man is aware of this hollow living and he yearns to achieve a more free, a more full life. Buber attempts to inspire man to want to be free. Man must manifest his whole being. Man must learn how to be really there as a whole in his situation.[174] This is the primary problem with which man must deal.

As has been implied, Buber desires man to risk and to dare to live, to rise above an anemic participation in life in which he becomes a pawn of fate.[175] The act of risking with an intensity of feeling, even if the person fails to achieve his goal, even if he engages in sin, is better than permitting himself to drift to and fro.[176] Explicitly, Buber avers that it is better to sin, by choice, than to fulfill the commandments of the Lord, not by choice.

Meaning is to be experienced in living action and suffering itself, in the unreduced immediacy of the moment. . . . Only he reaches the meaning who stands firm, without holding back or reservation, before the whole might of reality and answers it in a living way.[177]

If man sins as he risks, he can always reform.[178]

Man can always repent if he is evil.[179]

Repentance, the reshaping of one's pattern of living in action, is easier to accomplish than the stimulation of oneself from a lethargic, indifferent existence.

The prophetic voices systematically condemned man's indifference to Divine responsibility, and they did predict dire consequences if man did not reform; but underneath all valid prophetic utterances is an alternative that man may follow in decision if the message has penetrated to the core of his being.[180] God does demand righteousness and justice from man, and as one enters into a full relation with the Thou, one becomes saturated with the desire to live righteously and with justice. In risking and daring man has been challenged to live in accord with the ten commandments. The commandments are not generalities but personal commands to each individual, for they bear the personal 'thou'.[181]

Buber would not have man break down in what he would feel to be indecision because of an either-or nature of God's commandments. Man is obligated to do as much as he can.[182] No more can be expected of man; yet this requires everything of man. What man should do day by day, moment by moment, cannot be foretold in advance, he must only do what is fitting in the moment of his decision.[183]

The requisites for man's successful risking is first that he should stand still so as to not continue fleeing from himself. While standing still he will be able to pull himself together and become a unity within himself.[184] Next he must be reschooled in trust.[185] Finally, he must learn that the universe is an integral unity, and that there is meaning in life, and that there is a God whom one can depend on even though suffering the afflictions of Job. Man is panic-stricken if he cannot trust his universe, if he does not feel 'at home with life'. When man feels that there is meaning in his life, in the lives of his fellow man, he can then develop feelings of interest and concern with life as it exists around him. From these feelings of concern and interest man can enter into a feeling of fraternity with his neighbor; in fact, his neighbor becomes a neighbor.[186] Firmly rooted in the intimacy of fraternity and trust, man can enter into a dialogue with his neighbor. Being able to enter into a dialogue with his neighbor, man discovers a thou and from the thouness of his neighbor, man will not only be able to embrace the world, he will also be able to encounter the central Thou.[187] In this act man experiences human truth which is to be devoted to God's truth. If one should ask, "But what is God's truth?", Buber would say that it would be difficult to predetermine this truth except that it must in some way involve the community and its people becoming holy. The truth must be discovered in each moment of man's existence.

> We find the ethical in its purity only there where the human person confronts himself with his own potentiality and distinguishes and decides in this confrontation without asking anything other than what is right and what is wrong in this his own situation. The criterion by which this distinction and decision is made may be a traditional one, or it may be one perceived by or revealed to the individual himself.[188]

What is important in the experience being described is that this state of being produces purity of heart which aids in decision making.[189]

The Importance of Man's Relationship to Man

As a result of the eclipse of God, and the difficulty man has in his effort to relate himself to the central Thou, man's relationship to man takes on an air of crucial importance if he is to really find meaning in his existence. Existence, in itself, cannot be possessed by any man. It must be shared among all mankind.

Not only is life meaningless, to Buber, if man has not come

to know the 'thouness' of another, it is also meaningless unless he can experience love. Love felt for another is capable of drawing God closer to the world, that He may be known. It is not crucial for one to be loved, the vital thing is to love. The drawing power, the inspirational power, of love may be elicited in a onesided love affair.[190] It is for this reason that the individual must initiate love even though his love may not be returned. This means that the individual must love his neighbor and even his enemy who will not return his love.[191] Buber's concern for the enemy contains no reflection of pacifism. He writes explicitly that he is not a pacifist, and that man must resist aggression with aggression. While resisting aggression the individual still must feel a concern for his enemy and love him whenever possible.[192]

Love and trust are for Buber practically synonymous. One's love for God is an attitude which may be interchangeable with trusting God.[193] To learn to trust God, in an age of eclipse, man must first learn to trust his neighbor, the stranger and even his enemy. In no wise would trust of the enemy be a blind trust. The individual, (or community), who is functioning as a whole being can evaluate the situation, and know the motivation and dependability of a neighbor or an enemy. Still, where possible in interpersonal relations, the highest expression of respect for another is trust.

The need, which Buber stresses, to have dialogue with one's neighbor is not synonymous with love. Dialogue is communication, and involves a mutual sharing of being. It is possible for two people to engage in a dialogue without saying anything to each other. It is the ability to have a meaningful relationship with one another, to be able to converse with another, to be able to entertain the dialogue, which permits the individual to enjoy a fulfilled life.[194] In the dialogue, the party of the first part never treats the party of the second part as an object to which he talks; the party of the second part is viewed as a partner in a togetherness, and the conversation is a mutual undertaking.[195] In this mutuality man is ever mindful that he cannot walk in another's shoes. Each personality is unique and cannot be completely known by the other, no matter how many times the two have met in intimate dialogue.[196]

To Buber, it is not enough to say that all men are brothers. He prefers to state that "men become what they are, sons of God, by becoming what they are, brothers of their brothers."[197] The brotherhood of man must not be stressed as a mere idea; man must step into the relationship immediately with the fullness of his being. To find one's brother one needs only to meet the person who is next to him. As stated previously, Buber has found it difficult to write, because to write means to jump over people who are near to him for someone who is remote. Obviously the value of so doing, of reaching more people through the media of the printed page, has not escaped him. Still, the person is responsible to his immediate associates, and to the building of relationship and dialogue with those who are spatially the closest.[198]

In speaking of meeting another individual, Buber repeatedly stresses, that man cannot create a 'thouness' in the being of another person. He certainly cannot force himself to be a 'thou' for another person. All the individual can do is to meet each person with whom he comes in contact, with as much of his being as he possibly can, without objectively examining the other, without seeking to use the other, without seeking ulterior motivations within the other, and certainly without thinking of all the other things he might be doing. With this readiness he will find the thouness of others confronting him.[199] All the same, in our world of specialization the itness, the objectivity of the other, tends to engulf the 'thouness', and with this tendency man often finds himself lonely and isolated from being.

Modern life is split in two: what is thought reprehensible between two persons is thought commendable in the relations between peoples. This is contrary to the prophetic demand. . . . But that split naturally continues into the life of modern man as an individual: his existence is divided into a private and public one which are governed by different laws.[200]

The splitting of man into an ethically schizoid being by itself tends to isolate man from God, and even from his neighbor. Ultimately, to attempt to rise above this breakdown in man's being, some men seek power for its own sake. The will to power, described by Adler, concerns Buber deeply. To will power means that the individual will have to treat others as pawns to his personal advancement. Others become objects and the 'thouness' of the other becomes an impossible state for the person seeking power to realize. He is therefore cut off from the realization of his own full being, and he is made to feel that he is alone. In striving for power, Buber believes, one must eventually do something which will be harmful to one's neighbor. When one has harmed one's neighbor, one has harmed God. The man who strives for power, sins and becomes guilty of transgressing God's way. No matter how much man sins, no matter how bleak the forces of chaos appear to be, man is still not abandoned by God. God seeks him out, comes to meet him, and calls him to turn from the way he has chosen.[201] In the situation of the twentieth century, man's turning from his way will still not enable him to meet the central Thou. To use a figure of speech, man has gone around the corner from God. He must first retrace his steps to the corner, and then when he turns the corner he will encounter the Thouness of God.

As man becomes increasingly aware of the eclipse of God, and of his own solitude, the situation grows more favorable to man. Eventually, the pain of his despair, of his solitude, will force him to turn from his way, to reject faint living, and thereby to risk a fuller, more meaningful life.

It is in solitude that man can first really question the meaning of his existence. As he faces himself alone he is enabled to take the first step towards purification of himself.

If solitude is a place of purification, necessary even to the man who is bound in relation, both before he enters the Holy of Holies and in the midst of his ventures between unavoidable failing and the ascent to proving true--to this solitude we are by nature disposed.[202]

110

Once man questions the meaning of existence, following a period of profound reflection which often occurs when he is alone, he often realizes how meaningless existence is. As he is confronted with the mystery of existence he becomes aware of his awe of God.

> All religious reality begins with what Biblical religion calls the 'fear of God'. It comes when our existence between birth and death becomes incomprehensible and uncanny, when all security is shattered through the mystery.[203]

It is at this time that man searches for a force which will give meaning to life, which will permit man to re-establish a positive world view from the shattered pieces of his security. If man turns at this point, rather than slipping back into an aesthetic life; it he turns to some force which is supreme but whose name he does not know, then man will again begin to discover reality.

> If one dares to turn toward the unknown God, to go to meet Him, to call Him, reality is present.... It is not necessary to know something about God in order to believe in Him: many true believers know how to talk to God but know nothing about Him.[204]

A Basic Hypothesis — Freedom of the Will

Underlying much of the prophetic challenge of Martin Buber is belief that man is able to rise above causality and to choose freely which way he will follow. This emphasis is at the heart of Buber's discussion of man's entering into a relationship with a 'thou'; it is underscored in man's ability to turn and redirect his attention towards God, and it is stressed in man's ability to repent when he has sinned. Unfortunately, as far as Buber is concerned, man has forsaken his ability to choose and tends merely to permit things to happen. It is this tendency in contemporary man which Buber seeks to shatter.[205] To be certain there is a security in this form of behavior, for one tends to escape the feeling of responsibility for his actions when he

111

simply drifts along. Nevertheless, man is still responsible, and he must be made to realize the fact. Causality has an unlimited rein in the world of 'it'.

> Every physical event that can be perceived by the senses, but also every "psychical" event existing or discovered in self-experience is necessarily valid as being caused and as causing. Further, events to which a teleological character may be attributed are as parts of the unbroken world of 'it' not excepted from this causality; . . . The unlimited rein of causality in the world of 'it' is of fundamental importance for the scientific ordering of nature, but does not weigh heavily on man, who is not limited to the world of 'it', but can continually leave it for the world of relation. Here I and Thou freely confront one another in mutual effect that is neither connected with nor colored by any causality. Here man is assured of the freedom both of his being and of Being. Only he who knows relation and knows the presence of the Thou is capable of decision.[206]

To Buber man is not entirely animal because man has been created in the image of God. To be created in the image of God means that man has been given the freedom to decide and to choose whether he participates in relationships. As the world of 'it' eliminates, or eclipses, man's ability to approach a thou, then man's freedom disappears. At this point fate enters the picture.

> The only thing that can become fate for man is belief in fate; for this suppresses the movement of reversal.[207]

As long as man convinces himself he is fated, he has no force by which to make a free decision.

As stated previously, in making a decision man must bring his whole self into the act. He cannot permit just his intelligence nor just his feelings to decide the issue at hand. His feelings and his intelligence must work together in order for him to effectively decide.[208] Freedom to choose does not mean that man suddenly does something with no reference to anything which he has ever done. Experience is important in the forging of the decision.

> Here you do not attain to knowledge by remaining on the shore and watching the foaming waves, you must make the venture and cast yourself in, you must swim, alert and with all your forces, even if a moment comes when you think you are losing consciousness. . . . So long as you 'have' yourself, have yourself as an object, your experience of man is only as of a thing among things, the wholeness which is to be grasped is not yet there; only when you *are*, and nothing else but that, is the wholeness there and able to be grasped.[209]

Experience and action are important, but not if man is constantly reflecting upon his experience and holds himself apart from contemporary events. Experience becomes significant as a factor in choice when man is caught up in his experience and participates fully in it.

Buber's Main Goal of Writing — the Re-establishment of Faith

Buber is seeking a way to restore faith and trust in contemporary man who has grown skeptical and suspicious because he has trapped himself in an existence of lies which are of his own making. Faith, as Buber conceives it, is not a feeling in the soul of man but is an entrance into reality.[210] Faith involves a mode of life, and it is not merely a confession of faith as many attempt to make of it.[211] The Christians, to Buber, have changed the Hebraic idea of faith and trust by adding a basic Greek idea of hoping, "for things which are not seen." In the Judaic world, the Hebrew has seen, has experienced the resources of the God in whom he trusts and therefore he does not hope.[212]

It is in faith that man can look forward to the future with considerable anticipation, for

> the power of faith can experience perfection as something assured, because it is something guaranteed to us by someone we trust... .[213]

When one has faith in another, one trusts the other, and when one trusts the other, one believes what the other says. When God revealed to man that man could be perfect, man is able to believe this because he trusts the God in whom he has faith.[214]

Buber's Concept of Man's Relationship to the Creating God

Buber is very insistent that God created man to be a human and not merely to be an individual. As a human, man is expected to participate in community relations.[215] God created man in His (Divine) likeness. One of the major aspects of man's likeness to God is his ability to respond to the other, to the thou. Man is capable of responding to the other because he is a God-created unity who has a social concern.[216]

God does not just arbitrarily or fatefully operate in human affairs; He chooses to meet man, to challenge man, to set the divine example. Why God chooses to participate in human affairs remains a mystery.[217] God, as he participates in human affairs, lends himself as the superhuman model. Man feels that he, because he is in the likeness of God, can approach the model which God has set for man.[218] This feeling of being able to fulfill the divine intention gives status to man.[219] Although participating in man's affairs,

God does not allow himself to be limited to any form of revelation and He does not limit Himself to any of them...[220]

In the twentieth century Buber believes that God has suspended his activity in human affairs and that we are again in an era in which, as the psalmist said, God is hiding his face.[221] Buber as a religious man, is distressed by the absence of God's presence and he states that this is a burden which the faithful must carry until that which separates man from God has been removed.

The idea that God is hiding himself is of course anthropomorphic. Man thinks in these terms because he needs to preserve the concrete concept of God. The more abstract the God concept is, the more it needs to be balanced by the evidence of living

114

experience. For this reason, the mystic, who believes he has experienced God in nature or beauty or contemplation, does not need to think of God in man-like terms.[222] Our age, however, lacks the spiritual orientation to perceive God adequately and therefore must think of him in anthropomorphic terms. In the Christian faith, Buber writes, more people believe in the divinity of Christ, because of His concreteness, than actually believe in the Godhead itself.[223]

Buber's equivalent to Kierkegaard's apostle, or perhaps knight of faith, is the 'nabi'. The 'nabi' is one who has received the word of God. He is not a prophet in the sense that he has some type of clairvoyance of the future. It is the 'nabi's' duty to set before the people to whom his words are addressed the choice and the decision which they unconsciously know they must follow.[224] Their work differs from the priest's, for the latter's decisive movement goes out from the human person towards the realm of deity, while the nabi receives something from the divine sphere.[225] The nabi is not necessarily a leader. During the period of the Judges the nabi was granted military insight because the people needed his leadership in their direct conflict with an alien power. Although the leader labors under divine inspiration he still must choose and direct the course of the battle; he can not merely rely on God for deliverance.[226] Usually the nabi is isolated because the court, the ruling powers of the day, prefer to associate with men who are corruptible. Therefore the nabi, who is not corruptible, usually becomes a powerless opposition to the powerful, and may be cast into the role of a martyr.[227] It is the duty of the nabi to speak God's word so decisively that it will touch the innermost soul of the listener and thereby evoke a favorable decision on the part of the listener.[228] He, the nabi, is often caught up in his task. He finds that the spirit moves him and often he feels that it is not he who challenges the people, but that he has become a symbol of the voice of God.[229] The spirit is, to Buber, the 'betweenness' which exists between the I and the Thou. It is a force which is found in the relationship and from which the relationship exerts its force. Thus, while the nabi feels he has become a vessel for the message, he is still

115

participating directly in the shaping of the message and he is existing in the fullness of his being.

To conclude this section, it might be restated once more that Buber at times felt himself caught up in the type of relationship he has with his work in the same way that the nabi experienced his work. Buber certainly does not state that the work of the nabi was finished in the days of the Old Testament, but to the contrary insists that the nabi's voice is needed today more than ever.

Part III: Jean-Paul Sartre

Although Kierkegaard is known as the father of the existential movement, the name of Jean-Paul Sartre is practically synonymous with existentialism in the minds of the lay-philosophical public. The importance of Sartre in the tradition is based primarily on the fact that he is the movement's chief literary spokesman. His plays alone have won acclaim for him and have deepened the public perspective of existentialism throughout Europe. Sartre has not only interested himself in presenting the existential position through the media of drama, he has also sought to bring some system to the movement which many feel cannot be systematized. Although most of those who are identified with existentialism seek to analyze man in his realistic situation, Sartre has permitted himself to go beneath man's existential problems to ferret out the original nature of man's problems. In his *Being and Nothingness* Sartre presents an ontology of man. Still to be produced is another work that Sartre is planning which will discuss man's ethical problems.[230] Finally, Sartre has not taken the time to reject the label of existentialism as some of the other men in the movement have. He has even created one of the first real apologies for the movement in his small but concise book, *Existentialism*.

Man is What He Makes Himself

Sartre is keenly aware that the existentialist position must be subdivided into two categories of thinkers — the religious existentialists and those who are atheistically inclined. Sartre counts himself among the latter.[231] In spite of the disagreement over the influence of God in man's life, he avers that all existentialists begin with the maxim — existence precedes essence — and that the starting point of a search for a philosophical position must begin in subjectivity.[232] If there is no God, as Sartre believes, no absolute principles, man himself must form the basic "existent". If man is the basic "existent," then his existence must precede the concepts which he forms. To Sartre, man first appears on the scene and then, only after appearing, does he define who he is. Man chooses to transpose to the facets of his experiences his interpretations of these experiences which provide them with meaning and in turn their essence. Man acquires meaning when he chooses to make himself something. Man defines himself. When man is undefined he is nothing, for he has no meaning. Man creates his own meaning by choosing to interpret what happens to him as having meaning. If man is unaware of what is happening to him, then the event has no meaning to him. Not only is man what he conceives himself to be, and indeed nothing more than that, he is also what he wills himself to be after his first venture into existence. To summarize the position, the first principle of existentialism is that man is nothing but what he makes of himself.[233]

The idea that man is responsible for what he is may at first appear to be a harmless concept, but as the consequences of this freedom of man develops one becomes aware, as does Sartre, that existentialism is the most austere of doctrines and is intended strictly for specialists and philosophers.[234] Yet, paradoxically as may seem, it is the drama of Jean-Paul Sartre which has made existentialism the rage among certain groups in France, which has brought its interpretations of life to the masses--to those who are not philosophers and who have not specialized in disciplined thinking.

Man will be what he will have planned to be and therefore must be responsible for what he is.[235] There is no human nature because there is no previous mind which established the conditions for such a nature, such as the mind of God or some sort of Platonic ideals. Existentialism's first move, according to Sartre, is to make every man aware of what he is, and to make the full responsibility of his existence rest on him. Thus the existential voice is one of challenge, a challenge made to mankind. It is challenging each individual to realize that he creates himself and that there is no force, no ready made set of principles by whose criteria choices may be made. Not only do the existentialists emphasize man's responsibility for his own course in life, they also seek to point out that as man shapes his own destiny, so is the destiny of mankind shaped. Perhaps there is no other philosophical position more keenly aware of the fact that "no man is an island unto himself" than the existentialists. Existentialists stress that radiating from man's choice is a spiralling set of influences which expand over the entire range of mankind, both temporally and in the future. Each of man's actions precipitates at least a ripple in the pool of mankind which shall radiate out from itself until the whole pool has been traversed.

Sartre Emphasizes Subjectivity

Denied criteria for action, faced with the idea that man's existence precedes essence and that the quality of man's life will be based on each of his decisions, one is made aware of the second principle of existentialism, namely that it is impossible for man to transcend human subjectivity. Man cannot rise above his station in life and transport himself to some detached cloud from which he may objectively evaluate his situation in life or, for that matter, the choices which confront him.[236]

Even if there are permanent values in this world, man is so "earthbound" that he could not recognize them unless he himself were to choose that they are indeed values. He has no criteria for an evaluation of values. In fact, to Sartre, it is when man chooses that values themselves are chosen. To choose to be this or that is to affirm at the same time the value of what is chosen. Sartre assumes that man will never choose evil. In the first place Sartre does not accept the concept that there is an a priori evil. What man chooses may turn out to be harmful to himself, or to society, or if interpreted by a moralistic philosoph

118

may indeed appear evil, but to the chooser it is not evil from his perspective.[237] Of course man may choose in bad faith and thus find himself in a bad situation, but even here he has falsely convinced himself that what he has chosen is good for him and does not involve evil. Sartre believes that most people choose in bad faith[238] and this is the exact purpose of his writing. Sartre wishes to confront mankind with this fact and to lay bare the motives which precipitate choices which are made in bad faith. He then wants to make man aware of the possibility that he may choose authentically. To do this Sartre stresses that man must realize that when he makes a choice that choice becomes valuable. What is valuable for one man must be valuable for all mankind; if it is not so, then the choice may have been made in bad faith.[239]

Sartre's Interpretation of Man's Basic Anxiety

In the twentieth century various writers have emphasized that man is in a state of anxiety. To Sartre, man is not *in* a state of anxiety for there are no "states"; man is anguish, he is his anxiety. Man is anxious because he realizes that he is not only choosing the type of person he is to be, but in fact he is giving an example which will influence the choice of others. He is anxious because he cannot escape the feeling of his total and deep responsibility, for himself and for mankind as a whole.[240] He is like the military leader on the eve of a great military maneuver who wonders if he has made the right decision, if the men who are about to die will be sacrificed in vain, or in a shroud of meaning which will justify their deaths. In his mind will perpetually be the question – "Am I really the kind of man who has the right to act in such a way that humanity might guide itself by my actions?" Leaders know this anguish, but it doesn't keep them from acting. To the contrary, it is often the very condition of their action. For in their search for the correct decision they are made aware of the number of alternatives, and they know that from all these possibilities one has been chosen which forms the basis of their action, and they know that what they have chosen has received a special value.[241]

The leader may look for an omen by which to justify his decision. He may appeal to God for divine guidance so as to lift the weight of human responsibility from his shoulders, but to Sartre this is a vain hope. A forlornness settles over man, for he realizes deep within himself that God does not exist, and that he must face the consequences of his decisions alone. As Dostoyevsky wrote, "everything becomes permissible if there is no God", and man is left with nothing to cling to. He finds that he exists without the possibility of his finding values already made for him. Man is therefore alone, without excuse, with no possibility to alibi the reason for his decision. There are no values, for there is no source for the values beyond the choice of the man who searches for the security of a world with values, by which to legitimize his choices.[242] It is because eternal values, omens in nature, and other such forces offer man a media by which he can escape his personal responsibility for his choices, that Sartre equates man's freedom from these forces with condemnation. Man is condemned to be free, he is condemned to walk alone and bear his burden of responsibility for his choices.

This condemnation attitude does not mean that Sartre thinks that there is nothing of value in being free. The existentialist is aware that decision makes human life possible.[243] Even so, to the average man on the street, Sartre believes, it is better to have some means to rationalize one's own responsibility.

Sartre has noted the fact that existentialism is accused of inviting people to remain in a kind of quietism; that is, since no solutions are possible to one's problems, one might consider action in this world futile. Man might then end up in contemplation. Specifically, this charge has been leveled against existentialism by communist writers.[244] Much to the contrary, Sartre emphasizes that man is thrust into the world. Man is engaged in the world to such a degree that he must act 'before positing' his possibilities.[245] Even contemplation would be a definite act of choice for man is still involved in the world. He cannot step out of himself to view his world. In this situation man is totally free and in his freedom values find a unique foundation. It is man who determines what is valuable. It is man who determines what is to be destroyed. To Sartre, nothing is destroyed unless man is there to observe it. As man chooses his values he is actually aware that his values are those of his choice, and are not grounded in eternal stability. The very fact that he has chosen his values in one moment implies that he may "unchoose" them in the next. Man is anguished because he knows that any conduct on his part is only possible and that the motives for the present conduct will not necessarily be sufficient to sustain the choice in the next moment.[246] In fact, man in the next moment may become a non-being; in death his being may be separated from him, and then there will be no future. Anxiety is involved in the realization that one is not to be the same self in the next moment of decision that he is in his present moment of awareness. Man is anxious because he is aware that each past resolution is totally ineffectual in the future. Thus the decision that "I shall not gamble" made in one moment is meaningless in the next moment, unless it is reaffirmed. The previous declaration stands behind the individual like a "boneless phantom". It is for the individual in the moment of reality to give flesh to this phantom, to redesignate meaning to the choice.[247]

Man's Anguish and His Mortality

Not only is man anxious about the fact that in each new moment he will be confronted with new decisions, and that his past resolutions will not be sufficient to carry him into the future unless constantly reaffirmed, but he also doubts the efficacy of his own choice. He distrusts himself, and he wonders whether he has pulled the wool over his own eyes with each decision that he makes. He wonders if in the next moment he will be able to abide by the decision of the moment. This is man's genius. Man can detach himself from the world. He can actually question his own decisions. In systematic doubt one finds the possibility of man being able to detach himself from his real situation. This ability to question, according to Sartre, posits a nihilating withdrawal.[248] In terms of Sartre's ontology, this nihilating withdrawal from the being of man may be discussed in terms of being-in-self and being-for-itself. Being-in-itself designates real being — what must be — and it includes all that resides in the past. Being-for-itself is the force which provides man with his humanity and prevents him from being merely an inanimate object. It is man's ability to be restless in his own being, to feel the gnawing nothingness which permeates his being which enables him to reach out in order to obtain more being and to find a firmer foundation for one's being. The being-for-itself is a process by which man becomes detached from his being and reaches towards the future. Being-for-itself and being-in-itself are not opposites; no dualism is implied, not even a bipolar monism. Monism is still involved because being-for-itself arises out of being-in-itself and reaches for the nothingness of the future in order to fashion that nothingness into something. With each future moment becoming a past moment, the being-for-itself of that future moment, which then becomes past, once more becomes one with the being-in-itself. Therefore, in terms of time,

> what separates prior from subsequent is exactly nothing. . . . The prior consciousness is always there. It constantly maintains a relation of interpretation with the present consciousness; but on the basis of this existential relation it is put out of the game.[249]

In freedom, the human being is his own past in the form of nihilation. The individual finds himself in "a certain mode of, standing opposite his past and future as not being them."[250] It is in this mode that man finds himself in freedom. Freedom, as Sartre defines it, is characterized by a constantly renewed obligation to remake the self.[251] The act of remaking the self forces man to realize that, although he is familiar with his self today, tomorrow he may be a stranger to his today's self and may indeed be another self. As Sartre writes,

> I make an appointment with myself on the other side of that hour or that day, or that month. Anguish is the fear of not finding myself at that appointment, of no longer wishing to bring myself [or this decision] there. . . .[252]

Even in the quasi-generality of every day acts man is engaged, he is venturing and he is discovering his possibilities by actually living in the possibilities of his existence. As one realizes one's possibilities, one at once realizes that they are exigencies, urgencies of the moment, and instrumentalities leading one toward the next moment, and that they may be questioned at any time. Most of the routine tasks which confront man in his everyday life, which to the uncritical mind may seem imposed on the individual because of his life situation, become only possibilities of behavior which one is not required to ratify in the next moment of life. Concerning his own writings Sartre affirmed,

> Nothing, not even what I have been, can compel me to write. [I must discover my essence as what I have been.] . . . I apprehend my freedom as being the possible destroyer in the present and in the future of what I am.[253]

Man does not need to be who he is in this moment in the next moment of his existence. If man chooses to be in the next moment what he is in this moment, it will be because he has given value or meaning to whom or what he is in this moment. Thus, as indicated before by a slightly different approach, man is the creator and sustainer of values.

To summarize the discussion, Sartre emphasizes that man is thrust into the world, not just at the point of his birth, but in each moment of his existence. Man is engaged in existence. Man, at once, apprehends himself as both totally free and in anguish; he realizes that he is not able to derive meaning from life except as it comes from himself and the being he has chosen to be.[254] As a result of these conclusions Sartre permits himself to surmise that what really scares the critics of existentialism is that it leaves in man the possibility of choice.[255]

How Man Ought to Reach a Free Decision

Once Sartre has stripped man of his reliance on divine guidance, or of faith in a world of established values, he then turns his attention to other possibilities of how man might arrive at his decisions. In the first place, Sartre doubts that man is ever actually confronted with decisions when he becomes aware of the problem and begins to worry about its solution. Solutions to problems are made at the moment of the problem's occurrence. To illustrate the point, Sartre recalled an instant in which a young man came to him to ask his advice about whether he should join the French army in order to fight the Germans, or whether he should honor his mother's wish that he remain with her as he was her only son. Sartre recognized that the young man was torn with anguish over the apparent problem; nevertheless he insists that the young man knew the answer to his problem even before coming to talk to one of the prominent leaders of the French resistance. The counsellor is chosen who will arbitrate in favor of the decision which the individual has come to. He now seeks support to implement his decision, a force to blame the decision-making on if the decision should prove untenable. When one comes to a counsellor he already has within him the solution to his problem. The counsellor must make explicit what the individual has already chosen.[256]

There are those who feel that if existentialism denies the world of sustaining values, then man will be reduced to the world of instinctual living. Sartre himself writes that if values are too vague or too broad for the concrete situation, the only thing left for man is to trust his instincts.[257] However, one does not arrive at a decision by relying solely on his instincts. Man is not influenced by a set of instincts, if there be such, man would *be* the instinct, and the circumstance of man as instinct would be predicated on his choice. Therefore the act of choice determines the instinctual behavior of the person. The instinct is not prior to the choice, and therefore cannot be used as the criterion for the choice, for the choice has already been made. Regarding the concept of instincts, some hold the feelings of man to be important criteria for choice; one ought to act in accord with his feelings. Here too, "feeling is formed by the acts one performs; so I can not refer to it in order to act upon it." One feels according to the way he has chosen to feel. To sum-

124

marize, "I cannot seek within myself the true condition which will impel me to act, nor apply to a system of ethics for concepts which will permit me to act."[258]

Contemporary American psychology is predicated on the assumption that for every effect there must be a cause, and that if one knows the cause one will be able to predict the effect. The position is often defined as psychological determinism. Sartre rejects this theory as applying to man in the moment of his decision making. Psychological determinism may be set into motion after man has made the decision, and may be valid until a new decision is required but in the act of decision making psychological determinism is preceded by the act of choice.

> Psychological determinism . . . is first an attitude of excuse, or if you prefer, the basis of all attitudes of excuse. . . . It attempts to fill the void which encircles us and to reestablish the links between past and present . . . [It reduces us to never being anything that we are.] . . . But this determinism, a reflective defense against anguish, is not given as reflective intuition. It avails nothing against the evidence of freedom; hence it is given as a faith to take refuge in . . . [Its evidence is based on introspection, but is given as a satisfying hypothesis.] They admit there is a consciousness of freedom but debate its value.[259]

To Sartre, it is important to re-emphasize that "nothing, not even what I have been, can compel me . . ." to do something in the new moment. Psychological determinism may have an appearance of truth when based on hindsight--when one reviews the factual existence of being-in-itself. But the for-itself involves a consciousness or an ability to arise out of its own being, out of any determinism, and to bring itself into an unknown moment, one which is not determined until after it is lived.

Sartre also quarrels with the prevalent notions which are advanced by the adherents of the Freudian system concerning the concept of the unconscious and the mechanism of repression. To Sartre these are untenable concepts. Psychoanalytical theory attempts to substitute for the presence of bad faith the idea of a lie without a liar. It is an attempt to excuse individual behavior by removing from the individual direct responsibility for his action, and placing this responsibility in the hands of another. To turn over the responsibility of influencing behavior to the realm of the unconscious mind would not be unlike turning the responsibility over to the hands of a complete stranger, for indeed, a person's unconscious is a stranger to the conscious mind. The determiner of the matters which are to be delegated to the jurisdiction of the unconscious is the censor. Sartre pungently points out that in order for the censor to function with discernment it must know how to evaluate the situation and then be able to maintain an awareness of that which it is repressing. To Sartre, it is not sufficient for the censor merely to recognize the repressed drives, it must also re-arrest these drives as they try for expression once again in the conscious life from whence they had previously been banished in another form. Sartre asks, how may one discern the impulses needing to be repressed without being conscious of discerning them? The most plausible answer would be that it must be that consciousness is cognizant of the drive to be repressed at all times. The drive, however, must be repressed so that the consciousness of the person will not be conscious of it. This provides an irreconcilable dilemma as far as Sartre is concerned. What has consciousness achieved when it has been conscious of a drive which must be repressed and therefore represses it, but then must sustain a cognizance of the repressed drive in order for the drive to remain repressed? Obviously, there is a force at work which does so confuse man, but this force is a conscious undertaking and Sartre has labeled the force as involving bad faith. One does not need to establish a duality or even a trinity to understand why man will be found in the situation of bad faith.[260]

Sartre's Concept of Bad Faith

One who practices bad faith is hiding an unpleasant truth or presenting as truth an untruth which is pleasing. Succinctly stated, bad faith is a lie to oneself. Sartre dismisses the concept of Freud's unconscious by stating explicitly that the essence of a lie implies that the liar actually is in complete possession of the truth which he is hiding. In this sense, the person chooses to exist in bad faith and in any new moment may reverse the choice. Unfortunately, the liar is often victimized by his lie, and becomes convinced that it implies a truth.

The purpose of bad faith is to postpone the moment of decision as long as possible. Bad faith in itself attempts to make the person what the person is not. If a man chooses to be what he is, bad faith is forever impossible, according to the Sartrean analysis. A concept is often made more explicit by studying its opposite, which in this case of bad faith would be sincerity. Sincerity is the opposite of bad faith, but unlike bad faith, which attempts to objectify, it is not a state but rather a demand. It is a quality of living which is characterized by man simply being only what he is. Bad faith, which objectifies the person into something concrete and lasting, requires extensive role-playing. This role-playing often imprisons a man in a concept which he finds difficult to avoid. Thus a man is a teacher, a waiter; a good man or a bad man. The role in itself requires certain types of behavior which the individual must perform to the best of his ability. The waiter must be able to offer service, to recognize himself as having a definite position in the maze of life and to will to dress himself in some distinctive uniform.

It is not enough, for Sartre, to merely posit that man exists in bad faith. It is essential to explain the root of the lie. The lie originates because the individual is confronted by the fact of his impending doom, by the fact that he is to die, and by the fact that he may not be able to keep the appointment he has made with himself to meet himself at some future time. All of this is realized in sincerity, and in sincerity man does not like the tension, the anguish, or the forlornness of his condition. In sincerity he hopes for something better, and this hope is translated into a faith that there must be something better than what obviously confronts man. The problem of bad faith stems inevitably from the fact that bad faith is indeed a faith.[261] Bad faith does not contain the norms and criteria of truth as they are accepted by critical thought of good faith. Bad faith (or the person) apprehends the evidence, but is resigned in advance to not being fulfilled by the evidence, and therefore to not being persuaded and transformed in good faith.[262] The possibility of bad faith is due to the fact that the being of consciousness is a being which finds that its own being is in question. Therefore the being of consciousness does not coincide with itself.

It has been stated bad faith is made possible by the being of man sincerely realizing that its future terminates, or becomes objectified, in death. In death the very meaning of our life escapes man, for not only does he not choose the moment at which the account will be closed, but at that moment his meaning becomes a fact which is to be handled by those who succeed him.[263] From man's point of view, death is indicative of the fact that the final value of this life remains forever in suspense. Death is that which prevents meaning from being realized in life and in fact removes all meaning from life. Death is what transforms life into an existence which may be symbolized by the idea of the Lost Chord.[264]

Sartre's Interpretation of the Meaning of Death

The unique characteristic of a terminated life is that it is a life which the "other" makes himself the guardian of. The "other", that is to say, he who survives the death of another, reconstructs the deceased life according to his (the former's) own subjective appraisal, and the deceased cannot defend himself against the product of the insinuations. To be forgotten is to be made the object of an attitude of another, and of the implicit decision on the part of the other to not remember the meaning of the dead life.[265]

To appreciate death from another angle, Sartre points out that death ends the mystery of life. Up to the point of dying man is in suspense, he never knows what he will be in the next moment for what he is may be totally changed in the next moment. After death, man can no longer change his own being, he has no possibilities which are of his own choice. It is for this reason that there is no place for death in the for-itself which is continuously striving to be something other than what it is. The for-itself is a mode which therefore will seek to avoid the realization of death so that its movement will not be inhibited. This avoidance of death leads into a faith that the inevitability of death does not confront man and that he may perpetuate himself. From this step, one enters the realm of bad faith.

Death means that the "other" has triumphed over one. Paradoxicaly as it may seem, man would not even know of death unless the "other" exists, and brings the meaning of death to our attention by his dying.[266]

The individual longs for an answer to the meaning or purpose of death; but to Sartre, death, like birth, is an absurdity. As an absurdity it cannot be explained by the person who sincerely attempts to gain an explanation. For the person who can accept the absurdity of death, who sincerely realizes that death forms the final boundary of life, it is possible to transform death into meaning, for death makes the meaning of life. In death the final note is struck, and the melody has been completed. In sincerity the individual may concede that all of his life has been nothing but the preparation for death. In absurdity he was born and in absurdity he will die. Death viewed in this perspective is not permitted to remain simply human, "but in fact becomes mine."[267] My life is unique because in between the boundaries of birth and death, I choose the content, and this content may never be chosen again. Man must realize that he cannot wait for death for man can only wait for a determinate fact. The process of death is already upon us at the time of birth, and the process must be realized and not hidden away.

As a result of the existential emphasis on death, some have chided existentialism for being morbidly pessimistic. Sartre rejects this allegation and asserts that there is no way of thinking which is more optimistic than existentialism, for it grants man the ability to create his own meanings, to be honest with himself, and to guide himself freely. What may be even more important, if life is based on the absurdity of birth and death, this means that what meanings man makes out of his situation can not be less than the state into which man was born and from which he must die. This is to say that existentialism opens to man the vista which is summarized in the philosophy — he has everything to gain and nothing to lose as he meets each day.[268]

Sartre's Concept of Interpersonal Relations

It has been noted that the person would not know of his death, or the possibility of death if there were no other people through whom he could be introduced to death. The concept of the "other" is an important point of orientation in Sartre's philosophy. Without the "other", the individual would know absolutely nothing about himself.

> What I know is the body of another, and the essential facts which I know concerning my own body come from the way in which others see it [my body]. Thus the nature of my body refers me to the existence of others and to my being-for-others.[269]

The sensory apparatus of the organism perceives the presence of other people, of the other person, of the "other". One is made aware that the "other" is perceiving oneself. By studying how the "other" perceives oneself, one may come to know one's for-it-selfness as one perceives the for-itself-for-others role. Thus the "other" appears to the individual through the latter's sensory perception as an organized being who is not unlike the individual's own being.

> [the Other] is conceived as real, and yet I can not conceive of his real relation to me.[270]

While the "look" of the other person makes me aware that he is looking at me, and that I am an object for him, at the same time my look is objectifying him and yet I am aware that my objectification is incomplete for I may never know the real other, for I am never able to walk in his shoes, to abide in his experiences which have constituted his "being-in-itself". Nevertheless I bring an interpretation of his being and to the degree which the other is aware that I am watching him, to the point that he understands my communication, he realizes that I am interpreting him. By reversing the same line of thought, one also becomes aware that the "other" is looking at him, is making an object out of him which he will endeavor to manipulate in the same way that he manipulates all objects. Furthermore, one becomes aware of himself, of who he is, by how the "other" reacts toward him, thus affording him a reflection of himself.

> In the field of my reflection I can never meet with anything but the consciousness which is mine. But the Other is the indispensable mediator between myself and me. I am ashamed of myself as I appear to the other. . . .
> By the mere appearance of the Other, I am put in a position of passing judgement on myself as an object. . . . Shame is by nature recognition. I recognize that I am as the Other sees me. . . . Nobody can be vulgar alone. . . . Thus the Other has not only revealed to me what I was; he has established me in a new type of being which can support new qualifications. . . . But this new being which appears for the other does not reside in the Other; I am responsible for it as is shown very well by the education system which consists in making children ashamed of what they are. . . . But at the same time I need the Other in order to realize fully all the structures of my being.[271]

Sartre is contending that a given person may never know himself by observing himself for at all times he is himself. It is impossible for him to step outside of himself for self-observation. The only way in which man may become aware of himself is by studying the impressions that he leaves on another person in his environment. One cannot judge himself introspectively; a person can only judge himself to the extent that he studies the impressions he has made on other people.

The basic analysis of the Sartrean self-concept is not far removed from the development of the self-concept as discussed by the American psychiatrist, Harry Stack Sullivan.

131

. . . you must think of the self as the 'apparatus' — the bundle of processes, selected memories, knowledge of relationships, and so on — that is struck off the very rich and capable human personality by the necessity for feeling secure in contact with others, long before one can possibly analyze and make reasonable sense of the cultural prescriptions of behavior. Now I want to talk briefly about the beginnings of the self-system. It is said that from the experience of rewards, that is, of approval, parental tenderness, learning by the anxiety gradient, etc., there occurs in childhood an initial "personification" of three phases of experience, which will presently be "me", the "me" being invariably connected with some sentience of the body. The initial "personifications" as "not-me", "good me," and "bad-me".

"Good me" is explained as "the growing organization of experience in which satisfactions have been enhanced by rewarding increments in tenderness from the mothering one."[272]

To Sullivan how one perceives the behavior of his parents or significant people shapes the development of personality. One develops in accord with the interpretations of oneself which others have made known to the person.

One also finds in the theory of client-centered therapy the implied Sartrean position, namely that as the therapist clarifies and reflects the client's statements the client comes to know himself. If the therapist is a directive therapist, according to Carl Rogers, the client is still likely to accept the interpretation which the counsellor makes of the client's problems.

It is important to stress once more that the individual is not determined by the "other", for he still must be responsible for his interpretation of the other's estimation of him and also is responsible for the impression he makes on the other regardless of whether he interprets that impression correctly. Sartre often emphasizes "this is the world in which man decides what he is and what others are."[273]

It has been stated that through our own sense perception we become aware of the organization of the other's being. This still leaves a question open as to how our organism may perceive the Other as being of the same existence that we are and is not merely an object among objects. Also involved in this problem is how one consciousness becomes aware of another's consciousness. Sartre argues that the meeting of two consciousnesses forms an a priori in his system which must be accepted to provide common ground for discussion. The relationship between consciousnesses, to Sartre, is logically unthinkable.

The Other is an a priori hypothesis with no justification save the unity which it permits to operate in our experience.[274]

[Actually] we can never apprehend the relation of that Other to [ourselves] and [the Other] is never given, but gradually [man] constitutes him as a concrete object.[275]

Man does comprehend that the Other involves a radical negation of his experience, since he is the one for whom he is not the subject but rather is the object. The Other makes man realize that he (man) is not the manipulator, but rather the manipulated. Sartre believes that this threat of becoming an object subjected to the gaze of the Other overwhelms man and forces man to attempt, by whatever means at his disposal, to conquer the individuality of the Other, and make him his (man's) object. The organism is in the position of attempting to rise above, or to recrystallize, the essential being-in-itself. As the for-itself develops, man is aware that he is totally responsible for his being. In that the for-itself never has foundations, the for-itself is an insecure identity which strives for permanence. When the Other confronts the individual, the individual's being-for-itself is captured and objectified. This potentially hostile act must be resisted on the part of the for-itself at all costs. This means that the individual stands in opposition to the Other. At this point, one becomes aware of the radical alienation between Sartre and Buber. Buber suggests that the "I" finds fulfillment when it can approach another and speak to him as a "Thou". Sartre finds the situation so untenable that even the lover's gaze is threatened by objectification. The Other is in fact a serious impediment in man's self-realization. To defend oneself against the Other, the individual becomes oriented towards an attempt to influence the Other's feelings, ideas, volition and character. As man influences the Other, he reduces him to an object which he manipulates and he forbids him the possibility of influencing himself. To Sartre the sadist is an individual who attempts to reduce another individual to that of identity with his tortured flesh. If the tortured person identifies himself with his flesh then he is reduced to complete passivity, is made impotent and loses his freedom.[276] Even the act of loving involves the capture of the Other's identity.

> In caressing the Other I cause her flesh to be born beneath my caress, under my fingers. . . . The caress causes the Other to be born as flesh for me and herself. . . . The caress is designed to uncover the web of inertia beneath the action- i.e., the pure "being-there" — which sustains it.[277]

The Other does not influence me just by being present in my environment. It is his act of "looking" at me which establishes the relationship between us.

> I am absolutely nothing [until] . . . I become aware that someone is looking at me. . . . [When someone looks at me] it means that I am suddenly affected in my being and that essential modifications appear in my structure.
> . . . I see myself because somebody else sees me. . . . This means that all of a sudden I am conscious of myself as escaping myself, not in that I am the foundation of my own nothingness but in that I have my foundations outside of myself. I am for myself only as I am a pure reference for others. . . .[278]

> [By the] Other's look I shall remain forever a consciousness. But it is for the Other, once more the nihilating escape of the for-itself is fixed, once more the in-itself closes in upon the for-itself.[279]

134

The most pronounced rejection of the look of others is found in the attempt of lovers to find solitude, to escape the look of third parties. Lovers will know the eternal bliss only so long as they are not conscious that they are looking at each other. To Sartre, however, this "looking at each other" is inevitable for eventually even the lovers will objectify one another.

Sartre states explicitly that man cannot be evil while he is alone.

> I am not and cannot be evil for myself for two reasons: . . . I am not evil any more than I am a civil servant, or a physician. In fact, I am in the mode of not being what I am and of being what I am not. . . . If I were to be evil for myself, I should of necessity be so in the mode of having to be so and would have to apprehend myself and will myself [to be] evil. But this would mean that I must discover myself as willing what appears to myself as the opposite of my good.[280]

Ethics, therefore, do not originate with the individual, but are bestowed upon the individual by the look of another person. It is the Other who interprets my acts as being bad or evil, and these interpretations will be made from his subjective evaluations.

Not only are ethics shaped by the Other, but also the individual's emotional states are also influenced thus.

> Feelings themselves are nothing more than our way of affectively experiencing our being-for-others. Fear in fact implies that I appear to myself as threatened by virtue of my being a presence in the world, not in my capacity as a For-itself which causes a world to exist. It is the object which I am which is in danger in the world. . . . Fear is therefore the discovery of my being-as-object. . . . . it refers to the origin of all fear which is the fearful discovery of my pure and simple object-state in so far as it is . . . transcended by possibles which are not my possibles.[281]

Modesty about dress, according to Sartre's analysis, symbolizes our worry that to be nude indicates that we are defenseless before others as objects. To put on clothes is to hide one's

135

object-state; it is to claim the right of seeing without being seen.[282] Man's feeling of shame and sin before God reflects the same foundation, namely that by definition God is pure subjectivity, and this means that man is pure objectivity to God's weltanschauung, This reduces man to being what he is not striving for.[283]

While man may decide what he is and what others are, as previously discussed, he cannot alter the necessity of his existing in a world in which he must work to sustain himself and in which he must relate himself to other people. Furthermore he must accept the fact that he is not superhuman but is fettered by mortal limitations. These are objective facts because they are found everywhere that man exists, and yet they are subjective facts because man must "live" the conditions, and furthermore, man is nothing if he does not choose freely to live within these set conditions to the best of his ability.[284] In the determination of man's free will, he is limited by these universal conditions. These limitations Sartre refers to by the term *facticity*.

Sartre's Concept of Man's Freedom of the Will and Facticity

Man does exist within definite limitations or factual situations. What is vital to man, in terms of permitting him to exist, is the fact that he can affirm; he can choose to work within the limitations which are imposed upon him. Man can choose to be an existent among other existents, or he may choose to commit suicide and thus remove himself from the situation. Utilizing Heidegger's term, Sartre writes that

> although brute things . . . can from the start limit our freedom of action, it is our freedom itself which must first constitute the framework, the technique and the ends in relation to which they will manifest themselves as limits.[285]

Two men might find themselves confronted with identical bodily afflictions, yet it is what the two men choose to make out of their imposed physical limitations that permits them to create their own unique existence. In fact, freedom implies man's attempt to rise above, to manipulate definite restrictions, and to cope with a resisting world.

> Simple wishes if fulfilled in a dream need no choice. ... To be free does not mean to obtain what one has wished but rather by oneself to determine oneself to wish.[286]

The world, by coefficients of adversity, reveals to man the position in which he stands in relation to the ends which he assigns himself, so that he can never know if the world is giving information about himself or about the situation. Obstacles which the world imposes upon man, vary in significance depending upon whether they confront an amateur or a professional, a man who is sick or well, a man who is run down or is in good condition, a man who couldn't care less about the situation or a man who is concerned about the situation.[287] Even the idea of being a hundred feet from the top of a mountain must be interpreted against the expertness of the climber and the condition he is in as a result of the climb which he has already engaged in. As has been shown in mountain climbing, many obstacles which men have thought to be impossible to overcome have been conquered by men of great determination.

Man of necessity finds himself located in a definite place in the world. To be born, to quote Sartre, is to take one's place, or rather to receive it.[288]

> I exist my place without choice, without necessity either, as the pure absolute fact of my being there. ...I am neither free nor not free, I am a pure existent....[289]

> My place is defined by the spatial order and by the particular nature of the "thises" which are revealed to me on the ground of the world.[290]

There would be no place if there were not human reality; in fact there would not be any space or time either. Yet, human reality has nothing to say about space, nor time, nor place.

Man would not know his place in the world if it were not for his freedom.

It is my freedom which comes to confer on my place and to define it as such by situating me. The sole reason that I can be strictly limited to this being-there which I am is that my ontological structure is not to be what I am and to be what I am not.[291]

It is in the light of an end that my place takes on meaning. For I could never be simply there. My place is grasped as an exile. To be sure, when man is born he finds himself in a definite place, but he is responsible for the place which *he* takes.[292]

Another "facticity" which envelopes the individual is his past life. Each individual has a past, and his choices are going to be colored by the past through which the individual has lived. Sartre is very frank to admit that no new decisions can ever be made without reference to the past.[293] The meaning of the past to the individual is that of an immensely important backdrop which provides him with a point of view. Nevertheless every action in which the individual participates is an attempt to wrest himself away from his past and to assume new meaning.

To Sartre, the past is not something which is immutable or unchangeable. In each present moment the past is being reshaped. The creation of the past in the present is never more obvious than in the propaganda techniques which seek to create impressions. At one moment the Soviet Union may be an ally, at the next moment she becomes a mortal enemy, and the text books are rewritten. In order for the past to be finished, completed, human history must first be terminated. "The meaning of the social past is perpetually in 'suspense'."[294]

Sartre, the master of paradoxes, states,

I can not conceive of myself without a past; ... but on the other hand I am the being through whom the past comes to myself and the world.[295]

My past is a concrete and precise proposition which as such awaits ratification.[296]

Thus we choose our past in the light of a certain end, but from then on it imposes itself upon us and devours us.[297]

Once a past is chosen, once the end is chosen by which the past assumes meaning, at that moment, and at that moment only, the past assumes a sort of necessity which approaches a determination of behavior.

[Determinism, itself, fails to deal with the question of how a cause can be constituted as such in the cause-intention-act-end.] In order [for there] to be a cause, the cause must be experienced as such. ... The for-itself must confer on it its value as cause or motive. ... Causes and motives have meaning only inside a projected ensemble which is precisely an ensemble of non-existence.[298]

It is by fleeing a situation toward our possibility of changing it that we organize this situation into complexes of causes and motives. ... The result is that it is in fact impossible to find an act without a motive but that this does not mean that we must conclude that the motive causes the act, the motive is an integral part of the act.[299]

What must be understood in the analysis of free will as presented by Sartre is his dichotomy between being-in-itself and being-for-itself. Being-for-itself is not a part of being-in-itself which is the real substance of the person.

Man is free because he is not himself but presence to himself. The being which is what it is cannot be free. Freedom is precisely the nothingness which is made-to-be at the heart of man and which forces human reality to make itself instead of to be.[300]

As soon as consciousness is made-past however, it is what man has to be in the form of what 'was'. Consequently when man reviews his past deeds, his past consciousness, he finds that it preserves its intentional significance and its meaning as subjectivity, but, it is now fixed, it has become objectified for that which has been incorporated by the past becomes being-in-itself.[301]

How does man come to make a decision, how does he arise out of his essential being so as to view himself from a different perspective? Sartre answers these questions by positing that

> I am my own motivation without being my own foundation,
> the fact that I am nothing without having to be what I am
> and yet in so far as I have to be what I am, I am without
> having to be.[302]

This is to say, that the basic substance of human existence is
human motivation to arise from its own substance, its own
existence.

In that motivation is to be found at the basis of man's freedom,
and is identical with the upsurge of the for-itself characterization
of man's personality, it necessarily follows, according to Sartre's
logic, that freedom appears as an unanalyzable totality. The
totality includes causes, motives, and ends, as well as the mode
of apprehending same and then organizing them into a unity
within the compass of this freedom.[303]

Human reality is therefore free to the exact extent that it
has to be its own nothingness. ... It has to be this nothingness
first by temporalizing itself — i.e., by being always at a distance
from itself — which means that it can never let itself be determined by its past to perform this or that particular act; second,
by arising as consciousness of something. Nothing exists in consciousness which is not conscious of existing and consequently
nothing external to conciousness can motivate it.[304]

The for-itself is perpetually establishing itself as an entity
which is set over against the in-itself which is composed of
the previously chosen acts and the consequences which have
stemmed from the choices. Thus the person is perpetually engaged in choice and perpetually is conscious of the fact that
he, himself, can abruptly invert his choice and reverse steam.
Man projects the future by his very being, but his existential
freedom perpetually eats it away as he makes known to himself
what he is by means of the future but without getting a grip
on this future, which remains always possible without ever
breaking into the rank of the real. Thus he is perpetually threatened by the nihilation of his actual choice and is perpetually
threatened with choosing his identity and consequently with
becoming other than he is.[305]

The individual exists in a world which already provides him with meaning which he, himself, has bestowed upon the world, but which did not come from himself, but which he discovered he possessed. He takes a trip and sees a railroad sign; this he interprets, he gives meaning to the sign, but the sign already had the potentiality for the meaning. He is born a Frenchman or an American but he gives meaning to his nationality and makes the concept Frenchman or American real and meaningful. Indeed, every event in the world which an individual encounters is revealed to him only as an opportunity; the meaning of the opportunity the individual himself must bestow.[306]

Man finds himself limited by the natural world; in fact, in order to exist man must obey the laws of nature. The paradox arises however that because man obeys the laws of nature, he is able to command nature itself, and to order it to suit his convenience with increasing accuracy.[307] Ultimately it is man's choice which permits even nature to exist. In the absence of a witness to a storm, the storm is an impotent force which merely modifies and distributes the masses of being which have come within its wake. Under such a condition there would only be a beginning and an afterwards to the storm, but the storm would have no meaning. The destructive power of the storm must be witnessed; that witness must be man. It is then necessary to recognize that destruction is not related to the wrath of God, but that man destroys, for it is he who gives meaning through choice to the environmental configuration which after the storm would no longer exist in that form. Thus even the forces of nature are made impotent to the will of man. As a matter of fact, before man was alive, life was nothing; it is up to man to give life meaning, and the meaning which man chooses to give life is identical to the values which he finds in life.[308]

Some have charged existentialism with dwelling on human degradation; they accuse the existential writers of forgetting the smile of the child and of perceiving only human aloneness. Others worry that existentialism involves a denial of reality and the seriousness of human undertakings, since God's command-ments are rejected as eternal verities. Still others feel that existentialism's implied futility forces hedonism upon mankind. To Sartre, the allegations are false and are made in bad faith. He reiterates time and time again that existentialism never ends with analyzing human degradation whenever this is a subject for analysis, because man is never conceived as a finite being, but he is always in the making, and is always faced with new possibilities even though he be the most degraded person. A new dawn is set before any state of human degradation which brings hope to the individual who is mired in the muck. Certainly existentialism declares that every truth and every action implies a human setting and a human subjectivity, but to Sartre, this fact means that human life is made possible. Man is not a purely mechanistic force nor a puppet of some divine interest.[309]

Part IV: Karl Jaspers

The most outstanding German existentialist to have survived the Hitler regime and the war is Karl Jaspers. In many respects Jaspers' thought closely parallels Kierkegaard's point of view. In fact, it might be said that Jaspers has reworked basic Kierkegaardian themes, and brought them into twentieth century perspective. Furthermore his thought represents a synthesis between that of Sartre and Buber.

As did Kierkegaard, Jaspers finds that the harmony of mankind has been seriously imperiled by the rise of mediocrity.

Today we are living in an era of the most terrible catastrophes. It seems as though everything that had been transmitted to us were being melted down, and yet there is no convincing sign that a new edifice is in the making.[310]

Everything has become questionable, the substance of everything threatened. It used to be said that we were living in a time of transition, but now every newspaper is talking of the world crisis.[311]

To compound the situation, the author indicates that no simple solution to the crisis may be found.

It is of multiple causation, so that it cannot be overcome by dealing with this or that particular cause, but must be apprehended, endured and mastered as our world situation.[312]

Jaspers calls not for a solution, for an undoing of the crisis, but rather for an attitudinal change. Instead of resisting the world, man must accept the world as is and then take the material he has been given to work with and therewith fashion his own domicile.

To the deep concern about their era that men like Jaspers enunciate, their critics answer that other people have had their problems too. Jaspers is more than aware of this.

The feeling that the social conditions are hopelessly disordered, and that no firm abiding place remains is not new to History.[313]

Each new generation shudders at the prospect of ruin while regarding as a Golden Age some earlier period in which those who belonged to it were harassed by the same gloomy volumnations.[314]

One important difference between the feelings of crisis in former years as compared to the twentieth century crisis is that formerly the menace to civilization came from without, whereas now it is from within.[315] A symptom of the inner crisis of man is the fact that he no longer is capable of experiencing anything remote, mysterious or wonderful.[316] His sense of awe has been replaced by a fundamental analytical attitude which demands explanations for everything which is experienced.

With the rise of the machine age, the age of conformity, man has been thrust back into the narrow space of his origins, there to decide whether he will continue to exist as a man or to become an automatic man.[317] Man has experienced an enormous leveling process as the result of the unification of his planet.[318] No longer is he capable of expressing the rugged form of individualism, no longer is he capable of migrating to a sparsely populated area in order to live as he chooses. Instead he is continuously surrounded by people whose wishes he must take into consideration before he implements a choice.

> More and more do we find that what can only exist as the outcome of individual initiative is being transformed into collective enterprises.[319]

To Jaspers, unless the drive towards organization is held in check by some contraposing force, it will ruin what it seeks to enhance – man as man.

> ... the course of the world ... seems to him in many ways undesirable – a feeling of powerlessness has become rife, and man tends to regard himself as dragged along in the wake of events which ... he had hoped to guide.[320]

> The epochal consciousness has turned a somersault in the void.... Beyond question there is a widespread conviction that human activities are unavailing; everything has become questionable; nothing in human life holds good; that existence is no more than an unceasing maelstrom of reciprocal deception and self-deception by ideologies.[321]

Today, faith in ideologies has been shaken drastically because man has become aware that he exists in a historically determined, yet completely changing, situation. Man has been uprooted because he no longer feels himself to be completely in charge of his own destiny as did man a century or so ago.[322] The fact that the historical determinate is itself subject to change leaves man without a firm footing in this world.

To summarize the position in which man finds himself, Jaspers writes as follows:

> ... the problem concerning the situation of mankind has been growing ever more urgent ... in former days only a few were anxiously considering the dangers to which our mental world is exposed, since the war the gravity of the peril has become manifest to every one.[323]

In yester-year man's chief problems were related to sheer physical existence, in the twentieth century his ability to use his mind creatively and independently of controlled thought is in jeopardy. The outcome of the problem being discussed is uncertain. Man must find a way to create a reality in which human existence can find fulfillment and rise into what is infinitely open.[324] The concern here is for man to find solid enough ground so as to be able to express himself in terms of his own abilities optimally. Man must search for this stable space in which he can maximally realize himself. He yearns for guidance, but does not find guidance from forces which are external to himself.[325]

> So long as the process of disintegration continues, any valid answers can come only from individuals speaking with individuals from the depths of our historical foundations.[326]

In that a stable criteria for existence which demands only that man conforms to it is not ready-made, man must himself work out meaningful foundations upon which further decisions may be based. This process, according to Jaspers, can be worked out only in consensually validated situations.

In spite of the difficult dilemmas of the twentieth century, Jaspers maintains an optimistic attitude concerning the solving of the problems which face man.

> The stimulating characteristic of our present situation is that thinking about it helps to determine what will become of . . . [man's crisis].[327]

Even though man's mental existence is threatened by conformity, it still holds the possibility of overcoming man's difficulties.

> The mental situation of our day is pregnant with immense dangers and immense possibilities; and it is one which, if we are inadequate to the tasks which await us, will herald the failure of mankind.[328]

If man is to receive no guidance from set and established

ideologies, if he is to overcome the difficulties of the current period in consensual validation with other individuals, then man must himself develop some answer to the question of why he exists.

> If man is to help himself, today, his philosophy must take the form of a study of what is our present conception of human existence.[329]

As a result of the crises which have plagued man in the twentieth century he is being forced to think about his situation in the world.

> The desire to lead a philosophical life springs from the darkness in which the individual finds himself, from his sense of forlornness when he stares without love into the void, from his self forgetfulness when he feels he is being consumed by the busyness of the world, when he suddenly wakes up in terror and asks himself: "What am I, what am I failing to do, what should I do?"[330]

> By living philosophically man seeks to build up his own strength which is what his world no longer gives him.[331]

> As long as man is not able to discover on his own initiative the ideas that come to meet him in the world, he remains hidden from himself. This is especially true in a world which has fallen into decay, when his standard ideas seem to be dying.[33?]

> The essential problem in reaching a satisfactory solution to the crisis of our twentieth century is whether the masses of mankind can be democratized, whether average human nature is such as to enable each person to accept his share of responsibility as a citizen equally aware with all others of what he i doing, and ready, as a part of his daily life, to take his share in deciding fundamental political issues, as well as the directio which his own life is to take.[333] All of this assumption of responsibility requires an enormous mental effort which the average man, according to Jaspers, may not possess.

To Jaspers, Kierkegaard was the first to undertake a comprehensive critique of the modern period, and his critique is sti valid, writes Jaspers, for the mid-twentieth century.[334] The sum effect of Kierkegaard's work, according to Jaspers, is that he confronted man with the fact of his "nothingness". Jaspers picks up this Kierkegaardian theme and sets it against a more philosophical tapestry by stating that the fundamental predicament of mankind, or being as a whole, is that being has a crack running through it. Being is not a whole. All human life, activity, achievement, and success are doomed finally to suffer shipwreck. The finality of the shipwreck may be found in natural disasters and ultimately in the death and suffering of man.[335] Jaspers would separate the shipwreck which all human endeavor must eventually suffer from the crisis which the twentieth century is afflicted with. Through the latter crisis, philosophy will endure. "Philosophy endures in every catastrophe in the thoughts of a few men."[336]

However, the situation of philosophy in our day is not favorable. Philosophies such as Marxism are being embraced by a vast number of people who are devoid of all faith. As a result philosophy has become more and more a mere enterprise of doctrine and history.

> Since our age has not yet discovered a style for itself or become fully aware what it really wants, the utilitarianism of purpose is dominant.[337]

Even the sister force of philosophy — religion — has lost the power of creative expression in conformity with an actual present.[338] As a result of the rise of science amidst the ruin of many of the ideologies and beliefs of people, philosophy is tempted to conform to the new scientific attitude and to talk only about what is knowable, what involves point-at-ables. Jaspers states cogently that on man's

> ... limiting himself to determinate object knowledge, that is to scientific cognition, he ceases to philosophize, saying: "It is best not to talk of what we do not know."[339]

In attempting to philosophize, the individual must seek to find reality in the primal sources, to apprehend reality in his thinking attitude toward himself and in his inner acts, to open man to the "Comprehensive" in all its scope, to attempt the communication of every aspect of truth from man to man in loving contest and to patiently and unremittingly sustain the vigilance of reason in the presence of failure and in the presence of that which seems alien to it.[340]

The ability to integrate oneself through philosophy must be accompanied by definite attitudes towards the philosophical undertaking. The six attitudes which are important if man is to develop as an individual are as follows:

1. "Let us not pledge ourselves to any philosophical school or take formulable truth as such for the one and exclusive truth: let us master our thoughts;

2. Let us not heap up philosophical possessions, but apprehend philosophical thought as movement and seek to deepen it;

3. Let us battle for truth and humanity in unconditional communication;

4. Let us acquire the power to learn from all the past by making it our own; let us listen to our contemporaries and remain open to all possibilities;

5. Let us each as an individual immerse himself in his own historicity, in his origin, in what he has done; let him possess himself of what he was, of what he has become, and of what has been given to him;

6. Let us not cease to grow through our own historicity into the historicity of man as a whole and thus make ourselves into citizens of the world."[341]

Jaspers takes special pains to emphasize that these are philosophical attitudes and ought not be confused with philosophical doctrine. "For the philosopher has no doctrine if by doctrine is meant a set of rules."[342] In fact, true philosophy is not a instrument, is not a content, but rather it is awareness in the process of realization.

To Jaspers, as to Kant, man grew up during the philosophical period known as the enlightenment. He grew out of immaturity because he assumed responsibility for himself. To Jaspers it is important that all individuals approach life against the following principles of the enlightenment.

Man strives to understand what he believes, desires and does. He wants to think for himself. He wishes to grasp with his understanding, and where possible to have proof of what is true. He wants his knowledge to be based on experience which is fundamentally accessible to everyone. He seeks paths to the source of insight instead of permitting it to be set before him as a finished product which he need only accept. He wishes to understand to what degree a proof is valid and at what limits the understanding is frustrated. And he would like also to have a reasoned basis for the indemonstrable premise, which he must ultimately take as the foundation of his life.... Even in obedience he wants to know why he obeys. He subjects everything he holds to be true and everything that he does in the belief that it is right to this condition; he himself must participate in it inwardly.[343]

To Jaspers, "a valid philosophy arises only out of that revolutionary change in the way of contemplating human existence which is known today as existence-philosophy."[344] Existence-philosophy is the German counterpart of existentialism. In fact, Jaspers is very impatient with any philosophy of the contemporary period which has not taken cognizance of existentialism. The "most characteristic symptom of philosophical weakness knowing nothing of Søren Kierkegaard and not accepting Nietzsche as a philosopher."[345] In arguing in this fashion, Jaspers does not mean that one must accept what Kierkegaard deduced from his own experience. The value of studying Kierkegaard is that he stood in the midst of dilemmas of our modern age.

Even though he couldn't show what ought to be done about

the problem, he can make them feel that they are on the wrong road.[346]

Thus the value of Kierkegaard is in the stimulation of thought rather than in the finding of concrete solutions to problems.

It is obvious, to Jaspers, that the ability of an individual to exist fully is related to his ability to deal philosophically with life.

> The goal of a philosophical life cannot be formulated as a state of being, which is attainable and once obtained perfect. ...it lies in our very nature to be on-the-way.[347]

In agreement with Kierkegaard, Jaspers argues that man may never reach perfection; nor can he ever permit his soul to take a rest. He is constantly wrestling with whatever reality he is confronted with. In that this reality perpetually changes man's viewpoint of life must also be fluid.

Jaspers' Concept of Freedom

An essential ingredient in the ability of a person to cope with his situation is freedom. Man must have freedom of the will. "Philosophy mercilessly presupposes the possibility of freedom," . . . even though man secretly yearns to be taken by the hand and to live fraudulently in the freedom of obedience.[34?] Freedom means that the historical continuity of one's own being even though it is built upon the foundation of heredity and modified by experience, does not exist as a simple datum; "it becomes actual only as a power of selfhood when it is freely assumed and appropriated."[349]

> For human beings are what they are, not simply through birth, breeding and education, but through the freedom of each individual upon the foundations of his self-existence.[350]

It is given to man to work in freedom upon his empirical existence as upon a material. Hence man alone has a history, that is, he does not live only by his biological heritage but also by tradition. Man's life is not merely a natural process. And his freedom calls for guidance.[351]

Thus what man makes out of the world is decided by each individual through the way in which he comes to a decision about himself in the continuity of his own action.[352]

Not only is man capable of freedom of the will, he also knows he exists.

In full awareness he studies his world and changes it to suit his purposes.... He is not merely cognisable as extant, but himself freely decides what shall exist.[353]

What man himself becomes is the upshot of the way in which he elaborates the knowledge which the contemporary mental situation forces on him.[354] Man is faced with the problem of whether he will fatalistically submit to the sway of the mighty forces which appear to determine everything that happens, or whether after all, to search for the paths which are discernible along which he can walk on his own volition because on them the writ of the aforesaid powers no longer possess supreme influence.[355]

...Man must not abandon his freedom to the tangibles, authorities, powers of the world;... he bears responsibility for himself and must not evade this responsibility by renouncing freedom ostensibly for the sake of freedom.[356]

In other words, man must not give in to the temptation of delegating his obligation to decide in order to avoid time-consuming deliberation and the burden of possible error. Unfortunately man not only tends to believe that he is a pawn in a vast game beyond his ken, but he is also tempted not even to contest the issue of freedom at all. Too many men, according to Jaspers, live only from day to day, stirred only by their desire to occupy the best obtainable place in the every-day worldly apparatus.[357] In order to exercise his freedom man must exert considerable energy.

He only who uses an unbending discipline, sustained by an

urgent feeling for the possibility of true fulfillment, walks along the road proper to man as man.[358]

At each moment the individual ought to know what he really wants to do. This desire to know what he really wants forges an interest in the future which shall confront him.[359] Man must equip himself with the fullest attainment of knowledge to bolster his ability to make his own future rather than merely to contemplate it.[360] However Jaspers stresses that man must concern himself more with his immediate situation and the near future rather than any remote future which is only possible.

> All planning and all activity that relates to a remote future is unavailing whereas it behooves us here and now to create and inspire our lives. I must myself will what is going to happen, even though the end of all be at hand.[361]

As the individual confronts his immediate future he must be aware of the reality of the situation which confronts him and the fact that whatever he is confronted with in itself cannot be altered. It is his task, however, to take this material and to mold it to the best of his ability. Man is therefore not free to create his future but he is free to meet his future and to shape the materials with which his future presents him.

In that man must wait to experience the content which the future brings to him, it follows then that no forecast of man's future can be fixed and definite in character. His future can be nothing more than an open possibility.[362] Jaspers would agree with Sartre that man may only make an appointment with himself in the future. Of course, the nearer the individual is to the future the more relevant it becomes and the more accurately it can be forecast. The more accurately one is able to predict the future the more active one may become in shaping the material of the future and in interfering with its content.[363] The individual must not keep his eye fixed on what will inevitably happen, but must pay attention to what may happen; from this base of operation the individual must seek to mold the future into what he want it to be.

The individual is confronted with the demand to attain a knowledge of what it is possible for him to do in the next moment of his existence upon the basis of his knowledge of what actually happens in the moment. Destiny for man only exists when selfhood grasps life and takes life over by its activity, by its realizing itself and by its daring to influence courageously the future.[364]

Although when a future moment becomes the real moment and the individual experiences for the first time the new experiences which the former new moment holds, he finds himself in a definite situation, but the situation in itself has no meaning. It is the task of the individual to bring meaning to the situation by interpreting the situation. No meaning can ever be found in the future because the future has no reality. Meaning is present only in real situations. Meaning is given to the real situation as a result of an interpretation of the situation by the individual. In that the future has no reality and no meaning Jaspers refers to the future which confronts man as 'nothingness'. Kierkegaard was one of the first to call this fact to the attention of his readers.[365] Never since the beginning of his days, at least until Kierkegaard, did man realize that he is faced by 'nothingness' and that it is incumbent upon him through remembrance of the past to carve out a new pathway for himself in the current moment.[366] Man's situation does not lead automatically to something inevitable, but rather it indicates certain possibilities and the limits of what is possible.[367]

One result of man's ability to interfere with the processes which confront him may lead to arrogance and a feeling that he is the master of the world. He feels that he could mold anything; he knocks at all the doors of opportunity seeking ways to perfect his situation. Alas, the individual may only mold the situation to a certain extent, and as the situation slips away from his complete mastery, man feels a terrible impotency.

> How man is going to accommodate himself to this [dreadful feeling], and rise superior to it, is one of the most vital questions of the present situation.[368]

Man must learn to accept the fact that his original impulse to

153

comprehend the whole is foredoomed to shipwreck as a result of the whole's tendency to be shattered into fragments.[369] The individual must learn that "no mode of passion, of vital will or self-assertion is unconditional in the moment; all are relative and hence perishable."[370]

> As long as my understanding remains incomplete, I can only think of the situation as still working itself out independently of my contribution; but as soon as I become an active participator in the situation, I want reflectively to interfere with the action and re-action between the situation and my own existence.[371]

In spite of the fact that a decision man makes under one set of conditions may not be valid in the next moment, man must not be tempted to remain indecisive. To Jaspers, indecision is in itself evil. Yet, all men are tempted to be indecisive at times. Jaspers advises that "we must all continuously recapture ourselves from decision."[372]

Jaspers' Criteria for Decision Making

When the individual makes his decision it must not be made on the spur of the moment or made irresponsibly. His decision must be lucidly taken out of an unfathomable depth and in order for him to commit himself to his decision unconditionally, the individual must himself be identical to his decision.[373] Man must be his decision. When man is conscious of his freedom, he becomes aware of certain imperatives which are addressed to him and which demand action. It is up to the individual whether he carries them out or tries to evade them.[374]

The individual arrives at the truth in independent thinking only if in his thinking he constantly strives to put himself in the place of every other man. By doing this, the individual can come to know what is possible for man as a whole to accomplish and therefore can have more insight into what he is able to accomplish.[375] Ultimately, in his attempt to realize a true decision, a correct decision, or a good decision, the individual can only do his best and if necessary hope that something invisible within

154

him, even to the world, will in some unfathomable way come to his aid and lift him out of his limitation.[376] This force Jaspers identifies as "transcendence" which is his philosophical equivalent for the theological term "God". The transcendent force does not seek to influence man's decision in any way. Therefore, the medium in which man is guided is to be found in his own judgement regarding his own actions. This judgement, when given free rein,

> . . . restrains or impels, corrects or confirms.[377]

A third force which may be relied on for determining the value of a decision is love. "Whatever is done from an impulse to love within the realm of reason is bound to turn out well."[378] As stated previously, the individual's decision will be guided by the advice which he has sought from his family, his friends, strangers and indeed anyone who will communicate with him. Yet the judgement that is ultimately decisive for the individual is not even that of the men whom he respects, although this is the only judgement accessible in the world; only the judgement of God would be decisive for the individual and this judgement left the making of decisions up to the individual. In conclusion only the individual's decision is decisive because once the decision has been made in that moment it cannot be undone.[379]

If man is to act harmoniously upon the decision which he makes, he must act unconditionally. He must be completely identified with the choice. When the individual has chosen what he understands his decision becomes the substance of himself and he heeds the unconditional command to action.

> Only when man conquers himself and goes where his decision unerringly leads him does the unconditional come into its own.[380]

It becomes obvious in the writings of Jaspers that he does not favor any form of anti-rationalism in the formation of a decision. Man, to Jaspers, is mind, and the situation of man is a mental situation.[381] It is the mental ability of man which distinguishes him from the lower animals. When man utilizes reason, it is accomplished only by means of a decision to be reasonable.[382]

155

Reason is not developed automatically, nor does reason come about automatically but rather by active self realization of reason itself.[383] The decision for reason is a decision for freedom, truth and the unconditionality of existential decision. It is opposed by the forces of natural occurrence and necessity.[384]

In attempting to become himself, by means of reason, man is confronted by moral, ethical and metaphysical challenges. Morally man is obligated to himself to seek to base his decision on thought. Ethically he must rehabilitate himself from perversion through a rebirth of good will. Metaphysically, man must achieve awareness of being which has been given to him as a consequence of his ability to love his fellow man.[385]

Jaspers' Interpretation of the Crisis of the Twentieth Century

Independence in the modern age seems to be silently disappearing beneath the inundation of all life by the typical, the habitual and the unquestioned commonplace.[386] As independence diminishes during the crisis period, when all meaning disappears and all certainty vanishes, something arises deep inside man. This unfathomable force is man's yearning for the self-preservation of his essential identity.[387] Paradoxically, as the age precipitates hidden dissatisfactions, these very dissatisfactions may lead to the recovery of the authentic seriousness which becomes real only in existential awareness. As the crisis deepens, as authentic seriousness develops, the ruinous attitudes of those who take life as it is and do what they please are cast off.[388]

Selfhood, or self-existence, first arises out of one's feeling that his being is against the world even though he still exists in the world. As man becomes aware that he is a separate entity from the world he becomes enveloped by a strange feeling of solitude even though he is in the midst of a crowd.[389] As he realizes his solitude from the world in which he participates, he also realizes that he is a self, an existent, and that he is freedom. Therefore to grasp a situation, to realize the crisis, is the first step in the direction of its mastery for once an individual is aware that something is wrong he finds that his will is aroused to meet the situation.[390]

As man becomes aware that he is participating in the crisis and that he does have the ability to modify the situation, he experiences his first conscious awareness of guilt. After a distinct action has occurred in which the individual has participated freely, he realizes that it need not have occurred, and that he could have responded to the moment in a different fashion.[391] The guilty feeling which the individual must carry with him as a result of action is, for Jaspers, identical with existence.

> . . . My very existence causes misery. . . . Whether I act or not, merely by existing I infringe upon the existence of others.[392]

Deep in the structure of the individual is guilt based on an awareness that he could have done things differently and the realization that he is responsible for what he has done.

Whenever men see the question of guilt clearly, they conceive the idea of complicity in guilt. All men are jointly committed to and are jointly liable for human actions. The individual is responsible for anything which takes place in his world.

> I am responsible for all the evil that is perpetrated in the world, unless I have done what I could do to prevent it, even to the extent of sacrificing my life. I am guilty because I am alive and can continue to live while this thing is happening.[393]

Following this thesis to its logical conclusion in an applied situation Jaspers indicted the whole German people and ultimately mankind in general as being guilty of the Nazi atrocities. From this feeling of guilt, which means complicity in human endeavor, and which means that the individual realizes that alternatives are available to him when he makes decisions, Jaspers deduces that guilt begets the individual's destiny.

> A man who is wholly himself, he recognizes that there are alternatives, and then his action will not be a compromise. He will want to force a decision between the alternatives he has recognised. He knows that he may come to wreck . . .

and is aware that a sincere failure may but emphasize the reality of his being.[394]

Man Must Transcend His Limitations

As man is confronted by his limitations he finds it necessary to leave physical reality and "he builds for himself a second world, the world of mind . . . but in this soaring flight he transcends life."[395] In order for man to maintain himself in human destiny, he must advance by way of consciousness.[396] He must reflect on what should be done in the present in order to determine which course he should commit himself to.[397] Man becomes truly himself only through the avenue of reason.[398]

As man transcends his physical limitations and enters into the realm of reason he must not neglect nor become aloof from the practical aspects of living.

Our first duty in life is to perform our practical tasks to meet the demands of the day. But . . . we shall not content ourselves with practical tasks.[399]

In opposition to not contenting oneself with the practical tasks of living, man must not take things for granted. He must elucidate every experience so as to understand it fully. The individual must learn how to proceed resolutely but without being run aground by stubbornness. He must learn to test and to correct experience but not to haphazardly tear it apart. He must retain every experience as an effective force in his thinking for as man is confronted by new situations his reason will utilize that which it has mastered from previous experiences.[400] The authentic person will try to comprehend as clearly and as decisively as possible his own development.

Man's situation does not become a truly mental one until he grows aware of himself as existing in the real world and thereby confronted by definite limitations of existence. These limitations the individual feels are over against his personal desire to achieve orientation.[401] The situation in which man finds himself is limited

158

in three distinct ways. Man's being consists primarily of his existence in economic, sociological and political situations upon which in reality everything depends. Secondly, man's life as a conscious being lies within the realm of the cognizable. Man may only understand that which he is conscious of. Finally, what a man can himself become is determined by the other persons whom he encounters on his journey through life for these people bring to man their interpretations not only of life, but also of his particular being.[402]

The latter factor, the influence of other persons upon the individual, Jaspers stresses in several places.

> Man can live only when, using his reason and working in co-operation with his fellows, he busies himself about the ordering of the technical supply of mass needs. He must, therefore, devote himself with ardour to the cares of this world unless he is himself to perish amid its decay.[403]

The individual in cooperation with his fellow man must bring "a world of purposive order into existence by striving to transcend its limitations wherever he encounters them."[404]

The depth and the breadth of the individual's situation, which is illumined by reason, is dramatically furthered by his ability to love his fellow man, and by his ability to read the symbols of the transcendence correctly. If he succeeds in realizing these two conditions the individual is able to live as an authentic personality.[405]

Jaspers' Concept of the Authentic Personality

The person who is authentic can only want one of two things from any given situation — the good or the bad. He follows his inclinations or he does his duty. He lives in perversion or in purity of motive. Emotionally, he lives out of hate or out of love. When the authentic personality makes a decision these forces are clearly in focus and he knows that he must choose according to these concepts. The one thing he does not fail to do is to decide when confronted by a choice.[406] The authentic person becomes aware of himself in terms of realizing that whatever he himself is, he is because he chose to be and what he chose to be is what he felt he ought to be. This awareness comes to the individual very slowly; at first it is nebulous as one develops the authentic disposition the feeling of being what one ought to be becomes quite lucid.[407]

As man becomes authentic and acts in an unconditional way he realizes that his life is not the ultimate, and therefore he subordinates his life to something else.[408] This something else is God, or to use the term Jaspers normally utilizes, transcendence.

> The more authentically free a man is, the greater his certainty of God. When I am authentically free, I am certain that I am not free through myself.[409]

According to Jaspers, man does not create himself, nor does he make himself free. His freedom must be given to him. The authentic individual has unlimited devotion to the transcendence.[410] His devotion to the transcendence does not mean that he will neglect the more mundane aspects of life because he realizes that his freedom has been given him so that he can mold reality. As a matter of fact, he realizes that by devotion to reality in the world, he not only expresses his devotion to God by fulfilling God's desire, but he permits his own selfhood to grow.[411]

To summarize the main characteristic of the authentic person, Jaspers believes that

> Life becomes for the individual the responsibility of the human being aware of himself as being, and in addition and simultaneously, the experiment of the knower.[412]

What man does investigatively, purposively and constructively paves the road of endeavor on which he discovers his destiny and the manner in which he becomes aware of being. Although the authentic person grapples with reality, he does not have a firm grasp on his own reality.

For I am not what I cognise, nor do I cognise what I am. Instead of cognising my existence, I can only inaugurate the process of clarification . . . (of what I am).[413]

Not only must one clarify whom one is in each new situation, he must be willing to transcend physical reality through sustained mental effort. The authentic individual's mental effort is not derived from a source which is external to himself, but wells up from himself. The reward of one who attempts to tap the mental reservoir available within himself is too often that of enforced loneliness. The authentic individual does not conform to the usual standards expected of man by the masses; he does not permit the world to impose on him any sort of mission; nor does he take what comes to him passively. He himself chooses his course in his existence and the choice he makes is ultimately at his own risk. He cannot pass the buck, he has no scape-goats at his disposal.[414]

A real difficulty which confronts the authentic personality is the fact that he finds it a difficult task to be continually exerting mental effort in his attempt to become aware of whom he is, what he ought to be, or the alternatives which the situation has confronted him with. To overcome lack of concentration requires almost superhuman strength. Paradoxically, if he withstands the temptation to slip quietly back into the morass of the masses, just as he begins to make a real start towards the understanding of what he seeks, he realizes that time has slipped by too fast, and life is practically finished for him. Nevertheless the authentic person follows this pathway of critical discovery.

In that ultimate shipwreck awaits the authentic individual, even as it does for the inauthentic person, Jaspers believes the former to be a heroic figure. Perhaps better than the term heroic would be the concept tragic hero when describing the authentic man. The authentic hero is often inconspicuous because his activity does not necessarily bring fame. He may have the power of self-maintenance even when confronted by tragedy, but he probably will lack the confirmation of public approval. He is not capable of sharing in the idols of his time for he is not bewitched by false expectations or tricked by applause. He is unperturbed by resistance and disapproval, which he often meets. With a steady gait he follows his chosen pathway with a singleness of purpose that often precipitates loneliness. He feels his situation to be an antagonist and yet he never quite is able to come to grips with that which restrains him. He wants not disciples but companions, yet the former tend to associate themselves with him. He doesn't attempt to predict prophetically the future but he describes the alternatives which are open to man. Although he may find himself in a basically unfriendly situation, he himself keeps his peace.[415] He is truly an outstanding man without whom, Jaspers insists, humanity as a whole would be shipwrecked. This is the man, the only man, who will be decisive for new creation, who is able on his own initiative to seize the helm and steer a course of his own choosing, even if this course opposes the will of the masses. As a result of his forcing himself ahead, humanity itself is able to experience a richer meaning.[416]

The authentic individual is a humble person in the very best semantical meaning of the term. He maintains a courteous smile which brings tranquility to him and to those who know him. He avoids the haste and jostle of the machine age. He maintains a humorous attitude in strained situations. He refuses to be panicked. He feels that personal remarks are in bad taste and therefore he never insults intentionally. His self-discipline promotes order and easy relationships whenever people are assembled in large numbers. He is truly a forceful personality to have in one's midst.[417]

The authentic individual never reaches the stage completely, but is on the way towards authenticity. In that he exists entirely in his own historical time he can experience something of the eternal presence within that time. He understands humanity because he is a determinate man who realizes himself in specific situations. As he experiences the historic hour in which he lives, he accepts his era as his own and he comprehends that his era is a part of the unity of history and of an even larger comprehensive reality. He ascends the scale of philosophical understanding himself and he refuses to shift the responsibility of philosophical thinking to any other person. He ascends to authentic existence because he meets each historical situation and electively determines his own acts. He refuses to apply 'weltanschauungs' or glittering generalities to his situation.[418] His endurance, his love for humanity raise him up to the good. He is always growing in stature through the experiencing of life at its limits. Yet he is tempted by the darker side of his life to soar higher than he is able. His resistance, his stubbornness and his pride drive him from the good towards evil.[419]

Authentic Existence Contrasted with Inauthentic Existence

The inauthentic man too often seeks a situation which will completely free him from all tensions. Some exist in the mental illusion that they have overcome their limitary situations; their illusion may not crack until they come to know personal disaster. In a time of plenty, the soul too often relaxes and takes its ease.[420] Inauthenticity plagues the individual, for in his daily life he often evades ultimate situations by closing his eyes and choosing to ignore the fact that choices which involve unpleasant consequences exist. The inauthentic person is tempted to react to the world situation in one of two ways. In the first place he may perceive the world in terms of a vague whole which permits him to remain aloof from the passing scene and no longer actively cooperate with what transpires in his situation. Or the inauthentic personality falsifies his situation by regarding it as an absolute which he is not able to do very much about.[421]

Instead of choosing to be authentic, the inauthentic person too often prefers to renounce himself and to plunge into the busy-work of life as into the waters of oblivion. In this type of existence one does only that which is contingent and he makes no genuine decisions.[422] This kind of life, which is one that involves proceeding in a succession of passing moments until it comes to its term, has no destiny. In the life which has no destiny one finds that the present is nothing more than a momentary effort to achieve enjoyment of life.

Man wins destiny only through ties: not through coercive

ties imposed on him as an impotent creature by great forces that he without; but by ties freely comprehended which he makes his own. Such ties hold together, so that it is not frittered away but becomes the actuality of his possible existence.[423]

Man might tranquilize himself in the self-forgetful pleasures of life, fancying himself to have gone back to nature in the peace of the timeless.[424] In this attempt to relax and enjoy life man finds an immediate aid via television and the cinema.

Most of the hours spent in the picture theater have to be paid for by a peculiar and unexampled dreariness of mind which persists when the tension of viewing has passed off.[425]

The mind of man has not only grown weary, it has become like jelly.

The mind has ceased to believe in itself, as self-arising, and becomes a means to an end. Having thus grown fully mobile as a mere instrument of sophistry, it can serve any master.[426]

Mass production has been a force which encourages unauthentic existence. Industry has created a situation in which man finds himself to be only a cog in the wheels of industry.

Work and nothing but work performed day after day will, when performed, sink forthwith into the fathomless abysses of oblivion.[427]

Work is conducive to authentic existence only if the individual can actively perform his work under the influence of a long range view and is aware of the meaning of what he is doing.

Mass production also is capable of seducing man into a form of utilitarian living. Utilitarianism reduces the sense of man's responsibility for his actions by reducing him to a mere level of existence. Utilitarianism robs man of his subject existence by molding him into an object which must be manipulated. "If I accept utility as the ultimate standard of knowledge, I surrender my own selfhood therein."[428] Man's selfhood is surrendered

164

because selfhood demands the utilization of reason. Utilitarianism demands the presence of reason only when the individual is confronted with a problem which must be solved. Selfhood involves the will to know, not the desire to live the easiest possible way. The latter approach, that of utilitarianism, is conducive to animal existence, and is not meaningful for ". . . those who recognize a constant claim upon them and persevere in the way of freedom."[429]

Jaspers' Concept of Transcendence

If the individual's life is not to be diffuse and meaningless he must find his place in some orderly existence.

When we move amid the phenomena of the world, we come to realize that we possess being itself neither in the object, which becomes continuously more restricted, nor in the horizon of our always limited world taken as the sum of phenomena, but only in the Comprehensive which transcends . . . the subject-object dichotomy.[430]

The individual experiences meaningful order as he becomes sustained by the comprehensive principle. Only when he realizes that there is a force which is transcendent to himself, which makes comprehensible life as a whole, is he able to find meaning in an edifice of work, fulfillment and sublime moments, and gains in his attempt to escape shallow living.

Suffice it to say that the Comprehensive conceived as being itself, is called transcendence (God) and the world, while as that which we ourselves are it is called being-there, consciousness, mind and existence.[431]

To Jaspers, God is absolute reality and cannot be encompassed by any of the historical manifestations through which he speaks or has spoken to man. God is not an object of knowledge and therefore no compelling evidence can prove his existence. This means that in relation to God "what matters is not our knowledge of God but our attitude towards God."[432] In that God is not an object of knowledge, it follows that God is nowhere in the world. To Jaspers it is important for man to invest himself in that which is not of this world, to commit himself to the force which makes all meaningful, but which is not man-made.

> The precariousness of all worldly existence is a warning to us, it forbids us to content ourselves with the world; it points to something else.[433]

Jaspers is adamant in his denial of the activity of God in the world. He argues that even descriptive terms may not be used in an attempt to know God. Even the terms 'wrath', 'love', 'justice', and 'mercy' have violated the commandment to make no idol of God.[434] The God of faith is the distant God, the hidden God, the indemonstrable God. In fact God is so far removed from man in Jaspers' thought that he is able to state the following:

> Hence I must recognize not only that I do not know God but even that I do not know whether I believe.[435]

Although man cannot expect to discover in finite judgement God's final word, he must infuse his life with God's power.

> To live by God does not mean to base oneself on calculable knowledge but to live as though we staked our existence on the assumption that God is.
> To believe in God means to live by something which is not in this world.[436]

Jaspers advances on the narrow road of decision. God's guidance is to be found only in man's ability to make choices of his own volition. Man is so created that if he can evaluate his situation, his choice will not be alien to that of God's choice.

> The voice of God lies in the self-awareness that dawns in the individual, when he is open to everything that comes to him from his tradition and environment.[437]

God, according to this position, acts only through the free decisions of the individual, but if the individual is authentic as the decision is made he is sure that what he is doing is what he ought to do. When he is sure that what he does is what he ought to do he feels that he fulfills God's directive. Of course the individual is never sure that he has lucidly made a right decision and therefore he cannot demand of others that they follow him or seek to duplicate his decision. Not only might the decision have been wrong at the time it was made, but also "it is always possible that everything will look entirely different later."[438]

> The voice of God as judgment regarding man's actions has no other expression in time than in this judgment of man himself with regard to his emotions, motives, actions.[439]

God's speech, or man's decision, can only become clear historically; it cannot be generalized. One must understand the existential moment which brought forth the decision.

Jaspers is aware that Kierkegaard felt himself to be in the hands of God. About this experience he writes as follows:

> The guidance he received was not tangible, it provided no clear command; it was guidance through freedom itself, which knows decision because it knows itself rooted in transcendent foundation.[440]

Man is a being who exists in relation to God. Whenever he decides freely and conceives of his life as meaningful, he knows that he does not owe himself to himself.

> . . . In my freedom I am not through myself, but am given to myself, for I can fail myself and I cannot force my freedom. Where I am authentically myself, I am certain that I am not through myself. The highest freedom is experienced in freedom from the world, and this freedom is a profound bond with transcendence.[441]

> The man who attains true awareness of his freedom gains certainty of God. Freedom and God are inseparable.[442]

If the individual does not experience the miracle of an authentic selfhood, he needs no relation to God for he will be content

167

with the empirical existence of nature, many Gods and many demons.

In the twentieth century man has experienced an extensive despiritualization of the world. This fact is not the outcome of a faithless people but is the result of the mental attitude of the people who seek to ground themselves in utilitarian ethics.[443] The result of the despiritualization of the world has led man into a deep feeling of misery and tragedy. Into the vacuum of a despiritualized Germany came Hitler and the personality disposition to tolerate his rise to power.

The fact that the world is alienated from religion does not mean that new faiths are not developing, nor that the old faiths will not be rekindled.

> For man, to abandon and forget religion completely would be to end the philosophic quest itself. It would be replaced by unreasoning despair ignorant of itself, a life lived merely moment to moment, a kind of nihilism full of chaotic superstition.[444]

If one is to avoid a debauched life it is necessary for him to realize some form of spirituality.

> Only with his eyes to God does man grow instead of seeping away undamned into the meaninglessness of life's mere happenings.[445]

Whatever relationship man develops to transcendence he is still responsible for constantly testing the relationship so as to not reduce transcendence to an idol of thought. What the twentieth century has experienced is a complete criticism of idols of thought which formerly were unchallenged by illiterate men or were accepted for their utilitarian value in ages which could bring little peace and comfort to mankind.

Jaspers advances five principles of faith which summarize his religious attitude. These principles can not be demonstrated but must be accepted because by one's very nature if one is authentic, their truth cannot be eluded. The principles of authentic faith are as follows:

168

1. **God is.**

2. There is an unconditional imperative.

3. Man is finite and imperfectible.

4. Man can live in God's guidance.

5. The reality of the world subsists ephemerally between God and existence.[446]

Concerning the first principle it is enough according to Jaspers to say simply that God is. It is an affirmation which needs no further proof. When all the world is disintegrating, one thing will remain: God is.[447] The second principle reflects the fundamental attitude which the authentic person commits himself to, namely, the realization in action of "thy will be done".[448] The fourth principle, Jaspers illustrates in the following way.

> Bow down before that which defies understanding, confident that it is situated above and not below the understandable. . . .
>
> Trust in this basic attitude makes possible an all-encompassing sense of thankfulness, a worldless, impersonal love.[449]

It cannot be emphasized enough, however, that God's guidance involves no other force than the freedom man is capable of exerting.

In that God encompasses reality, is reality, according to Jaspers. Karl Deutsch who introduces Jaspers' book *Tragedy is Not Enough* interprets that "every stone, every event not merely exists in itself, but can also function as a symbol, a code, or — in Jaspers' term — as a 'chiffre' or cipher, corresponding loosely or accurately to some pattern in the encompassing reality." Man may fear and tremble that he may have misread the cipher and misunderstood the message, but nevertheless all being, all existence contains within it the message of God's process.

One of the most successful ages of mankind to have interpreted the ciphers of the encompassing, the meaning of the universe, was when the spiritual foundations of humanity were laid by the Greek philosophers, the Hebraic philosophers and the Oriental-Indian faiths between the period of 800 to 200 B.C. This period Jaspers discusses as the axial period of history, and its importance will be discussed in the section dealing with Jaspers' educational implications.[450]

Jaspers' Discussion of the Crowd, the Masses and the individual

The individual's ". . . existence has become so dependent on the masses that the thought of them must control his doings, his cares and his duties. He may despise them in their average aspects; or he may feel that the solidarity of all mankind is destined someday to become a reality; or he may, while not denying responsibility which each man has for all, still hold more or less aloof: but it remains a responsibility he can never evade.[451]

The masses disinclined to tolerate aloof independence and greatness, it is prone to constrain people to become as automatic as possible. Life within the mass is unspiritual and inhuman because the mass as a whole has no spirit or being. In the mass, man's individuality is sacrificed to the fiction of a general equality.[452] The individual is permitted to undertake only those actions which in some form or other will be regarded as useful by the mass.

The masses themselves are influenced by the fact that no one knows what each individual component contributes to the situation. The convictions of the masses seldom are founded on sound judgment and are more likely to be swayed by insincere promises and unverifiable illusions.[453] In terms of convictions which are of an enduring nature the mass is not capable of producing the same for it seldom knows what it really wants save to consistently demand average conformity.[454]

People 'in the mass' would seem to be guided by the search for pleasure and to work only under the crack of the whip

170

or when impelled by a craving for bread and for dainties; yet they are bored when they have nothing to do, and have a perpetual craving for novelty.[455]

Love of nature or human being wanes and disappears in mass perspective. The machine-made products vanish from sight as soon as they are made and consumed. New commodities are in constant demand and they too will be destroyed.

The technical level of the twentieth century and the rule of the mass are closely related. The huge machinery of social provision must be adapted to the peculiarities of the mass.

Today it is taken as a matter of course that human life is the supply of mass-needs by rationalized production with the aid of technical advantages. The assumption seems to be that the whole can be reduced to perfect order by reason alone.[456]

In no other age has man belonged more to the masses than he has in the twentieth century.

It seems as if the world must be given over to mediocrities, to persons without a destiny, without rank or a difference, without genuinely human attributes.[457]

To Jaspers, the masses are an inescapable fact with which the individual must reckon.

Men do not exist as isolated units, but as members of a family in the home; as friends in a group; as parts of this, that, or the other 'herd' with well-known historical origins.[458]

It is the task of the authentic person to be something more than a mere member of the mass, to make untransferable claims upon himself and not to merge in such a way with the masses as to forfeit his right to independent existence as a human being.[459] Although many of the existentialists emphasize the importance of the individual walking in a lonesome valley, Jaspers is keenly aware of the importance of other people to the individual.

Actually no man can ever be fully and definitely satisfied

with himself; he cannot be entirely self-contained in his judgment of himself: He requires the judgment of his fellow men concerning his actions. He is particularly sensitive to the judgment of those he respects. He is less moved by that of the average and the crowd, of inert individualized institutions, but even here he is not indifferent.[460]

Even independent thinking does not spring from the void but develops from the thoughts of civilization.[461] In thinking man is necessarily dependent upon his experience which not only includes what has been taught to him, but what has been developed as a result of his communication with others. As one communicates with others one not only learns about the world around him, he also is able to learn about himself. Thus man's independence may develop only from his enmeshed existence in the world.[462]

It is the irresponsible type of independence which manifests itself in intellectual opportunism. No authentic discussion with such a person is possible for the two only are able to talk back and forth about perhaps a variety of interesting things.[463] The existential task of life is to establish real communication between people. This living communication will arise only "in the depth of their struggles from their continuing love for each other, and the mutual bonds which it creates."[464]

The Goal of Philosophy Is the Development of Communication

Philosophy demands that the authentic person "seek constant communication, risk it without reserve and to renounce the defiant self-assertion which forces itself upon you in ever new disguises."[465]

Communication, then, is the aim of philosophy, and in communication all its other aims are ultimately rooted: awareness of being, illumination through love, attainment of peace.[466]

Truth, itself, is bound up with communication. If one can

172

not communicate a truth that he possesses, Jaspers would strongly argue that what one possesses is in fact not truth. "The truth begins with two."[467]

The power of communication originates in love, which, of course, requires two for itself to originate. Man is worthy of love not as an instant of life, but as a possible existence. This possibility of existence is the nobility which is present in each individual and which makes it possible for him to be worthy of love.[468] Although communication founded on love is an essential ingredient in the development of the authentic person,

it is impossible for us men to live solely by love, this force of the highest level, for we fall constantly into errors and misunderstandings.[469]

Everyday complications of a technical world make it necessary for man to master these complications in the environment and to be distracted from communication.[470] Man has no choice but to follow the way of technicalization, he cannot turn back the clock. It is necessary for man to obtain food and shelter and for this he must cooperate with the technicalized world. He must live and respond to men not of his own choosing. He must make it possible to live at peace with such men and to do this he must build a body of mores and to structure a community. The reality of the world cannot be evaded. There is no existential ivory tower into which the individual may escape; nor is this even desirable in existential thinking.

To play an active part in the world even though one aims at an impossible, an unattainable goal, is the necessary precondition of one's own being. What we have to endeavor, therefore, is to live at harmony with the powers of this world without being absorbed by them.[471]

Authentic independence implies a particular attitude toward the world which is "to be in and yet not in it, to be both inside it and outside it."[472] Man's ability to straddle the double necessity of being in the world and rising above the world is not due to his intellectual ability nor to his self-discipline evolved

173

from reason. It is rather due to his ability to love, which permits him to get in touch with all reality, even that which is above the time-space continuum.[473] In love man becomes aware of his responsibility for his fellow man. In fact, true nobility is not found in the isolated person; it is based on one's interpersonal relationships with other persons and it is based on one's ability to realize his own potential. The nobility of love exists in the interlinkage of independent human beings who are aware of their duty to discover one another and to help develop each other.[474] When one has isolated himself from his fellow man he is overcome by anxiety.

> The sufferer from anxiety has confidence in no one; he will not enter into absolute ties with any other person. One who fails to participate in what others are doing is left alone.[475]

As a result of being left alone man is faced with a life of misery. Whether man succumbs to misery or not, as previously stated, is related to how authentic he is. The more authentic a man is, the more he is aware of why he finds himself in his situation. The more he understands about his situation the less likely it will be for him to suffer the agonies of misery. Misery is reserved more for inauthentic man who does not understand what is happening to him at all.

Man's Situation in the Twentieth Century

There have been periods in history in which man has felt his world to be durable, and in these man has accommodated himself to life as he found it. Today the individual is regarded with indifference. No one is indispensable. People have no more genuine individuality than one pin in a row; they are mere objects of genial utility. The worker at the machine concentrating upon immediate aims has no time or inclination left for the contemplation of life and his personal meaning in the scheme of things.

Daily affairs are carried on in conformity with fixed rules

174

and habits. The desire to act in accordance with general conventions, to avoid startling anyone by the unusual. . . .[476]

is dominant in everyday life.

The individual who passes forty begins to feel that the world has no more use for him, and that he is enmeshed in some sort of dread which is beyond his ken. The dread of life is demonstrated by people who demand medical treatment far beyond what is regarded as reasonable from the medical and scientific point of view.[477] Man has an awareness of imminent ruin which is tantamount to dread of the approaching end of all that makes life worth living. In some cases this dread is of world war and nuclear destruction; in most it is the growing awareness of the slowing-down process of age itself.

There is a tendency toward positive gratification of the mind without personal participation or effort; one seeks to promote efficiency in living, and fatigue and recreation are strictly regularized. Immediate self-will is what primarily moves man since he has become a mere replaceable cog in the machinery.

The divorce of labor from pleasure deprives life of its possible gravity: public affairs have become mere entertainment. . . .[478]

Such an impulse towards contemporary self assertion culminates in a trumpeting of the present, a glorification of the passing show — as if there could be no shadow of a doubt as to what the present really is.[479]

Those people who become successful in the technicalized society, and who force their way into the front ranks, enjoy more advantages in terms of luxuries, but they too, according to Jaspers

are the slaves of their functions, which merely demand an alerter intelligence, a more specialized talent, and a more lively activity than those of the crowd.[480]

The would-be climber must be able to make himself liked by others. He must persuade, and at times even corrupt himself

175

as well as others. He must be serviceable enough to give him self the appearance of indispensability. He must learn to hol his tongue while being adept at rationalizing grudges. He mus be ostentatious, yet modest. For a climber it is necessary to hav a readiness to appeal to sentiment on occasions, and to be cap able of working in a manner that pleases his superiors. Abov all, the climber must avoid showing independence except wher it is expected. This is the formula for the successful man, bu not for the authentic man.[481]

The externals of the twentieth century betray its decay. Home into which the masses are herded, resemble barracks which ar to be escaped on weekends whenever possible. The home itsel is transformed into a mere sleeping place. Public education, in stead of merely supplementing education in the home, usurp the primary role and takes children away from parental in fluence. People are no longer horrified at divorce and the poly gamous tendencies of our society. Abortion, homosexuality an suicide are rampant. Women are being denied their roles a mothers by their emancipation, and their growth in economi independence.[482]

On the broader scope, reality is divided against reality. Trut opposes truth. Every moral imperative is tainted by guilt for i must destroy others equally moral and equally imperative. It i the nature of the age to crush the greatness it finds in man.[48]

> . . . We may define our human situation by saying that no reliance can be placed in worldly existence.[484]

Hard labor, old age, sickness and death cannot be done awa with no matter how modernized man becomes. They haun man and they initiate the dread of life which is to be foun deep in the foundations of every man's style of life.

> I must die, I must suffer, I must struggle, I am subject to chance, I involve myself inexorably in guilt.[485]

These are inevitable situations which every man must experience and must acknowledge and accept if he is to become authentic The dread with which a person faces these ultimate situation may be unconsciously effective and may influence the individual even though he is not aware of what force is molding his personality. To the existentialist it is essential that man be made aware of these forces so that he might cope with the anxiety produced more creatively.

Man knows that he is situated in a definite place in this world. As Jaspers writes

> My place is, as it were, determined by coordinates; what I am is a function of this place; existence is integral; and I myself am but a modification, or a consequence, or a link in the chain. My essence is the historical epoch and sociological situation as a whole.[486]

The place of mankind is his own peculiar place, his unique situation. What is important for man, however, is not his situation but what he chooses to make of it. Strictly speaking, only an individual can be said to be in a situation, for each situation is unique, and what is made of that situation is dependent on the individual.[487] Man's inviolable property in this world is the narrow space he possesses. It is this possession which enables him to share in the totality of life which he is a member of. The situation in which man lives is not a final one, for the next moment creates for him a new space in which he must exist. Even the negative world situation of the twentieth century is not final, a new situation is perpetually forthcoming.[488] Western man is too impatient to await the changes which must take place in his era. As a result, he too often feels himself to be abandoned to this world and to all its misery. He has no escape from threatening disaster yet he still reaches for deliverance.[489]

> By watching the doom of what is finite, man witnesses the reality and the truth of the infinite.[490]

Man is forced to realize that every configuration within being doomed to failure. However failure is not necessarily all black, all negative. "The way in which man approaches his failure determines what he will become."[491] Failure encourages man to seek redemption at the very least.

That man is not God is the cause of his smallness and un-doing. But that he can carry his human possibilities to their extreme and can be undone by them with his eyes open — that is his greatness.[492]

As man realizes that he is in a definite situation there arises something in him which demands purposive behavior in regard to the problems which confront him.

The grasping of a situation modifies it, insofar as the grasp-ing of it renders possible the adoption of a definite attitude towards it and an appeal to the tribunal of action.[493]

Jaspers' Concept of the Tragic Dilemma

Throughout Jaspers' philosophical discussion one is aware that much, if not all, of what man does is destined to be destroyed. Man is not immune to destruction. The more aware man is of his being, the more he is aware of the fact that he himself will be destroyed. Jaspers' tragic point of view "sees human need and suffering as anchored in metaphysics."[494]

Without such a metaphysical basis, we have only misery, grief, misfortune, mishap and failure. The tragic, however, is visible only to a kind of knowledge that transcends all these.[495]

Tragic awareness is capable of redeeming man from his potential state of worthlessness and misery. Tragic awareness permits man to understand what is happening to him and opens to man the possibility of identifying with the suffering state. When he is able to identify with his suffering state, when he is able to know the reasons for the conditions which befall him, the indi-vidual becomes capable of struggling with his situation. By struggling with his situation man often finds himself able to transcend the misery he feels and he may even transform the tragedy. As man wrestles with the tragic one of two thing happens —

178

Either the tragic remains intact, and man liberates himself by enduring it and transforming himself with it, or else tragedy itself is, so to speak, redeemed; it ceases to be; it becomes past.[496]

However, not all men rise to the knowledge of their tragic situation in life because they content themselves to live in mediocrity. Those not aware (consciously) of this tragedy which afflicts life tend to be wiped out indifferently during the disasters of life just as any natural obstacle is eventually destroyed.[497] Whenever the tragic sense appears, something extraordinary is lost, this is man's sense of security, his sense of being at home in the universe. The man who experiences tragedy, in the sense of realizing the gross limitations which constantly shackle him, experiences a catharsis of the soul.[498]

It is an experience that touches the innermost being of each man. It makes him more deeply receptive to reality, not merely as a spectator, but as a man who is personally involved.[499]

The authentic man realizes that he will be and in fact is confronted by unanswerable questions.

Human life understands itself in terms of its potentialities and perils, its greatness and nothingness, ... its sheer joy of being alive and its bewildered terror at failure and destruction, its love, dedication, and openness of heart, and then again its hatred, narrowness and blindness. All in all, humanity sees itself confronted by an unanswerable problem, by the ultimate collapse of every effort to realize its promise ...[500]

The alternative to tragic awareness is the abolition of human awareness of the alternatives which confront man.

The tragic hero finds himself heightened by his awareness and physically he is intensified. He is a man who fulfills himself in goodness but cancels himself out in evil.

179

In each case his existence is shipwrecked by the consistency
with which he meets some unconditional demand, real or
supposed.[501]

Against this shipwreck which perpetually confronts the authen
individual, Jaspers stresses that there is a counterweight.
is not futility.

> ... there are in the world things worthy of faith, things that
> arouse confidence; there is a foundation which sustains us:
> home and country, parents and ancestors, brothers and
> sisters and friends, husbands and wives. There is a foundation
> of historical tradition, in native language, in faith, in the
> work of thinkers, poets and artists.[502]

Even these factors however are not absolutely reliable for all.

> The essential task for man is to learn to live which means r
> only that he must learn to die, but that he must learn to li
> with the tragic of life. Only as he is capable of living under t
> shadow of death and in the reality of the tragic will m
> appreciate life.
> Certainly man is not satisfied with existing under the shade
> of uncertainty. He has a great inner drive towards deepeni
> his being, enlarging his understanding of the eternal in order
> give him a more firm foundation. The drive gives rise to t
> philosophical attitudes of wonder which leads to knowledge,
> doubt which leads to certainty and of forsakenness which leads
> the self. How this drive is expressed in each generation depen
> on the degree of communication between men which is possil
> in that era.
> To Jaspers, one might conclude, there is truth, not truth
> an absolute, but truth as a process.

> Truth lies rather in a process of continuous questioning and
> critical appropriation ... it means an incessant searching,
> trying, and risking all in a state of ignorance.[503]

CHAPTER IV

THE EXISTENTIALIST'S APPRAISAL OF THE CHILD
AND HIS EDUCATION

art I: S∮ren Kierkegaard

Although S∮ren Kierkegaard felt that he was perfectly suited
r the role he was to play in history, he disparaged his child-
ood and thought that his experiences were hardly a model
be followed in bringing up children. To gain a clearer under-
anding of Kierkegaard's suggestions pertaining to the education
a child, it is necessary to examine his own childhood for his
periences ought not be replicated in the lives of other children.

It is terrible when I think, even for a single moment, over
the dark background which, from the very earliest time,
was part of my life. The dread with which my father filled my
soul... and all the things in this connection which I do not
even note down.[1]

hen Kierkegaard's father was a child he had cursed God be-
use of an intense feeling of loneliness while he was shepherding
me sheep on the lonely, rugged heaths of Jutland. As a result
this impiety he became convinced that he had committed the
pardonable sin. Eventually he moved to Copenhagen where
became quite successful in the wool business. When all was
ing well, his first wife died. He interpreted her death as
rtial punishment for the sin of his childhood. Before the
riod of mourning was over, the father was forced to marry
cousin who was a maid in his house at the time of his wife's

death, and their first child arrived within eight months. Th
father became full of dread and sank into a deep melancholy
for he believed he could find no forgiveness.[2]

Søren Kierkegaard was the youngest of the family. The gir
in his family babied him, but his father saw in the young chil
a religious possibility. The father assumed the role of Abraha
and his boy became Isaac; and the father, according to Kierke
gaard, stood ready to sacrifice his son to prove his devotion t
God and complete repentance. This does not mean that i
reality the father ever considered infanticide, but as far as Søre
Kierkegaard was concerned his father murdered his childhood

> I never knew the joy of being a child. The terrible agonies
> I suffered disturbed the calm which is the constituent of
> childhood, of having it in one's power to be industrious,
> to please one's father; for the unrest within me resulted in
> my always, always being outside of myself.[3]

The resulting melancholy which he experienced not onl
deprived him of his feeling of youthfulness, it also denied hi
the child's normal enjoyment of immediateness and spontaneit
He was rarely allowed the privilege of going out to play wit
his peers. Instead, the father, who was retired, would take hi
into the garden and ask him where he would like to trave
Then the father would create a travelogue of the chosen countr
so complete with detail that it carried the boy off into a worl
of vivid imagination. This was the training period for h
imagination which he was to use so effectively as an adult writer

Not only did his father refuse him the opportunity of pla
with other children, he also dressed him inappropriately fo
school which made him look ridiculous to his peers and cause
him to be ridiculed. Kierkegaard would strike back with h
wit, which was sharply developed at an early age, and as
result often suffered beatings at the hands of his clas mate
"Humanly speaking", he wrote, "it was a crazy upbringing.
His experience with his own crazy upbringing led him to observ
that nature endows the child richly so that he can survive th
way parents mismanage the upbringing.[6]

From childhood, Kierkegaard was encouraged to develop his remarkable imagination. In terms of the stimulation which the father gave the boy, Kierkegaard became convinced that he could do anything except stifle his deep feelings of anguish. Although Kierkegaard's father dominated his son and demanded absolute obedience, the father did not nag his child. When Søren Kierkegaard went to school his father simply said that he expected him to place third in the class. He never inquired about his son's progress in school beyond a casual interest for he was confident that the boy would live up to his expectations. Kierkegaard placed second in his school.[7] As a boy, nonetheless, Kierkegaard idolized his father; he later explained, "adversity draws men together."[8] It was most important for him to be successful in his educational endeavor. Eventually he even completed his theological examinations in order to please his father. Yet he was aware of the tragedy in his father's life. He perhaps even knew more than what his father told him. Young Kierkegaard took great pleasure in the fact that he had deceived everyone, and that no one knew just how unhappy and melancholy he felt.[9] To explain this feeling of dread and anxiety he wrote,

There is no greater emotional torture than to be ashamed of one's father, ashamed of the man one loves most, and to whom one owes most, than to have to approach him with back turned and with averted eyes in order not to witness his dishonor.[10]

Kierkegaard, upon becoming a youth, was responsible for copying his father's letters. When he refused to do this, his father would not scold him but would merely say that he was going to do them himself, and the guilt-stricken boy would immediately be willing to assume the task. He longed for a scolding because then there could have been a row, and perhaps he would have avoided the tedious work. His father seldom scolded him. One occasion when he did receive a scolding was when he upset a salt shaker. Søren protested that this was not as bad a deed as that committed earlier by his sister when she

183

had broken a vase but who had received no scolding. The father responded that one does not need to scold another who has done something terrible, for then they know what they have done. One needs to scold another over a trifle to make an impression.[11]

As well as being responsible for copying his father's letters, Kierkegaard was also asked to copy the sermons of Bishop Mynster. For this deed he was paid. Once his father offered to quadruple the pay if the boy would write the sermon from memory. He rebuked his father for trying to bribe him into matters pertaining to religion.[12]

To Kierkegaard, his father's chief error in raising him was not lack of love, but it was mistaking a child for an old man.[13]

Kierkegaard's Suggestions for Child Development

Kierkegaard states that strictly speaking he was most severely trained in the Christian faith as a child. He thinks that humanly speaking this "bringing up was a species of madness, for my earliest childhood was made to groan under impressions too heavy even for the melancholy old man who laid them on me."[14] Kierkegaard was weighted down with adult problems beyond his ability to cope with them. In his *Journals* he noted that if a horse is harnessed to too great a load and then required to pull that load, it will try with all its might and then will fall down. His reflections about his own childhood convinced him that children should not be given responsibilities which normally would slow down an adult. Children should be given only those responsibilities which they are mature enough to assume and still maintain their child-like state.[15]

He feels that it is wrong to force the life of a child into conformity with decisive Christian categories, no matter how benevolent the adult authority.[16] Kierkegaard states that it is impossible to cram Christianity into a child, for the child will merely transform the faith into an idyllic mythology which in turn may blight his spiritual growth at a later time of maturity. To the melancholy Dane, the child's life should be one of play

184

and jest.[18] The child ought not be offended by too many ceremonial responsibilities.[19]

The child's life is a simple life and the child abides in a state of innocence. Innocence is a "state which can very well endure, and therefore the logical haste to get it annulled is out of place."[20] A child should not be forced to grow into manhood too fast, for upon attaining manhood, if indeed not before, he will become guilty and a sinner. Once innocence has been transformed into guilt, Kierkegaard strongly emphasizes, it cannot be recovered; for as one wishes for it, it is lost and it — the person's guilt — becomes compounded because added to it would be the sin of wasting time.[21] To Kierkegaard the child will only too soon find his innocence compromised by a feeling of boredom, and with the feeling of boredom his life becomes complicated.[22] The child is not born in sin, for he is born in ignorance, and therefore has not had the chance to assume or choose sin; thus he is innocent, and one will find him in an intimate, immediate unity with his natural condition.[23] It is because the child is innocent that Kierkegaard felt that infant baptism is inappropriate, and he rather admired the Irish whom he heard kept one arm of an infant out of the baptismal ceremony so that the growing person could eventually love a girl, do some fighting, and in general commit a few sins.[24]

Not only must one not accuse a child of being sinful, one must indeed be very circumspect to never believe the worst when a child does a misdeed, for the ill-timed suspicion, revealed perhaps by a chance remark, will induce in the child a state of anxiety in which the child's innocent, but weak, soul may be tempted to believe himself guilty, which in turn may reduce the child to spiritual impotency.[25] The concept that negative attitudes on the part of the parent may negatively influence the child has been suggested over a long historical period. Quintillian accepted this thesis, Harry Stack Sullivan also subscribed to the theory. The Danish theologian avers that the child does not know what the dreadful is, what the idea of sin is, what it means to be 'sick unto death'. The imperfection in the child is not in his being sinful, or even in not knowing what the dreadful is, but it is

185

just the opposite; namely that occasionally he shudders at that which does not involve sickness unto death and thereby is carried away from the experience of immediacy which his life hithertofore is characterized by.[26] Actually, it is the parents' duty to not permit the child to come into close quarters with a feeling that he is a miserable sinner, or that any preventable guilt infects his freedom to grow. The art of parenthood is to "be constantly present and yet not to be present, to let the child be allowed to develop itself, while nevertheless one has constantly a survey clearly before it."[27] In a discussion of the seducer, Kierkegaard pointed out the seducer's delight at the fact that his victim had been brought up strictly and in seclusion, and that she had not learned the pleasures of the world. This had made her proud, but it also forced her to disregard what other girls were enjoying. The result of this isolation meant that she lived in a world of dreams, and thus would be an easy mark for the seducer. Yet the Danish bachelor knew that it was not easy to say when one ought to let the child walk alone and be independent. Nevertheless, the child must be so freed.[28]

Kierkegaard responded enthusiastically to 'the possibility' which is in the child.[29] Any child may become an Apostle of the faith. Kierkegaard warned fathers that it is necessary for them to realize that a child is a trust.[30] The child must not be treated just as another object in the household, and certainly he should not be kissed in the way a cat is petted; nor must the parents wrap their ego in the child so that they prove their own excellence by showing the child off. A father should think with profound seriousness about the responsibility he bears for the child.[31] One responsibility which the father has is to treat the child as a person, and not as an object to be observed. He deplored family situations in which the father is unwilling to curse his son, with all his parental authority, as much as he did the family situation in which the son will not defy his father. When the father displays anger at his son's disobedience and defiance, the occasion arises for a reconciliation, and the condition is set for the intimacy of forgiveness.[32] The feeling of intimacy which arises from the act of forgiveness is one which broaden

186

and deepens the child's personality. To Kierkegaard, many people are no longer close enough to each other within their own family bond, for they tend to observe each other as one might do in a game, rather than being intimate, one with another. There must be spontaneity in the family situation. In this relationship it is necessary for there to develop a feeling of duty, on the part of the child, to realize the parental aspirations for him.[33] It must be borne in mind that the parent must not do everything for the son, for this would be to deny the son any objective existence, and would cause him to become "shut-up" in his father's love. On the other hand, the parent should not keep the child emotionally disturbed by making a series of demands for him to conform to.[34] It is important that the child learn a lofty quietude towards the parent, which later on will be shifted to God.

How a father treats his child affords a casual observer a chance to gain deep insight into the father, for the child, with all its possibilities, still remains an unstructured experience. What the child becomes is a reflection of what the parent has precipitated in the child's being. Although Kierkegaard was not a father, he sensed that there is truth in the Chinese proverb, "Bring up your child well — thus you will know how much you owe your parents."[35] To state this in another way, Kierkegaard argues that the highest thing one can owe another is life. This becomes even more poignant when he goes on to assert that, "a child may owe still more to a father for in fact it does not receive life pure and simple, but it receives it with a definite content."[36]

Kierkegaard, in his discussion of marriage, writes that it is the duty of the married couple to have children.[37] He himself liked children. Occasionally when he visited his sister he would play with his nieces who looked forward to his infrequent visits. He was intrigued by the stiff examination that children can put adults through by insisting on answers to their searching questions.[38] His heart was warmed by the affection and love which mothers show their children. He writes with tenderness about the techniques of Danish mothers who blacken their breasts at weaning time in order that they would not still be

187

the same to the eyes of the infant, and would even give the infant a taste so that he will not have to feel too great a disappointment. Yet during this process the mother's "eyes are as full of love and as gentle as they were before." He also noted how fortunate the child was whose mother, at the weaning time, could provide her child with stronger food so that he would not perish.[39]

Kierkegaard esteemed the energy and devotion which children display.

> I may smile at a little urchin of five years who takes hold of a thing so passionately, and yet I assure you, I have no greater wish than that at every time of life I may take hold of my work with the same energy, with the same ethical earnestness as they.[40]

Kierkegaard realized that it takes a long time before a child learns to separate himself from the objective world, to realize that he is not a part of his surroundings but that he is a separate identity. Erik Erikson indicates that this experience is discernible at about the age of two and a half, but that the youngster is not confident of himself until he is four.[41] In that the child does not have to wrestle with himself as an individual, Kierkegaard felt that his life is calm and that this calmness permits an industriousness which the child engages in to please his father.[42] Erikson also states that after the age of five the child becomes industrious so as to release pent up oedipus tension, but also to please the father.[43]

Kierkegaard holds that all unhappiness can be related to false impressions received during childhood.[44] Although he writes about the responsibility of parents towards children, he was quite aware of his own previous experiences, and he observed other instances where the family failed the child. As stated previously, he became convinced that Providence endowed the child richly because He knew in advance what could befall the child who must be brought up by parents.

Kierkegaard shares an interpretation of the contemporary psychoanalyst, Harry Stack Sullivan, who states that the person is essentially what he is going to be by the time that he is ten years old.[45] This does not mean that childhood experiences determine what the person will become, but such experiences have formed the resources which will influence future human growth and development.

Kierkegaard's Concept of Youth

Kierkegaard uses the terms youth and child to distinguish two age groups. He does not indicate the actual age range which he is thinking about when he uses the terms. As was just mentioned, he believed that the person is what he is going to be by the age of ten; the middle school in Denmark begins at the age of eleven, therefore it might be safe to conjecture that youth centers from the age of eleven to a year or so after puberty.

As with the child, Kierkegaard does not become serious about the condition of youth. He indicates that theirs is an age in which one should make love and dance. He observes that,

> Our first youth is like a flower at dawn with a beautiful drop of dew in its cup which reflects all the surroundings in harmonious and melancholy terms. But the sun rises above the horizon and the dew-drop evaporates.[46]

Youth to Kierkegaard, although capable of reflecting that which is in his surroundings, usually has little conception of reality and its suffering, or of what it means to become authentic. The Danish thinker had no desire to precipitate a change in this status. Kierkegaard was even favorably impressed by his observation that youth hold the illusion that the future holds something extraordinary for them.[47]

Kierkegaard's Own Experience with Education

Kierkegaard was sent to the School for Civic Virtue at the age of eight. He looked forward to going to school because he thought it was his duty to go and to master his lessons.[48] When given assignments to memorize Latin he took care to be sure that

189

the task was successfully carried to a conclusion. He even reviewed his lesson to his sister in order to guarantee to himself that he knew what he was supposed to know.[49] His teachers, however, never commented on him in terms of his being an outstanding pupil. Nevertheless he was recommended for each level of education offered in Denmark.

Kierkegaard seemed to be favorably disposed towards his professors. Professor Nielsen, who was in charge of the elementary school, especially impressed the boy. Kierkegaard felt that the professors should be treated with great respect and he was astounded, in secondary school, at the fact that fellow students would not give a suitable expression of respect to their teachers.[50] Kierkegaard was not completely under the thumb of his teachers. One time a class was so disturbing to a professor that he said he would go to the school master about the unruly situation. Kierkegaard calmly asked him if he were going to tell the headmaster that all of his classes were like the one he wanted to complain about. The teacher did not go. The source of the teacher's irritation was that the students were eating sandwiches and drinking beer.[51] Croxall, a Kierkegaardian authority, also points out that Kierkegaard undoubtedly pressed his teachers, and often led them into inconsistencies.

Kierkegaard's school experience was not pleasant. He had no close friends or pals, and he was ridiculed for his odd clothes. His wit often defended him against insults but this only precipitated fights for which he was ill-prepared.[52]

From secondary school he went to the University. He passed his first examinations in Latin, Hebrew, religion, geography, geometry, arithmetic and German. He did well on examinations in Danish, Greek, history and French. One of his teachers observed that Kierkegaard had his own ideas about how he should be taught. In *The Present Age* Kierkegaard comments,

> Among the young men of today a profound and prodigious learning is almost unthinkable; they would find it ridiculous.[53]

Kierkegaard himself reacted to his studies with a light heart. He was known for his card playing, beer parties and quick wit.[54]

His first position was with Neilsen's school where he was employed to teach Latin. He taught Latin for two years and then quit. He did not give an account of why he resigned save to observe that it wearied him and he thought of it as a waste of time. In *Either-or,* which contains semi-autobiographical material, the young man who quit teaching Latin said, "I resigned a teaching position in which I was perfectly suited for I had everything to lose and nothing to gain...."; the young man then continued that he joined the circus in which he had everything to gain. This latter remark was not autobiographical.[55]

After Kierkegaard became an author, he was a sought after commencement speaker. For this task he usually prepared a half page of notes and then went to the rostrum. Thus, his interest in education was never broken.[56]

The Implications of Kierkegaard's Thought for Education

One of the most surprising facts in Kierkegaardian literature is that he does not discuss education to any great extent. It is true that his primary interest was in aiding adults to become Christians by challenging the lethargy of Christendom. Nevertheless, he found time to write about most of the contemporary personalities and he commented on practically every significant event of his day. He discussed the training of the clergy, journalism, public opinion, marriage, political parties, the relationship of the individual to the group, the psychology of the masses, the rise of democracy, and several of the major systems of philosophy which carried an impact in his day such as those of Schopenhauer, Hegel and Kant. His *Journals* are filled with notes about small things; the men and women of his day, and the problems of children, which have already been examined. His writings are filled with biographical accounts of himself, but even here he does not go into detail about his formal education. The fact would perhaps not be too important save for the fact that educational problems were at the forefront of awareness in Danish, as well as European, society. Rousseau, Pestalozzi and Fichte were all advocating the liberalization of

191

education. In Denmark there was an educator who might have become as famous as John Dewey had he not written in the Danish language and remained loyal to his small country. His name is Bishop Nicolai Grundtvig who was born in 1783 and died in 1872.

Nicolai Grundtvig was a prominent leader in the revolutionary movement in Denmark. He was an advocate of constitutional reforms. He realized however that in order for the people to become self-governing they must first be educated. He was thus the founder of the "Folk-School", which in time became popular throughout the Scandinavian countries. He insisted that classical education ought to be buried for it was dead, and he advocated the teaching of Danish culture and history as well as the Danish language; his primary purpose was to develop great patriots imbued in pride of country and Danish traditions.[57] He sought a curriculum which would bring culture to the masses. He insisted that education must include not only the humanities, but also manual subjects which would teach students to create with their hands. Above all, he wanted children to be permitted to stay young while they were young and not to be ushered into manhood prematurely. Education must be adapted to the child's needs.[58] To Grundtvig, childhood is a fantasy time, and education should communicate to the child through images, myths, and stories which make life graphic. Education should not be thoroughly immersed in reason and emotion. The school's purpose is not to instruct man in the art of reading books, but is rather to awaken man, and he felt that spirited and interesting lessons are a necessity.[59] Concerning Christianity, he felt that it is not the task of the school to make children into Christians; the task of the school is to prepare them to be men, and then after they have become men one may hope that they will become Christians.[60]

Grundtvig's Christian policies were liberal, and as a result he seriously alienated Bishop Mynster. Mynster was Kierkegaard's confessor, the most trusted friend of his father, and the one man who replaced his father in the life of Kierkegaard after the father's death. It is more than probable that Kierkegaard

elt obliged to defend the old man (Mynster and indirectly
his father) against any attacks on his person or thought. As a
result of this attitude Grundtvig and Kierkegaard came into
conflict. The twentieth century followers of Grundtvig have
found it difficult to forgive Kierkegaard for his attacks on their
reform leader. If, however, one examines the attacks of Kierkegaard on Grundtvig's thought one will find that they are
associated with the latter's understanding of religion. One time
Grundtvig preached a sermon in which he asked the question,
"Why is the word of God gone from the house of God?" Kierkegaard felt that this was inappropriate and preferred the question
to be, "Why has the power gone from the preaching of the word
of God?"[61] At another time, Grundtvig expressed his approval
of the tolerance towards religion which he had found in England.
Kierkegaard needled him for not realizing that the tolerance he
praised was in reality indifference, which is the profoundest
falling away from Christianity.[62] Kierkegaard was also disturbed
about Grundtvig's politics, for the former distrusted the masses
and preferred to be ruled by a small coterie of qualified people.
Not once does Kierkegaard attack Grundtvig for his educational
reforms; in point of fact he tends to agree with every point which
previously was discussed as being the educational policies of
Grundtvig. Kierkegaard's silence in the matter may well have
been that he so opposed Grundtvig's religious and political affil-
iations that he could not bring himself to saying anything kind
about the man. Or, again, he may have been so loyal to his friends,
Mynster, Neilsen and Clauseen — all three of whom were feuding
with Grundtvig — that he did not want to betray them. Finally,
it may be observed that Kierkegaard was not a man of action;
Grundtvig was, and in general the time was ripe for his educational reform, and he didn't need too much help from the
melancholy Dane for the Folk-School was an established fact
at least two decades before Grundtvig died.[63]

There is some evidence that Kierkegaard did back Grundtvig
on at least one occasion. Grundtvig was trying to convince the
king and the Danish assembly that the royal school at Sφro
should be turned into a school open to the young people of

Denmark who were eighteen to thirty years of age. He wante these people to be able to enroll without examination and the be able to take whatever courses they wished. The courses woul all be in the humanities and many of them would be dedicate to furthering the students' patriotic spirit. The King waverec the assembly (even though composed of Grundtvig's party favored classical education.[64] At the time of this discussion Kie kegaard had an audience with the king. As their conversatio proceeded they talked about what to do with the masse Kierkegaard advised the king to stand fast against the politics reform movement. The king agreed, and then Kierkegaard sai that "what the whole age needed was education." This is replication of Grundtvig's argument. The conversation continue about education for a little longer and then the king came t the point of his concern, which was to ask Kierkegaard to assum a teaching position at Sφro. Kierkegaard, who was not intereste in marriage, the ministry or teaching evaded the question an it dropped.[65] The important point is that Kierkegaard believe in the education of the masses, whom he felt were an ignorar lot. This was not a meaningless conversational item but was a essential ingredient if a person is to be raised from the masse into being 'the individual'. As stated in the third chapter, all pe sons can become 'Individuals', but they must first experience th full knowledge of the universal. They must be fully developed i the ethical stage. The person who is a constituent of the masse must be made aware of man's possibilities, by studying th accomplishments of man throughout history. He must be taugh that past history is conditioning him in his present situation an that he may influence his future by assuming responsibility fc his decisions. He must be made conscious by education that h has a soul or a self. This awareness can be stimulated throug poetry, knowledge of the Bible, or study of the great literatur of the ages. The education of the masses, to Kierkegaard, mear that the adult population also had to be educated which wa exactly the emphasis made by Grundtvig. Kierkegaard's goa would be to stimulate adult thinking and by so doing bring ther to an awareness of their inner-most self, which would eventuall lead them to the ability to make responsible choices. Once the adult would learn to make intelligent choices, Kierkegaard assumed that he would choose God. The teacher can not force an adult to assume responsibility for himself and become 'the individual', but the teacher can open vistas for the adult which will enable him to think more creatively. While Kierkegaard was most concerned with developing a certain type of morality in people, he was aware that morality can not be taught in the same way that a person can learn language, art or handicrafts in general.[66] He firmly believed though that the individual must go through a stage in which he would believe that he could learn to differentiate right from wrong and thereby discover the ethical. This optimism he believed is doomed to failure for the ethical cannot be generalized or reflected on; when one learns this fact, the insight will then serve as a catalyst for the dread which is likely to induce the person to choose himself as being responsible for making good or bad situations. Dread is accrued by the individual who seeks to know truth but finds that the more he knows, the farther he is away from truth; the more ethical concepts he understands, the more unethical he becomes.

The greatest danger which Kierkegaard foresaw in adult education was the possibility that the student would lose personal involvement in the educational process, and that instead he would become a mere observer. To become an observer of the educational situation means that the person tends to compartmentalize learning to such a degree that it has no impact on his ethical consciousness. This is particularly evident in the rise to prominence of science. Kierkegaard was not opposed to science as such, but he was opposed to science when it became more important than ethical concerns. When science becomes the highest criteria of judgement it does away with religion.[67] Science, writes Kierkegaard, reduces everything to calm and objective observation. By removing passion from life, the author feels, an essential element in freedom of choice is denied. Not only will science negatively influence faith, it will also deny freedom.[68] When science emphasizes the importance of doubt, it then becomes a force which will slay the learner. Eventually, according to Kierkegaard's logic, the learner must doubt that he doubts, and if all scientific learning is based on doubt, then the learner will realize he can not learn because he doubts that he doubts, which is to deny the agreed point of departure into the learning process.[69]

Kierkegaard did not launch a formal attack on classical education as such. He did specifically state that 'the Individual' will not waste time; he himself ceased teaching Latin, and whenever he writes of school subjects, Latin and Greek are omitted from his list. To bring the individual into the height of the ethical stage classical learning would not be as valuable to the student as would his undertaking to learn the humanities.

In summary, Kierkegaard favored the education of the masses which to him also meant adult education. The purpose of education, especially when it is geared to the adult population, is to deepen the ethical understanding of people in terms of helping them to realize that they are capable of structuring a portion of their future by their current choices.

Another purpose of education would be to bring the aesthetic person into an awareness of his relationship to the whole of mankind, and that his joys and sorrows are associated with problems which confront man as a whole.

The educational system, to Kierkegaard, would lose its value if it were too scientific or if it were too classical, for then it would not bring the person into a situation where reflection of his being was of paramount importance. By implication of Kierkegaard's writings, and as indicated by a study of his library, he should favor a humanities curriculum if he is to be consistent.

Kierkegaard would not generalize a specific curriculum for all levels of the school system. He felt that the educational purpose for adults would not be the same as for children. The child should be allowed to remain young in spirit as long as he is a child. Innocence is a state which the child can well endure, and thus any haste to make the child grow up psychologically would be out of place. Kierkegaard deplored the education which is designed to make little men and women out of children. His emphasis that children should be permitted to remain young and carefree as long as they are actually children chronologically, is also emphasized by Heidegger, who concluded his book, *An Introduction to Metaphysics,* by quoting Hölderlin: "For the mindful God abhors untimely growth."[70]

Hölderlin states exactly Kierkegaard's problem. If one could guarantee that one could "christianize" a child, Kierkegaard would certainly prefer to do so; however, he realized that children do not have the capacity to understand the Christian faith, and therefore they transform it into an idyllic mythology.[71] Kierkegaard was aware that while the child can not profit by premature religious instruction, he can be irreparably lost by it. If the child should misunderstand the anguish and dread of religion, the condition may well be established whereby the faith will be repugnant to the grown person.[72] For this reason, the child should not be exposed to melancholy old men whom they might admire, for they might come to believe that God is unjust, and therefore be driven from God.[73] It is important to select teachers who do not have a morbid personality to teach young children. The child's life should be gay and enjoyable. He ought to have a teacher who also knows how to enjoy life.

Kierkegaard's zeal to encourage significant people to permit children to enjoy their stage of life presented him with a problem. He also believes that the basic personality of a person is formed by the age of ten. By ten the youngster must be exposed to a series of significant experiences which will encourage him to seek for a knowledge of God's love as he grows up. Kierkegaard's emphasis on the age of ten as being the critical age is alien to orthodox Freudianism, but is fully acceptable to Harry Stack Sullivan who also sets the critical age this late.

Kierkegaard wrote that what one learns is not as important as how one grows.

What is really important in education is not that the child learns this and that, but that the mind is matured and that energy is around.[74]

Kierkegaard was critically aware of the fact that knowledge by

197

itself does not guarantee wholesome attitudes in life. "Every one knows a great deal, we all know which way we ought to go and all the different ways we can go, but nobody is willing to move."[75] It is the quality of energy which must be preserved in the growth of the child. Spectatoritis must be avoided at all costs. The child will eventually be brought close to God only if he has access to an abundant supply of energy which will permit him to react passionately to the religious challenge. The adult must retain the childlike ability to throw himself into whatever he does with enthusiasm and sustained interest. The school curriculum must then be associated with the interest of the child as well as with his readiness to master the material. The child must not be forced into a learning situation for which he is ill-prepared. He must be provided with a learning atmosphere which will invigorate him and permit him to adequately express his energy without having to learn to repress rigidly his feelings. The school should provide a curriculum which will lead the child into action, both physically and mentally, and which will prevent him from assuming an observer's role to the ongoing process.

Although Kierkegaard stressed the importance of spontaneity in the child's life, he must not be permitted to be carefree at the expense of honesty or truthfulness when he does confront reality. Honesty was so highly cherished by Kierkegaard, that he once expressed how he would champion the cause of a critic of Christianity if he were really honest. The adult should be honest and truthful with the child at all times.[76]

On the superficial level this would mean that subjects such as death, sex, or money would not be tabooed topics, as they usually are. The adult authority would not seek artificial means to discuss these problems with the child, nor to educate him in these matters, but he certainly will not accept the attitude that these subjects may only be hinted at. Kierkegaard did not favor the creation of artificial problems for the child. The curriculum should be designed so that the child will not be aware of the tragedy of life, or the sexual side of life, until he is cognizant of these forces and he, himself, raises questions pertaining to the problem. When the child does ask questions, his questions must be frankly and honestly answered. Kierkegaard opposed the teaching of historical Christianity to a young child because he may be stimulated to ask too many questions about the crucifixion of Christ. Kierkegaard depicts a child who is unspoiled by learning, but who in a series of story-pictures is exposed to the crucifixion scene. The child's mood will change from one of unspeakable delight with the lovely pictures to one of sorrow and anxiety. The child will ask who it is on the cross and what he did to deserve such a brutal fate. He will be told that he was the most loving man who ever lived. The account of His suffering will make such a deep impression on the child that he will not be in the mood to hear about the glory which triumphed. He will forget the other pictures for he will have something to ponder about. The child will even entertain a desire to avenge this good man, little realizing that there is an eighteen hundred year span between their lives. This, to Kierkegaard, is an example of misplaced honesty. The child is incapable of understanding or accepting the victory of the crucifixion regardless of adult attempts to explain it. In the act of pondering the meaning of the situation and worrying about it, the child loses his enthusiasm and energy for the lighter things. He is forced to grow up and become responsible for his actions prematurely. The honest answers had to be given, the picture did not have to be shown.

Kierkegaard insists that the adult world should not give the child an opinion of himself which is fallacious. This would mean that parents and teachers should never imply that the child is cleverer than what objectivity dictates; nor should they ever infer that the child is more inadequate than he is. One sometimes finds a teacher pondering what grade she should give a student. Kierkegaard would want the concept of school failure carefully considered, for the child must never be allowed to shy away from a valid awareness of himself.

The teacher must not permit the child to hide relevant information from himself. It is the teacher's responsibility, as previously indicated, to motivate the child to become active. It is just as important for the teacher to prevent his thought from escaping into some hiding place where it might become obscure to him, whether he can understand it or not, with him . . . the teacher will penetrate every irregularity, until if he does not have it, there is but one single expression which explains his failure — that he did not will it, . . . this he cannot endure.[77]

An implication of this searching of the child's personality in an effort to bring to light anything which he might wish to repress is that Kierkegaard would encourage the teacher to break through the child's 'idealized self' if at all possible. The teacher would seek to aid the child in the child's attempt to reaffirm his real self.

For a parent or a teacher to interfere in the child's life one requisite must be met; the adult must have the ability to love the child. The child must be loved by someone else so that he will know he is lovable. After the child realizes that he is lovable and is worthy as an individual he will no longer be ashamed of himself. Because the child will have no need to be ashamed of himself, he will not have to defend himself by developing a false, idealized personality. He can afford to be his real self. He will be able to examine himself because he will be confident that nothing will be discovered which will devastate him. As the child comes to know himself, he will come to know the knowledge of God's love which dwells within him. Once he has found God's love he will have firm ground under him so that he will be able to invest himself enthusiastically in life.

It becomes important, in terms of Kierkegaard's concept of love, that the teacher who is introduced to the child have a loving disposition. The teacher must himself feel secure enough that he will be able to shower warmth and affection on the child. To Kierkegaard, the opportunity for a child to bask in the warmth of love may be one of the more profound experiences of his life. However, in agreement with Bettelheim, Kierkegaard holds that love is not enough. Kierkegaard writes that he felt that he was loved by his father and his biographers report that his mother loved him, yet he was made old by other emotional states inherent in the personality of his parents.

Perhaps the most significant implication of Kierkegaard's philosophy for education would be in the area of teacher selection. In that the child's being contains manifold possibilities, it is essential that the teacher be aware of her obligations to the child. As a matter of fact, the teacher may have more responsibility for the guidance of the child than the child's parents. The parent is responsible for the child because he did the original act which caused the child to come into being. He did not choose the child who was thus derived. The teacher, on the other hand, chooses to influence the child. She has assumed responsibility for the children whom she would teach. The school system is obligated to employ only those teachers who have a sense of responsibility for what they do, who are capable of warmth and love, and finally who are capable of honesty.

Kierkegaard does not spell out the type of person he thought would be a good teacher. One may only infer the type of person he would favor. To complicate the problem, Kierkegaard would probably insist that the teacher of the elementary school child should be a different type of person than the teacher of the adult. In all probability, "The Individual" would be Kierkegaard's preference for a teacher regardless of the grade level. This person radiates the honesty and the love for others which Kierkegaard deemed essential in the personality of the teacher. "The individual", who does not owe allegiance to a static ethical system nor believe that he ought to demand that others duplicate his thought, would be most relaxed with children, and would permit them to retain their spontaneity as long as possible. In terms of content knowledge, he would bring to the teaching situation much learning, for he has progressed through the advanced ethical stage in which he would have studied very diligently. On the debit side of the ledger, "The individual" would have difficulty working with people who demanded conformity to ethical patterns or to standardized procedures. He probably would have considerable trouble with the administrators of the school system, if the administrators were assuming close supervision of the teaching process. The problems which the teacher has with the administration supervising the teaching situation probably diminishes as one ascends the teaching scale. It might be that 'the individual" would be most effective teaching adults and least effective teaching on the elementary level. Effective in this sense means the degree to which he will adjust himself to the school's administration. It also becomes more necessary that the adult student be exposed to 'the individual' because he would be able to challenge him to know himself and would provide a more permissive atmosphere for self-evaluation. Besides that, the adult is already within the ethical sphere of existence and would be more in need of a teacher who has already resolved for himself the ethical crisis which the adult must face. Of course there is an assumption upon which this discussion is based and that is that the purpose of adult education is for self-knowledge and not to train oneself in a field of learning. In the latter situation an ethical teacher would be more appropriate because he would tend to be more subject matter oriented than would "the individual".

Certainly Kierkegaard would advise against the employing of a person who is still in the aesthetic stage to teach children or adults. This person would have no sense of responsibility either in terms of preparing his lessons or in terms of meeting his educational responsibilities. He would be most unreliable.

Kierkegaard was aware that not many persons advance beyond the ethical stage. There would not be enough individuals who have reached the religious stage to fill the educational vacancies current in contemporary education. It is necessary to select the majority of teachers from the ranks of the ethical. This would not necessarily be ill-advised because the ethical teacher would have a better chance of working closely with the supervising personnel in his school system. In that most children are at the aesthetic level of experience, the teacher who is ethically oriented is able to encourage growth in the child. One must not select a teacher who is in the process of ethical deterioration because too much melancholy will accompany his personality. The ethical person who would be best suited for the teaching profession would place somewhere in the first standard deviation of a mythical continuum which plots the depth of one's ethical interest and achievement.

There is considerable danger that the ethical person will attempt to mold students according to her own preconceived notions. This attempt to mold the child might also place considerable strain on the child which would not be wholesome in terms of the child's existential growth and development. The teacher in this stage could only partially foster honesty in the child because the teacher has not learned to be honest with herself. The lack of self-knowledge which plagues the ethical person may also plague her teaching experience because critical self-evaluation may be blunted, or emotional blind spots might be present. To solve these problems Kierkegaard would probably suggest that one would have to consider the quality of ethical concern of the teacher about to be hired. One's ethics are partially learned according to Kierkegaard and therefore they themselves would be amenable to being structured. Kierkegaard's desire to maintain the child in a permissive atmosphere, to love him, to not prematurely expose him to adult problems, to encourage his spontaneity, to be honest with him and to avoid melancholy would certainly be endorsed by the advocates of John Dewey's educational approach. It would seem that Kierkegaard might well stand ready to approve a teacher who would be ready to implement John Dewey's philosophy of education on the elementary level and possibly even on the secondary level.

At all grade levels, the relationship of the teacher and student stands out as being the most important quality in the educational encounter. The teacher must throw her own personality into the teaching process. She must avoid reducing the curriculum she has to offer to mere doctrine which must be memorized. The teacher must realize that her personality is inseparable from the content which she has chosen to teach.[78] Not only must she blend her personality with that which she desires to teach, but she also must create an atmosphere which permits her subject matter to become vital and stimulating. If she is discussing a historical personality, that person must assume contemporary meaning. In the teaching process the teacher must also assume responsibility for what is being taught. She must not teach what comes easy. As Dewey indicates, she is responsible for what she thinks is important enough in the culture which she selects to present to her class. She is a responsible mediator of culture. She is also responsible for the methodology she chooses to use when presenting the material. If a child does not learn in her class, she is responsible for this fact because she chose the method of teaching which apparently was not successful.

Kierkegaard would aver that in courses which do not involve mere training or the presentation of basic facts the teacher ought to utilize the Socratic method. While using the Socratic technique the teacher must share the feeling of oneness with the student which means that she must have a feeling of equality with the students. She must have the ability to come down to the level of her students' ability and start from where she finds them.[79] In this endeavor she will often find that she is learning as much as her students learn although perhaps not the same things. The Socratic approach of Kierkegaard also involves pointing out to the student where his mistakes are and then permitting him to correct the mistakes without further guidance.[80] Kierkegaard disapproved of any technique which spoon-fed the child. He also argued against any attempt on the part of a teacher to create for herself a following, to encourage discipleship.[81] To the Danish philosopher, the main task of the teacher is not to permit the student to treat the subject matter or life in general irresponsibly. The teacher must be a force who continuously challenges the students to meet life enthusiastically and responsibly. The second task of the teacher is to enlighten the student whenever he makes an erroneous judgment, especially if he errs in evaluating his own potential.[82]

Implied in some of Kierkegaard's epistemology is the Socratic theory of innate ideas. The good teacher will elicit what the student already knows. He will then encourage the student to reconstruct his experiences in much the same fashion that Dewey would recommend.

The first act of teaching is for the teacher to learn.[83] Teaching begins with the teacher learning where the student stands, and then seeking the student out at his own level. To do this the teacher must be secure enough in her own personality to try to empathize with the child, and to view the world from where the child is and not from the adult vantage point. Not only is it essential for the teacher to place herself in the student's place, so that she will understand what the student understands, but she must be willing to let the student examine her so that he will become convinced that he is understood by her.[84] Carl Rogers states that this experience of empathy, of the counsellor beginning where the patient is, and of the patient's testing the counsellor is necessary to successful counseling.

Paradoxically, the intimate relationship of the teacher towards the student does not mean that the teacher must remain descended on the student's level as a pal or a confidant. To Kierkegaard it is essential for the teacher and the student to feel a certain distance between each other.[85] They must realize that one is an expert and the other is a novice and that the two do not blend well together. This distance between the teacher and the student ought even to develop a little awe of the teacher on the part of the student. Without awe the student is likely to be disobedient. What to Kierkegaard would be worse than disobedience, without awe of the teacher there is a tendency to transform the purpose of the school from teaching and transmitting culture to one in which students observe the educational process and make comments as to how the school should be run.[86] As stated in the third chapter, Kierkegaard was not an adherent to the concept of democracy. He believed in efficient, well run organized government.

The student should not build a fear of the teacher to the point that the student suffers emotionally. The student should experience a tension with his teacher which will precipitate in him the following reaction:

> The student must experience a tension ... which exhausts life itself and the fire of that enthusiasm and inwardness which makes fetters of dependence and the crown of do-

minion light ... which gives recognition to the ... student ...
occasion to learn.[87]

This essential tension between teacher and student results from
the necessity of reconciling their meeting on the latter's level,
in order to initiate the educational process, and their being held
apart by the former's indispensable aloofness. The teacher must
see to it that the student has it clearly in mind that he is the
teacher, the master of the situation, and that indeed he has
something of significance to offer the student even if it is no more
than pointing out the errors of the student's thinking, yet all the
while providing the student with the objective example of
someone who has worked through the same problems with which
the student is now wrestling. Harry Stack Sullivan defines a
similar role for his concept of a therapist and he describes this
role as one which involves expert-participation.

Kierkegaard is also mindful that the teacher must have his own
private personality, which will not be exposed during the school
day, into which he can retreat for self-stabilization. He must be
able to relax, in solitude, free for a time from the downward pull
of the student's problems. Not only must the teacher have some
privacy, he must also be free from extensive committee obligations. Kierkegaard believes that committee after committee is
formed by people who passionately want to do and be what they
ought, but who do not want to commit themselves.

Part II: Martin Buber

Like Søren Kierkegaard, Martin Buber does not write extensively about children. Both of these men are more interested in
challenging the adult world to turn towards God, and in encouraging them to exist really. Nevertheless, what comments Buber
does make about children permit one to assume that, to him,
childhood is a pleasant state.

Buber believes that the conditions for the I-Thou experience
(as discussed in the second chapter) precede the formation of

the ego concept of the child.[88] From the womb experience and earliest infancy the child is not one who responds very often to the world of "it"; rather he responds with the fullness of his being to the stimuli which impinge on him.[89] Harry Stack Sullivan writes that the child is at first an undifferentiated whole in terms of his reactions to his environment and that only as he matures will he learn to react specifically to the environmental stimuli. This is close to Buber's concept of the I-thou which exists between the mother and the infant, only Sullivan would define the experience as one which involves empathy.[90]

Buber rejects any theory that the child is born evil or, for that matter, even into a neutral state. The child is full of virtue at birth and indeed is innocent of any hereditary sin. As unpremeditated as it is, the child's innocence or virtue is as meaningful as the virtue which the adult might experience as a result of the calculated decision to approach the Thou. The fullness of the child's being permits him to develop a feeling of basic security. The child, however, is not responsible for the security which he feels and as a result he faces many pitfalls which will disrupt his security. It is the task of the child's parents and his teachers to foster in the child an ever growing awareness of true being.

To Buber, there are three persons who most influence the child. The first two are the child's mother and father, the third is God.[91] How the latter influences the child, Buber declines to discuss, save for the observation that God is constantly creating in the child the possibility of his turning back when he goes astray. The mother offers the child the invaluable initial experience of I-thou, as well as his first experience with I-it.

. . . The child that calls to his mother and the child that watches his mother — or to give a more exact example, the child that silently speaks to his mother through nothing other than looking into her eyes and the same child that looks at something on the mother as any other object — show the twofoldness in which man stands and remains standing.[29]

The act of silently relating to the mother is the initial act in the development of an I-thou experience. The act of objectifying the mother's being forms the basis of the child's developing capacity to relate to the objective world. The child also learns of the thou through his father in whose presence he finds security:

> More precisely, as in the dark a father takes his little son by the hand, certainly in order to lead him, but primarily in order to make present to him, in the warm touch of coursing blood, the fact that he, the father, is continually with him.[93]

Buber offers no hint that he has experienced parents as being the type of threat to the child which Kierkegaard thought they were. The parental experience is a vital one and is one which builds security, trust and the ability to react with the fullness of one's being.

The child lives his experiences without reserve. He is spontaneous in that which he does. He lives in a world of concrete objects but he does not objectify his world, instead he almost personifies the objects of his encounters as he himself reacts to them as a thou. Buber holds that the intimacy with which the child reacts to the world is an argument against psychoanalytical theories that those who turn to God are compensating for inner psychological conflicts. Buber insists that the ability to approach God is predicated on one's ability to live in the I-thou encounter which exists prior to the conflicts which psychoanalysts (for example Scheler) use to interpret such expressions of being.[94]

Buber, like Kierkegaard, insists that the child is certainly a reality of his own. As a reality the child is capable of entering into a relationship with the world which is full of meaning. This is to say: "in every hour the human race begins."[95]

> Across the whole extent of this planet new human beings are born who are characterized already and yet have still to be characterized . . .[96]

The child is born into a historical situation which will not only shape him as he develops but which he will be able to shape as he develops. It is the task of education and parental upbringing to not squander the creative ability the child has to bring an effective force into history.

. . . what has not been invades the structure of what is, with ten thousand countenances, of which not one has been seen before, with ten thousand souls still undeveloped — a creative event if ever there was one, newness rising up, primal potential might. This potentiality, streaming unconquered, however much of it is squandered, is the reality child: this phenomenon of uniqueness, which is more than just begetting and birth, this grace of beginning again and ever again.[97]

This concept challenges the educator to take these new beings and to aid them in their growth and development so that their creativity will be effective and so that their potentiality will be channeled into the most meaningful existence possible.

Youth is a period in growth and development and transition. The youth is leaving the feeling of unity which is the possession of the child, but he has not acquired the independence of an adult. In this case the child's physical maturation is slower than his mental development. Youth are capable of tremendous insight and because of this often find themselves worried about problems which are beyond their level of effective solutions.[98]

Buber believes that adolescence is a period of storm and stress, as G. Stanley Hall would say. Buber describes it as a frightening period and one which often involves the person in bitter disappointment.[99] This is a period when the person needs an understanding adult to bolster him in times of doubt. The teacher's personality stability will be of tremendous value to the adolescent.

For the adolescent student, the teacher can be of most service by aiding him to become increasingly aware of the sterility he suffers from identifying himself too closely with his peer group, or as Buber might phrase it, with the "party". He can help the student to perceive that something is lacking, that there exists a hollowness in his life which will not be filled in by fast living nor by hiding oneself in the crowd. This assists the student to develop clarity of consciousness, brings him to the point of a decision to assume responsibility for himself.[100] As indicated before, it is important that the teacher have both faith in himself and trust in the meaning of life, so that it can be transferred to the "quaking student" and thus enable him to bask in the confidence of the teacher. In this way "he can awaken in young people the courage to shoulder life again."[101]

All ages are educable. The personality is never frozen solid according to Buber. One may always change, one may always learn, one may always turn from the direction which one is going. It is the teacher's responsibility to encourage the student to change with each new fact which pertains to his situation. It is the teacher's responsibility to encourage the student in the growth of awareness that he is responsible for what he is and that he can choose to be something else.

Buber believes that it is a sad fact that most people are surrendering their rights to experience reality and to make their own decisions. This can only be a consequence of the dissipation of their childhood potentials which must be re-integrated. It is for this reason that Buber argues that the world must be re educated and that each civilization must initiate a thorough program of adult education.[102]

The essential curriculum of an adult education program ought to be based on either prophetic tradition and Greek philosophies or on Zen Buddhism. Buber, representing the Judaic tradition, would prefer that adult education be based on the prophetic teachings. It is the task of twentieth century educators to adapt the teachings for this current age, and to not permit the material to become out-moded or antiquated.[103]

The age must be schooled in trust. People must be brought to trust the God who has been trusted by countless people throughout the ages. The teaching which fosters this attitude will be highly personal and will involve no generalities.[104] All one can hope to do for his students is to prepare an attitude

n the mind of the adult which will be conducive to the making
f courageous decisions when he is confronted by his need to
rust God, or to make ethical decisions.[105] The teacher is a guide,
n experienced person who can lead another just so far, and
hen can only point the way. It then becomes the student's task
o traverse the terrain alone.[106]

The teacher is also a guide for children. Usually she is able
o guide the child quite a distance through the educative pro-
ess. It is advisable however for her to stop and point the way
o her students so that they might learn to develop their own
owers to explore reality. In this case of course, should the
tudent become lost, the teacher will be able to find him again
nd once more point the way. The effectiveness of the teacher
s a guide is dependent on how much the child trusts her.
Therefore she is intent on being trustworthy in her relationship
vith her students.

Buber explains that the content of a lesson is important to
earn, but this must take second place to the student's gaining an
nderstanding of the how of the lesson.[107] It is the how, not the
vhat, which must be communicated to children. In the develop-
nent of faith in the child, it does not matter to Buber what
ontent is learned in the development of faith but that the
hild learns how to develop faith in another person. To imple-
nent the development of faith, it is necessary to provide the
hild with an I-thou atmosphere.[108] It is difficult to establish
iis relationship whenever one wills, about all the teacher is
ble to do to foster the attitude is to stress the act of developing
utual relationships between her and her class, and among
ie students themselves. The teacher is obligated to be "fully
iere" in the teaching situation. She must permit her entire
eing to meet the being of the student in such a way that the
tudent might be stimulated to react in the same way as the
eacher. The teacher must always challenge the student to
ee beyond isolated facts, to the meaning of facts themselves.
le must challenge the student to relate himself to the "person-
lity" of the book, or of a historical figure in much the same
ay as an individual relates to an eidetic personality as de-

211

scribed by Sullivan. All of this means that the curriculum mus[t] not be contrived but must be of vital concern to the studen[t.] It must be understandable and presented at the time in whic[h] the student is both motivated and ready for the material. Th[e] most significant lesson which the teacher attempts to brin[g] students at all ages is the art of conversation. Students must b[e] encouraged to converse with one another. The teacher must b[e] constantly ready to encourage any spontaneous and unpredic[t]able conversation which is based on the vital concern of the st[u]dents. She will not merely organize this conversation into "story hour" which comes at a specific time but she will b[e] sensitive to opportunities in which full enthusiasm of the chil[d] can be brought into being as the result of his entering into real conversation.[109] No matter what the school board polic[y] is, barring one which refuses the students the right to talk, th[e] teacher can always be alert for real conversation, and then e[n]courage it. In this way the teacher can also foster the art of re[al] listening which Buber declares is vanishing from the worl[d] scene today. The teacher can encourage her students to be co[n]cerned about what fellow students are saying, and for th[at] matter, as a teacher be concerned with what the student says.[1]

Not only is conversation needed, as well as the developme[nt] of the art of real listening, but the teacher must also aid th[e] student in his attempt to enter dialogue. The ability of man [to] meet man is one of the needs of our age. Buber believes th[at] this has been one of the failures of the school system. The st[u]dent must be encouraged to participate fully in the moment [of] learning. One way of encouraging this is by the enthusiasm [of] the teacher who fully participates in the moment herself. T[o] stimulate the student to be fully functioning in the teachin[g] situation the teacher must be willing to use all of the audi[o] visual aids which will further the student's participation, n[ot] only by hearing, but by seeing, talking, doing and feeling.[1] The teacher must not insist on blind acceptance of her instru[c]tion. As a matter of fact, she will encourage the common testin[g] of the views which are being aired in the classroom. Not onl[y] will the testing prove beneficial to the student in terms of d[e]

212

eloping critical thinking, but also the common testing will lead
nto the aforementioned conversation and will develop in the
tudent the need for dialogue so that he might examine together
vith others all of the issues.[112]

Buber writes that the educator does not work in a vacuum.
. person always knows something before he learns something
ew. It is the task of the teacher to discern where the student
, what facts he has at his command, before the teacher can
resent new subject matter to the student.[113] Much of what the
udent knows preceding the teaching experience is, of course,
ained directly from experience. In some cases the student may
e aware of new information which is gained from a charismatic
xperience. The educational authority must start from where the
udent is and then help him to reconstruct his experience on
ae basis of the curriculum experiences.

The work of education has a twofold influence upon the
adherents of the world-views: a founding one and a postu-
lating one. First it helps each to take its root in the soil
of its world through enabling him to experience this world
widely and densely. It provides him access to, exposing him
to the action of its working forces. And, secondly, it educates
in each his 'world-view-conscience' that examines ever anew
his authentication of his world-view and opposes to the
absence of any obligation to put his world-view into effect
the obligation of the thousand small realizations of it.[114]

he school must give the child as wide a knowledge as possible
out the world he lives in, yet it must not do this at the ex-
nse of a thorough examination of the important aspects of
e. The curriculum must be designed so as to permit the stu-
nt to dig deeply into fields of personal interest — to spe-
alize — so that he can get close to the subject matter which
of concern to him. The school authority must follow this up
continually challenging the student to re-evaluate critically
s viewpoint and his understanding about the meaning of life.
goes without saying that this is most applicable to adult
ucation, which is what Buber is most interested in.

213

Buber realizes that education "is the great implement which is more or less under the control of Society; Society does not however, know how to utilize it."[115] The great task of the era is to educate men in living together; man must be educated so that he will be capable of living with man.[116] The school experience must therefore be a community experience for the child Buber looks forward to the time that education, in its social form will arouse and develop in the being of its pupils the spontaneity of fellowship "which is innate in all unravaged human souls and which harmonizes very well with the development of personal existence and personal thought." However, Buber is not optimistic that this freedom in education will be realized because of the political systems existing today which dominate education.[117]

The teacher must be continually awake to his own tendencies to slip out of the sphere of the I-Thou experience which he may have attained to and not re-enter the sphere. A person who follows an "intellectual profession" must pause from time to time and interrupt his more mundane activity to become aware of the special problems which confront him. He is greatly tempted and in fact necessarily so, to occupy himself in intense yet dispassionate reflection on the problem with which he is concerned. In this act, the intellectual person dips into the I-it stage of experience. When an intellectual person ventures upon a problem he hesitates and then begins to grope for a solution to the problem; while groping he wrestles with the problem in its isolation, he then tends to succumb to the world of I-it. When this happens he must overcome his surrender and become whole person once more. In this progression he will actually become more of a person than before tackling the problem, for he brings into the I-thou experience an illumination of the problem which he gained during the process of thought.[118] Upon the individual's returning to the I-thou experience he again integrates his being. There are some people who enter an I-thou encounter only in privacy following an act of inwardness. Buber would counsel against employing these people as teachers be

214

cause one must have an outward concern for one's students and the subject matter which is to be taught.[119]

One gains a little insight into the way of the teacher through Buber's discussion of Jesus and His teaching technique. One time Jesus asked his disciples who men said he was, and eventually asked them directly who they believed He was. Concerning this event Buber writes as follows:

> To whom else shall a teacher, who not only no longer has a teacher himself but evidently neither a friend who really knows him, direct the question than to his pupils? If anybody could answer him, they could; for from the unique contact which such a relationship produces they have acquired the experience from which alone the answer could be made.[120]

The one who really can tell who another is, is one's teacher. The teacher of another knows what goes on in his student's being. It is ideal, according to Buber, for one to have a teacher to whom one can always turn when in confusion. However, when no teacher is available for the teacher, the latter must turn to his students who also have been exposed intimately to his being. The teacher must gain some insight into his being from his students. He must not remain indifferent to their perspective of whom he is. He must learn from his students whether they think he is accomplishing his goals; he must seek their self-evaluation of his teaching ability. Teachers must realize that they are influenced by their students, that their personalities are molded as a result of student contacts.[121]

Buber's second educationally relevant idea of Jesus is His rebuke of the man who called Him good. Jesus said that there is none good but God. To explain this unexpected retort, Buber observes the following:

> God teaches His doctrine for all, but He also reveals His way directly to chosen people, he to whom it is revealed and who goes in it transfers accordingly the doctrine into

215

personal actuality and teaches therefore 'the way of God' (Mark xii. 14) in the right manner of man. So Jesus knows himself to be a qualified means to teach the good Master's will, but he himself does not will to be called good: . . .[122]

Once again it is not only the content which the teacher has to offer, but it is the 'how' of his life which is important and which challenges men to decision. Jesus would not permit the man to call Him good for this might permit the man to excuse himself from following the way because he knows he is bad. To Buber, this becomes even more clear when Jesus refuses to teach the young man who came to him to learn of the truth. Jesus said merely, "Follow me."[123] Whenever someone asked for the 'how' Jesus invited that person to follow Him and to experience for himself what he sought.

> . . . What is required of those who follow: it is a question of 'abandoning themselves', getting free of themselves, 'self' meant as the epitome of everything to which a man is attached; this is the proper expression for the surrender, to make one's self free. No general verbal definition of the way leads beyond this preliminary condition of following, but only the way itself.[124]

The teacher of ethics cannot lead a student by words into the way which Buber would have the individual travel. The teacher can give the student the example of one who is relaxed from attachments which tend to split his personality in half. He can encourage the student to also detach himself, and thus prepare him to enter the not only ethical, but verily the religious stage. In this way, one can understand a most provocative statement Buber makes: teaching itself demands nothing of the student, it does not insist on conformity. What teaching does is to proclaim itself and to lead the student into an experience which designed to open the door for him to walk into a dialogue and a thou relationship.[125]

216

One of the most important courses which Buber would include in the curriculum for any age level would undoubtedly be history. Buber is more than aware that if the prophetic message is to be fostered, history must be taught. To Buber, a great religious teaching is bound to a historical situation. The religious insight is concerned with the particular moment of its announcement. It is meant to affect the lives of those who hear it first proclaimed. Once the teaching has been rendered it becomes available to the memory and tradition of the generations which are to come. It is the task of each generation (of the historians of each generation) to extract from the historically fixed revelation the counsel and the encouragement, the exhortation and the comfort it has to offer the new era. In this sense it is the duty of the historian to not only record the facts, but to interpret them against the needs of his contemporary hour. The historical interpretation is needed, for a historical teaching, once given, penetrates existence and stands there available for use. Each generation, however, must reforge its meaning.[126]

In terms of philosophical speculation, one ought not merely think about profound subjects, events or social situations. The philosopher, writes Buber, forever stands on the threshold of decision and thus must be ready to decide and then act on his decisions when contemplating important problems. As one thinks about philosophical problems, one must make evaluations which might lead to the solution of the problem on the basis of the available information at hand. Once the evaluations have been made the true philosopher must stand ready to criticize what he finds, if the situation calls for such action, and he must stand ready to demand that society change its way if a social problem is involved. He must not shrink from the task even though the society in which he lives may reject him.[127] In this way one would not find a course in philosophy to merely be introductory. Philosophy courses would always be, according to Buber, applied philosophy. By this interpretation, existentialism would be emphasizing social reconstruction. However, one must not first set himself to be a social reconstructionist. He must not condemn his society as being in need of reform until after he has studied the problems which his society is concerned with.

In reference to science, Buber believes that the true science teacher would be an individual who is caught up in his work, even as should a true scientist.

> True science is a loving science. The man who pursues such science is confronted by the secret life of things which has confronted none before him; this life places itself in his hands, and he experiences it, and is filled with its happening to the rim of his existence. Then he interprets what he has experienced in simple and fruitful concepts, and celebrates the unique and incomparable that happened to him with reverent honesty.[128]

In no way is Buber opposed to science when it is entered into with enthusiasm. As one reads his description of the loving science and the man who participates in its mysteries, one finds no suggestion which would militate against the objectivity which is being demanded of modern science. However, one finds in Buber that he insists that a quality of warmth and of being must be inserted into the usual coldness of the study.

No matter the subject field, Buber advocates that the teacher should encourage the student to meet the subject, to personify the subject matter if necessary so that he may relate to its content, and not merely treat the material as an object, another 'it' to be manipulated.[129]

Part III: Jean-Paul Sartre

Sartrean philosophy may be directly related to educational problems in the following ways: 1. Implicit in Sartre's thought is how the child should be viewed and treated by school authorities, especially the teachers. 2. His philosophy contains explicit principles as to what type of person should be engaged to teach children. 3. Sartre's philosophy contains a form of epistemology and 4. Sartre's theory suggests what subject matter is important, certainly at the high school, if not at the elementary level.

It has been stated that the first principle of existentialism is that "man is nothing but what he makes himself."[130] Although to Sartre this principle contains a seed of optimism about the nature of man's existence, he feels that others choose to interpret man's freedom in despair. As a result of the existential emphasis on choice and upon the problems of anxiety and death, critiques of the philosophy have indicated that Sartre has forgotten the smile of the child. Actually nothing would be more foreign to the mind of Jean-Paul Sartre. His wish for the child is that he be able to maintain his smile as long as possible.[131]

"Children should be encouraged to exist their place, to observe their facticity."[132]

One must always avoid placing demands on children which would make them grow old before their time. As previously stated, existentialism is a philosophy for specialists, for men who have undergone severe philosophical training.[133] Children are not specialists, nor are they equipped to assume existential responsibilities, because they are dependent upon their parents. They must not be burdened with too much responsibility nor with existential awareness. How cruel it would be to place the child in the dilemma of being aware of his freedom while being fully dependent upon the choices of his parents for his very existence.

Although Sartre would encourage children to live their lives to the fullest, he is aware that the shadow of uncertainty will befall them once they enter school. Upon entering school, the child encounters "the educational system which consists in making children ashamed of what they are."[134] The educational system takes the initiative to make children become aware that they are to be expelled from their place as they transcend childhood towards future manhood, and even more simply towards the future. Although the child will not relish becoming ashamed of what he is, it is a necessary experience for him in order that he may fully realize all of the potentialities of his being.

The shame which Sartre discusses is often felt to be one's

original fall from innocence. It is the child's awareness that he has fallen into a world of things, that indeed he is a thing, and that in order to express his spontaneity and to be what he is, he needs the mediation of the educational system.[135] According to Sartre, the preschool child is almost wholly a pure subject; he does not perceive himself as an object among objects.[136] As a matter of fact, being subject, the child is absolutely nothing (because he has no independent identity) until he is aware that someone else — the teacher, the principal, his fellow students — are looking at him. As he becomes aware that he is being observed, that he is being studied by others, he becomes increasingly aware that he is an object.[137] This awareness suddenly affects the child's deepest being. The experience brings to the child the possibilities of pride and shame. However, as the child enters school there is little chance that the initial educational experience will bring him a feeling of pride, and thus he begins his education in shame.[138]

As subject, he was not aware of himself as an object for the manipulation of others; in school, as object, he finds that the teacher — his teacher — comes to organize his experience, and to mold him into the traditions of humanity. As discussed in the third chapter, that which the child knows of himself will come to him from the significant people who influence him in his environment. To be certain the child's parents have brought to him considerable objectification of whom he is. Sartre believes that the teacher continues the process. In that the teacher molds the child's personality, and participates actively in the child's defining of whom he is (which is accomplished as a result of seeing himself through the eyes of his teacher), it is obviously important to select carefully the teachers to whom society will entrust the task of furthering the child's self-concept.

In school, the teacher's look causes the child to be born again. The teacher's look fashions the internal structure of the child's personality, and sees through the child in a manner that the child himself will never have access to introspectively.[139]

Socrates challenged man to "know" himself. Sartre validates the Socratic position, but then enlarges on it with the observation that one may only know himself to the degree that he is aware of the impressions others have given him of himself.

It has been stated that the educational experience brings to the child an experience of shame. Feelings such as shame are nothing but man's way of effectively experiencing his being-for-others.[140] School phobias may be related to the child's discovery that he is being made into an object for others and that his control of himself is being stripped away from him. The shy child may be embarrassed by his own body for he realizes that "it is my body as it is for the Other which embarrasses me."[141]

The young child, according to this existential analysis, is never destructive when he breaks things around the home. This is so because the toddler does not perceive meaningful organization in that which has been broken. In the act of breaking a toy, the child has merely rearranged nature.[142] The educational authority, if not the parents, will quickly teach the child that there is order in the universe, and that this order is essential to the child's well-being. From this point on, the child will be aware that he is destroying whenever damage is done; he will be looked at by some significant authority, and he will become ashamed of what he has done.

Significant people bestow on the child the concept which he shall have of himself. He finds himself reflected in the mirror of another's reaction to him as an object. Thus to Sartre, the child is not born evil anymore than he is born anything else.[143] This suggests that the child will not have to undergo severe discipline in school in order to correct his tendency towards waywardness. Parents and teachers must not assume that the problem child is naturally evil. The degree to which he is a problem will be directly correlated with the image he has received of himself from other people. Should he ever encounter a teacher or a counsellor who follows the Rogerian method, who can adequately reflect confidence in the child, the child's problem may dissolve.

As stated, the child comes to school enveloped in his subjectivity and his sincerity. The pre-school child does not try to mask his true feelings, but is refreshingly open and frank, and is overflowing with sincerity. In school the child learns that he is and object, looked at by other people. The greatest danger that he faces is that he will acquire an attitude which drives him to attempt to conform to the defining images of the teacher, of the parent, and of any significant person he meets. They may tempt the child to lie to himself as he strives to be what he sincerely feels that he is not. The consequence of this experience may be exemplified by the child who assumes the pose of a good student and strains to be a model, but who may expend so much energy in his role playing that little is left for the acquiring of new learning.[144] The child must at all times be encouraged to not objectify himself permanently. The educational system must attempt to help the child preserve the child's subjectivity and sincerity; if the school fails to do this, the child will tend to reject the educational process. He will be threatened with the danger of being "possessed" by the look of the Other, perhaps even of his teacher.[145] He will realize intuitively that either the Other will possess him or he must possess the Other. This attitude is one of conflict between student and students, teacher and students, and student and teacher. Sartre's theory may be the source of some teachers' difficulty with fourth and fifth grade students. The fourth grade atmosphere is often a transitional one between the freedom of movement experienced by students in the primary grades and the more academic situation of the higher grades. The student finds himself being treated as an object with increasing constancy and as a result increasingly resists the trend. It is most obvious that the students will not be able to resist the educational authority for a long time. Eventually he decides to hide from the look of the teacher. He attempts to force the teacher into becoming a 'this' among 'thises'. He forces the teacher to be nothing but a teacher, an expounder of facts, an educating machine. He forces the teacher into a mold and in this way he hopes to keep the teacher's look from capturing him.[146] This means that the teacher must be rejected as a person; he must be objectified at all costs. Or, perhaps a reaction formation takes place on the part of the student which motivates him to become nothing but a student, to identify completely with the role while in school, so that the teacher will have access to only a part of himself and will not become acquainted with his subjective self. The student assumes a role which is not in harmony with his true being, he is no longer sincere, and he will continually be haunted by his real self which has been contained. As the student accepts such objectification he often finds himself in roles which are not conducive to good scholarship, or success in the educational process. To Sartre, the child, regardless of his previous experience, can always be helped by the sincere teacher. Sartre rejects any psychoanalytical attempts to argue that the child's personality is permanently solidified at any age; the child is always capable of being helped, for he is not psychologically determined. When the child performs in a manner which is delinquent, or which involves failure when he really is capable, he is living a lie which he has consciously convinced himself is true.[147] He nevertheless is aware that he is living a lie and should a sincere teacher permit him to face his situation the lie may be overcome. Sartre's approach to a problem child is not essentially different from that of Carl Rogers when he counsels such a child. Both assume that the child has within him the ability to choose a new course of action if he is confronted with an atmosphere which is trustworthy.

It is necessary for the teacher, who wishes to facilitate the growth of the child into the experience of being true to himself, to understand that much of the child's anxiety, which produces bad faith, is his fear of not finding himself to be what he is. Simultaneously with his fear that he will be unable to keep the appointment he has made with himself to be himself — the same person — in the near or distant future, the child is suffering also from the anxiety that he might be frozen into his present personality, which he is not ready to abandon, but which he knows must be transcended. Once aware of this conflict, the teacher can expose the child to the predicted human growth and development cycles which would enable the child to know just what to expect the future to bring or that he will transcend his childlike state because of maturation. Of course the child must be made aware that no one can predict what the future will bring, but that one normally expects a person to follow definite patterns in both the maturation of one's physical self as well as the personality reactions to the changes of one's physical being. Sartre declares that there is a great danger that society may oppress the child because of his dependent nature, and seek to be his guardian. In this situation the growth of the child is impeded, for he is being fixated into a role of a child. To Sartre, a severe education treats the child as an instrument since it tries to bend him by force to values which he has not admitted. Liberal education does much the same thing; it chooses a priori principles and values by which to guide itself in the education of the child. The child finds himself being compelled to learn. Each attitude that the philosopher of education or the administrator adopts, with respect to the child, interprets his being, and thus limits his freedom.[148] Sartre aligns himself with Rousseau and Freud to the degree that he argues that society, the school, and the teacher impinge on the freedom of the child, and define for him his being no matter what the original attitude or outlook of the child is.

It cannot be stressed enough, according to Sartre, that the teacher has a profound influence on the child. He will help define the type of person the child will become.[149] The decisions the teacher makes in behalf of the child will have cosmic significance. This is to say, that any person influences not only himself, but countless others in an expanding circle. A neurotic anxiety may be precipitated by an awareness of this fact that one influences so many as he decides how to teach and what to teach a child. The teacher is condemned to carry the burden of the child's being upon his shoulders, he also must carry his own burden too. To feel responsible for the growth of the child is to feel that one is the incontestable author of an event in the child's life. The teacher is responsible for the way he acts towards the child; this way will form the basis of the objectification by which the child will come to know himself, and will orient his style of life around. The teacher will often feel abandoned and lonely.[150] Some may even leave the profession in order to find less noxious roles in life, where their personal responsibilities for the development of mankind, or any other person, will not be so clearly discernible. The teacher will often find himself alone as he determines his method of evaluating students and then applying his approach to his students or as he selects meaningful material to teach from prescribed curriculums. Although his past experience may guide his current decision, the decision which he makes is his own and he is responsible for its consequence. The good teacher will accept this fact and will find himself unable to tear himself away from being responsible for doing whatever he can for his students. In teacher recruitment, only the teacher who is capable of assuming personal direction of her life by conscious choice should be considered. Furthermore, only those individuals who are capable and are aware of their responsibilities in the teaching profession should be employed. Finally one should employ only those teachers whose lives radiate the quality of being to which one wants the student exposed.

It is important that the teacher not shirk his responsibility in choosing what he will do in the educational endeavor. Even if the school board adopts a policy which instructs the teacher to do some specific act, or teach in some specific way, it is the teacher's responsibility to decide if he will conform and choose to do what the school board or the administration desires, whether he will go his own way in the teaching process, of whether he will resign. The teacher must never pass-the-buck for he is responsible for what he is doing if he is doing anything. Even the teacher who adopts a laissez-faire attitude has committed himself in a decision and must hold himself accountable.[151] The teacher must also guard against the tendency not to re-evaluate his choice in each new moment. No prior decision is automatically acceptable in the new moment. The teacher must be flexible and always alert for new possibilities inherent in each moment.

The teacher shares the same confidence that the military leader experiences whose reaction to critical decisions was indicated in the third chapter. The teacher cannot help but wonder if he has done the right thing as he puts into effect his program of learning. He will wonder whether he will waste the talents and capabilities of the young people who are exposed to his influence. If the teacher is at all aware of her existential possibility she will be confident of her decision because she knows that she has chosen her course on the basis of the best available information she has at her disposal and she has not just been pushed into the decision by any ill-wind. Unlike the military leader, where a militaristic chain of command exists which demands adherence without questions to orders, the teacher cultivates spontaneity and critical thinking among his students. He wants to be questioned, he wants the students to be able to understand the material at hand. He does not want to weld his group into a colorless mass. He does not want a crowd of students. He realizes that he will have a colorless mass or a crowd as a result of the way he "looks" at his students.[152] To avoid this he would seek to encourage his students to be themselves and he would not demand that they abandon their identities. To prevent his students from becoming a crowd, the teacher must not permit the look of the students to forge him into a leadership role which they might then surrender themselves to. The teacher must not be molded by his students or by his administration; he must retain his spontaneity and be flexible at all times.

It may be true that some people will reject the teaching profession because too many grave responsibilities would threaten the person. Some people might not teach unless they could be told what they are to do and have this act in some way relieve them of their responsibility for accepting what they would do. The teacher must not feel that he is compelled to teach nor should the teaching profession attempt to pressure a student to become a teacher against his will. One becomes a teacher because one wants to be at the origin of concrete existence.[153] The teacher chooses to be responsible for the new existent which he is helping to create. The explorer and the artist likewise share this desire to be at the origin of new endeavor. One might critically comment that actually the teacher does not create a new existent, but rather is the midwife, as Kierkegaard spoke of it, to the formation of new awareness. The teacher is not ultimately responsible for the child's intellectual and personality development, for the child himself bears this responsibility. He chooses to use what the teacher brings to him; he also chooses to reject some of the material the teacher has to offer. The teacher is responsible for what he has chosen to stimulate the student with, but the student works with the raw material himself. Sartre thinks that too many people blame the school and their educational attainment for what they are. Nothing is to blame for what a person is — not education, not physiological constitution, not heredity, not one's mother. While these forces may factually confine the individual, it is what the individual chooses to make of these raw materials which matters.[154] When the child comes to school he is more than being in-itself, he is also a being-for-itself. What the teacher presents to the child is important because it is absorbed by the being-for-itself which is itself being transformed into being-in-itself. The teacher is responsible for the being-in-itself of the child because his material is part of the make up of that being. The child who is now possibly the man is transcending his being-in-itself, he is being-for-itself which has been constituted independently of the being-in-itself which the teacher influenced.

In the educational process, one must be careful to not force the child into premature closures concerning the nature of being nor of his goals in life. The student must not be allowed to define absolutely himself in terms of a concreteness which cannot be changed with new choices. The child must himself be encouraged continually to make his own meanings out of what is perceptually being presented to him.

In that decision making is a vital ingredient in the life of a person who is authentic, it is important not only to encourage the child's perceptual development, but also to encourage him in the act of decision making and problem solving. The child should be presented with only solvable problems so that he will not become discouraged and refuse to try to solve future problems. On the other hand the child should not have too easy problems to solve because he may then be devastated by life's harder problems. In the act of stimulating the child to make decisions, one must take care to enlighten him that "to be free does not mean to obtain what one wishes but rather by oneself to determine oneself to wish." The child must not come to believe that all of his resolves will be favorably developed. The stress should be placed on the child's ability to wish as often as he desires to wish, and that he should take appropriate action to realize his wishes. As soon as it becomes feasible, the child must assume responsibility for himself and be encouraged to realize how important his choices are, not only in his own existence, but in the existence of others.

The ultimate interest of existential education is to make the child aware that even educational inquiry must be based on a choice to inquire, and must result in choices to act upon the newly gained insights.[155] In an existential system of education great stress would be placed on methods which are designed to bring to light, in strictly objective form, the subjective choices by which each individual makes himself a person. The educator would stand ready to guide the child into this learning process.[156]

For the child, as for the adult, existence precedes essence. The child is a child, and then he acquires acculturation. As the child grows up he will learn that he is entering a world already "possessed" by others, and that it will be useful to him, as an existent among existences, to discover how others possess the world. The child finds himself not only engaged in a world possessed, but in a world which already has potentials for meanings.[157] It is essential for the child to learn that meaningful potentials may be useful in his own development.

The meanings which the child finds have developed from the past experiences of man. To Sartre, past motives and causes, present motives and causes, and future motives and causes, all organize into an indisssoluble unity by the very upsurge of a freedom which the individual is, and which is beyond causes, motives and ends.[158] In that the past is "homogenized" into the present, it is impossible for the individual to make existential choices without reference to the past of mankind and more importantly to his personal past. It is important, therefore, to study the past, and thus history forms an important ingredient in the curriculum. The past must not be presented as something concluded, but as something which is dynamic and which is being re-defined in each new moment. The student must be made aware that the past does not have any other meaning than

228

what individuals in the present choose to bestow upon it. Furthermore, the past must not be taught as an end in itself. It is necessary only for the facilitation of contemporary choices. As Sartre writes: "There is a past only for a present."[159]

In the study of history, of one's past, one is likely to become discouraged by man's apparent lack of progress. The student should not be permitted to dwell in despair about man's inhumanity to man.

> The history of life, whatever it may be, is the history of a failure. The coefficient of adversity of things is such that years of patience are necessary to obtain the feeblest result.[160]

Students must be confronted with the evidence that results are gained by man's efforts to cope with life even though they may be feeble. Sartre emphasizes that when nothing is ventured then nothing is gained.[161] Even the smallest gains would not be accomplished were it not for the determined action of individuals.

As developed by Sartre several times, freedom of the individual does not mean that he may operate independently of the natural order of life. In fact, nature forms a facticity which limits man's range of choices. In spite of this limitation, man has within his grasp the command of nature, for he has learned that by obeying it, he is able to command it.[162] It is therefore important to study the laws of nature; the existential curriculum would include courses in scientific fields.

Not only would science and history be included in Sartre's educational program, but mastery of language would be very important. Sartre agrees with Heidegger who declared, "I am what I say."[163] It is necessary to master language before one can realize one's own potentials. Language, originally, is a form of being-for-others.[164] One does not just devise a language for no purpose, one develops language in order to communicate with others and to receive their impressions of one's self. Sartre contends that language exists for people, and not people for the language.[165] While it is true that language fraught with meaning confronts a child, still it is for the child to use the language, and not be used by it in an objectified form. One ought not make a fetish out of the language's grammar, nor demand conformity to a definite grammatical structure.

Not only in Sartre, but in all of the existentialists mentioned listed on the chart in chapter two, one finds an extensive, yet facile, ability to use words and an expectancy that the reader will also be agile with these existential terms. In addition, existentialists such as Sartre draw upon a vast field of literature. To understand fully existential writers, a knowledge of the literature of the world is almost a necessity. There is little doubt that Sartre would include language arts in the school curriculum if he could define its courses.

Aesthetics would also be included in an existential curriculum because Sartre argues that "beauty which is implicitly apprehended gives a totalization of ourselves."[166] Beauty, which to Sartre means excellence of form, has qualities which bring wholeness to the individual. To be certain, the young child may not be impressed with the wholeness of pattern because he focuses too much upon details of the art which he can handle in his young and inexperienced mind. As the child becomes acquainted with himself, as he develops an integrated personality, he develops aesthetic appreciation.[167]

On the college level, Sartre would undoubtedly favor philosophy. It is important for the teacher to be aware that the student is in possession of all the meanings of being although the particular exemplifications are yet to be developed or ushered in by the skillful teacher. In the field of philosophical-ethical considerations there is only intuitive knowledge.[168] It is the teacher's task to help the student recognize that which he already intuitively knows. The best methodology for this development is that recommended by Socrates.

Sartre would advise against any curriculum approach which would encourage the child to approach the subject matter in a dispassionate way. An individual, even a child, must be encouraged to have a point of view about what he is undertaking. It is, furthermore, impractical to talk about pure knowledge because all knowledge, to Sartre, is engaged in the life process. A person's emotional matrix, his style of life, his point of view are engaged in the person's activity and thus can not be distilled from his intellectual life.[169] Sartre agrees with Dewey that knowledge involves action; one must learn by doing, but when one does, one reacts with his total being. Because pure knowledge is impossible in Sartre's belief, it is necessary constantly to reconstruct experience and to test one's engaged knowledge.

The act of knowing carries with it almost mystical powers according to Sartre, for "to know is to cause being to be there."[170] If one did not 'know' a city was destroyed, then to Sartre the city would not be destroyed, but matter rearranged. Once one knows of the city, it could be completely leveled before the eyes of the person and still the city's presence although absent would be influential. Before one knows, the unknown object has not given up the secret of its being. When one knows, the unknown object has been penetrated to the core of its being and it becomes known. Learning therefore is like a hunt; it is a search for the meaning of the object, or, it is a search for the essential being of the object which is to be known. In the hands of a skillful teacher, the learning situation would be exciting to the child, for he would be transformed into a hunter stalking his prey.[171] Knowing is not only a discovery of the being of another object, it is also the appropriation of that object. To know is to take over the being of the object, to incorporate it within the schemata of the individual's interpretation of life. The truth discovered, writes Sartre, is like a work of art, for as a piece of art is my creation, so knowledge is also my creation.[172] Knowledge, therefore, is an assimilation of the facts in question. It is not something which the individual or the child may approach and then attempt to keep at arm's length. He must drench himself in that which he seeks to know. The student transforms the known into himself; it becomes a part of his thought. To borrow Dewey's phrase, the known is "reconstructed into the individual's being" and becomes engaged in his life's endeavors.[173]

Once one has reconstructed experience, once one has assimilated knowledge, then one may develop memory. Memory is not something which is dormant in the child. It is a live and an active force which not only is a recall of past events, but is a living entity which awaits recall in order to help shape the individual's future.[174] Donald Hebb refers to memory as involving cell assemblies in the cerebrum which await relevant perceptions to become active again.[175] This may provide physiological evidence for Sartre's theory.

Finally, when all is said and done, perhaps the whole existential approach to education might be summarized in the statement that existentialists will never consider man an end in himself, but as a being who is always transcending himself. It is the teacher's task to help the child become aware of his own intuitive knowledge that this is so, and the teacher must resist any attempt on the child's part to define himself permanently or stabilize his life inflexibly.[176]

Part IV: Karl Jaspers

Jaspers' Interpretation of the Nature of Children

As in the case of the other existentialists, Jaspers' writings contain an expression of positive warmth towards children. To Jaspers children do not distort reality but react to the events which encompass their lives with natural simplicity. They are endowed with the gift of being spontaneous but unfortunately tend to lose the ability as they mature. "With the years we seem to enter into a prison of conventions and opinions, concealments and unquestioned acceptance, and there we lose the candour of childhood."[177]

Jaspers writes that children are natural philosophers. Their questions are not of an extrinsic nature but are concerned with the task of seeking further knowledge of themselves. He recounts the story of one child who summarized the main motif of Jaspers' philosophy when he said, "I keep trying to think that I am somebody else, but I'm always myself."[178] Jaspers comments, "This boy has touched on one of the universal sources of certainty, awareness of being through awareness of self."[179] It follows, then, that Jaspers would advocate an educational system

232

which would encourage the child's philosophical tendency, and which would not force him at too early an age into the prison spoken of above. He would not be in favor of imposing any artificial standards on the child. The child's spontaneity must be encouraged. One has nothing to fear as a result of permitting a child to be a child.

The Purpose of Education

"Education is dependent upon something that at once over-rides it and is its source — upon the life of a spiritual world. Education cannot derive from itself, but serves for the trans-mission of the life which manifests itself directly in human behavior. . . ."[180] According to Jaspers the transmission of cul-ture is the most important purpose of education.

> He who . . . has absorbed the writings of the classical poets, philosophers and historians, has gained familiarity with math-ematics, has studied the Bible and some of the great imag-inative writers of his own country, will have entered into a world which, in its infinite expanse, will have endowed him with an intrinsic inalienable value and will have given him the keys to other worlds.[181]

It ought to be the desire of educational authorities to encourage and develop the student's ability to think clearly and meaning-fully.[182] To best foster the student's ability to think he must be introduced to the historical foundations of man's thinking. Only through the presentation of an historical attitude can man deepen his insight into what has been preserved so as to utilize the stored solutions to problems which confront man ever anew.[183] (Stored solutions do not refer to ethical insights, but to the 'facticity' of existence, such as where mineral deposits are, how to manufacture equipment, etcetera.) It is the voice of the past which will make the student aware of his own existence, and the student's own life will transmit that voice to the future.[184]

> No reality is more essential to our self-awareness than history. It shows us the broadest horizon of mankind, brings us the contents of tradition upon which our life is built, shows us

standards by which to measure the present, frees us from unconscious bondage to our own age, teaches us to see man in his highest potentialities and his imperishable creations.[185]

It is essential for each person to learn that he has not just hap pened, but that even to the tiniest detail of his daily life he supported and surrounded by his origins; he must accept the fa that his life is guided by these foundations, and that the onl way for him to become truly himself is to take possession mo decisively than usual of these foundations.[186] The aim of an hist rical curriculum is to foster the unity of mankind and to encou age boundless communication not only between men of th present, but between man now and man of the past. Throug successful realization of this communication man will find himse closer to a harmonious existence which is free from violence.[1] Through historical study students are able to become acquainte with historical personalities. By analyzing the historical hero, th student is capable of recognizing his own potentials and he be comes inspired to stand fast no matter what happens to hin "When a hero stands the test of doom, he gives proof of man dignity and greatness."[188] Even as one studies men who ar known to be historical failures one may be inspired.

> One person's failure may acquire transcending symbolic sig-
> nificance for the thought or conduct of others; and it may
> lead to new possibilities even for the person who failed. . . .[189]

It is essential, in a sense, to help students interpret the meaning c failure, and to help them to see that one failure need not con pletely cripple the individual in the next moment.

However Jaspers does not recommend that the educationa curriculum focus only upon the past, for it is the present which i the most important to the student.

> But in concrete historical form no knowledge can be timeless
> and universal. In every case, man must acquire it anew to
> bring its truth to life for himself.[190]

That material which is selected must be translated into an understandable matrix and not be allowed to remain merely content which must be memorized. Educators are remiss in their duty if they permit students to lose themselves in either the past or the future.

Only through the present reality of their situation will they gain access to the timeless and to reality itself.[191]

A student's life becomes richer only when the past and the present illumine each other.[192] Thus, it is the task of the educator to not only acquaint the student with the dynamic past, but to also introduce to him the scope of the present situation. A knowledge of the student's own world provides the sole means whereby he can first of all become aware of the extent of the possible; secondly, shape sound plans for the moment and form effective resolves; thirdly, acquire the outlooks and ideas that will enable him to interpret his human situation as a manifestation of the transcendent.[193] As soon as the student has become aware of what means, and within what limits, knowledge is attainable, he has no choice but incessantly to strive towards an understanding of his time and situation.[194] It is very important that the student be introduced to reality and encouraged to analyze it, to appraise it, to accept it, and then to go on from reality to modify the situation, wherever possible according to what he believes it ought to be. The student learns to know through his daily association with people, especially his teachers, through his handling of tools and through technical knowledge gained in and out of school, and finally through his contact with organized groups.[195] The term 'reality' has special connotations as Jaspers uses the term. Reality is a description of the factual situation which man finds himself in. The description is of man's own making. It is true that man finds himself within the bounds of definite situations, yet in terms of permanency, 'reality' is not real, does not exist, but has to be grasped by a cognition which involves an active seizure.[196] In other words, the student must be made aware that what reality is to him, is precisely what it means to him for as he interprets his situation he creates the reality of the situation. "All knowledge is interpretation . . . all being is for us an interpretation."[197] It therefore behooves the educational authority to convince the students of the necessity of their making accurate perceptions and interpretations of that which they are dealing with. Jaspers' belief in the enormous importance of teaching students to sharpen their perceptions and mental acuity in evaluating the evidence is made apparent by the following quotations.

> . . . All knowledge in the world refers to particular objects and is acquired with definite methods from definite points of view. Therefore it is wrong to make any knowledge absolute.[198]

"What I comprehend is . . . merely one of a number of obtainable perspectives of orientation therein."[199] Although the idea that one must not generalize the particular is sound, as far as Jaspers is concerned, he nevertheless concedes that this principle is very difficult to achieve wholly. To escape absolutism one must take a leap into the imageless, unobjectifiable, self-impelling source of one's own self, which is reason.[200] Man, to be himself, must be encouraged to live by his reasoning ability.

Jaspers argues stongly that reason in its most uncompromising form is indispensable to the authentic man: "Reason appears as the outline of man's life, as we hope he will be and in so far as it lies within our power to create him."[201] Because of the obvious significance for educational theory of this belief it would be proper to go into his concept of reason a little more fully.

> Where Reason provides a space, illusions disappear, frenzy and ferocity pass away.[202]

> Reason strives to avoid the sin of forgetfulness and self-deception, losing the One in a harmony that is only apparent. It presses on constantly to the place where unity is broken through in order that in this break-through it may grasp the truth that is in it.[203]

Reason does not exist by nature but only by decision.[204]

The decision for Reason — which is also a decision for freedom, truth and the unconditionality of existential decision
is against nature, occurrence and necessity.[205]

By Reason "life becomes existence, devoted to a purpose related
to Transcendence."[206] Thus, if Jaspers is correct, the most important thing education can do for the child is to show him how
to develop his reasoning power and give him every opportunity
to solve his own problems by reason. Reason is not identical
with intellectual ability, although it can take no step without
some intellectual ability.[207] Reason is capable of going beyond
intellectual ability for it is able to transcend intellectual acuity.[208]
Thus all children who are in school, have the ability to reason
and to solve problems. Jaspers is keenly aware that a person's
ability to transcend intellect is limited and that the attainable
limits of knowledge vary from person to person. Objective
knowledge has been more developed than subjective knowledge.
For subjective knowledge to develop, the individual must will
the knowledge into existence. In that this will is not ripe in most
people, the majority remain incapable of a spontaneous urge
towards fundamental knowledge.[209] The child, on the other hand,
has access to this subjective knowledge, but finds it blunted by
objective learning in the school system. There may come the day
in which the educator will seek to develop the child's subjective
ability more than he does now.

Jaspers would defend the idea that the educational system
will be helpful to the child only if it permits a growth of his
ability to reason.[210] To do this the school must encourage a
program which will challenge the child's resources, will encourage
him to actively participate in the learning process, and above all
will not suggest that reality is a closed system causally influenced.
Reason has no assured stability for it is constantly on the move.
Therefore the school authorities must never be satisfied with any
level of attainment of their children. Once a reasonable position
has been gained, the child must be encouraged to press on and

to criticize the conclusions he has reached. The teacher must tak
care to help the child differentiate between creative criticism an
mere capriciousness. Creative criticism leads to self-knowledg
and knowledge of one's horizons, and therefore develops in th
person a profound sense of humanity. The teacher must discourag
any signs of intellectual arrogance. To assist the child in the pat
of reason it is necessary to encourage him to learn how to liste
and be able to wait for the clarification of reason itself. This mear
that impatience and surrender to anxious passions should b
discouraged. Leading the student into the path of reason, thu
defined, will make him dissatisfied until he has considered ever
last shred of evidence; he will not prematurely seek the goal c
unity which may precipitate fallacious knowledge.[211]

The student must be encouraged to never take things fo
granted but to think for himself. As he begins to think for himsel
he will realize that he has serious responsibilities.[212] Existentia
education would therefore be non-authoritarian and would retur
to Socratic principles of education in non-technical subjects. A
the child would be encouraged to analyze, criticize and gen
erally investigate everything, the educational authority woul
seek to counter any tendency on the part of the child to be se
duced by the whisperings of irrationalism.[213]

"Science is an indispensable constituent of reason."[214] It i
impossible for reason to function adequately without recourse t
the scientific method. Jaspers would have the school curriculun
heavily saturated with scientifically oriented courses. Genuin
science is a knowledge of the methods and limits of knowledge
Jaspers states:

> Without science truthfulness in philosophical thinking is no
> longer possible today. We profess an unconditional belief in
> modern science as the way to truth.[215]

The scientific method, according to Jaspers, is perhaps the greates
event in history since the creative axial period from eight hun
dred to two hundred B. C.[216] Even today the sciences continue
to achieve the most extraordinary results. However, the science

nust not be taught as though these were the only courses that mat-
ered. Natural science lacks a comprehensive view, for its basic
otions are more of the nature of experimental recipes than
uths which have been definitely demonstrated.[217] Furthermore, science suffers from a paradox of achievement. For
istance, as the medical world conquers a disease it is some-
mes at the expense of human immunity from another disease.

Technical advances do not create a perfected world, but at
every stage introduce fresh difficulties and therewith new
tasks into an imperfect world.[218]

t is the duty of educators to help the student identify the
omplicating tasks which science brings with it into the world.
To understand science, one must participate in it.[219] It is
ecessary not only to formulate abstract courses to introduce
science to adolescents, but to provide them with laboratories
here they themselves may conduct scientific experiments, and
ome to know what it means to study science first hand. Of
ourse, man's scientific knowledge can only go as far as reality
grasped by man's methods and enclosed within his categories
f study.[220] Science would also be offered to elementary school
aildren, but extensive laboratories would not be required.
A good science education teaches young people that nothing
nould be indifferently reacted to, but that every fact, even
te ugliest fact, must be taken into consideration. Secondly,
science should give to the child the attitude that nothing is
nished, but that everything is in progress. This also includes
ae concept that the universe is too broad for a few simple
xplanations or interpretations of its meaning. Thirdly, modern
science should increasingly become more interdependent rather
aan tending towards specialization. This should encourage
ae young mind not to scatter itself over a wide range of
ompartmentalized endeavor, but to try to synthesize its ex-
eriences. In the fourth place, science helps to instill in the
oung intellect the concept that little value should be attached
possibilities of thought. The emphasis is upon definite and

concrete knowledge after it has proven its worth in action Finally, scientific education ought to encourage the attitude of inquiry towards all phenomena. It encourages the mind to transcend itself and to seek understanding through reason.[221]

Jaspers is aware that at times an inauthentic type of science over-extends itself and claims universal validity. This science is a powerful tempter of young minds and can neutralize some of the positive values of the proper science possibilities. Insofar as a science puts forth the claim to an absolute status as a picture of life in its entirety, it has become, so to speak, a creed or a faith.[222] In this case science has been seduced to serve the will to power rather than the will to truth. Authentic science encourages students to embark on the road to truth.[223]

Unfortunately, science too often is adapted to please the crowd. In this case, instead of serving for fundamental research it is bent towards technical advancements in the civilization When science is bent to serve the crowd only its immediate practical results are emphasized, and it is incapable of opening for the student new horizons, of setting him on the way to truth.[224]

History and science are not enough for man. He basically wants more than either of these two forces is capable of giving Man is faced with a fork in the road of existence. One side leads to the darker side of life, and involves the individual in the occult and the irrational. The other side involves the person in an attempt to prove the origin of his existence through reason.[225] It is the second road which leads man into the field of philosophy. Philosophy forms the third triumvirate which should be throughout education. Philosophy actually emerged before any science, goes on beyond the scope of any current science, and is present whenever man seeks awareness of himself. In philosophical matters almost everyone believes himself capable of judgment. In this it is unlike science because science requires specialized training. Living is sufficient to train man in the philosophical quest.[226] Therefore philosophical questions may be raised at all levels of the educational system and to all levels of mentality. Children and the insane are quite

240

apable of valid insights in philosophical endeavor.[227] As a matter of fact, no one can escape the philosophical quest; it s always present. The question is only whether a philosophy is onscious or not, whether it is good or bad, muddled or clear. t would be the purpose of educational authorities to aid the tudent to obtain a conscious philosophy which is good and lear.[228] Philosophical thought must spring from free creation. very man must arrive at this method of thought and its onclusions by himself.[229] This too would suggest that Jaspers avors the Socratic methods of teaching.

In the relationship between philosophy and science, philosophy s more than any scientific methodology.

> ... The essence of philosophy is not the possession of truth
> but the search for truth ... Philosophy means to be on the
> way. ... We can determine the nature of philosophy only
> by actually experiencing it.[230]

cience, on the other hand, while it is to be on the way too, cuses its attention more on what it has observed, what ality has already encompassed in order to break it down into nderstandable components and analyze it by its rigorous methdology.

> The certainty to which ... philosophy aspires is not of the
> objective, scientific sort, which is the same for every mind;
> it is an inner certainty in which a man's whole being
> participates. Whereas science always pertains to particular
> objects, the knowledge of which is by no means indispensable
> to all men, philosophy deals with the whole of being, which
> concerns man as man, with a truth which wherever it is
> manifested, moves us more deeply than any scientific knowl-
> edge.[231]

In the teaching of philosophy one must perpetually guard gainst absolutizing an approach and against the presentation of

an historical form of philosophy which is without current applic
tion or interpretation.

> To take a past philosophy as our own is no more possible
> than to produce an old work of art for a second time. At
> best we can produce a deceptive copy.[232]

The teacher must remember that his philosophy, although vit
perhaps to him, is potentially old to his students, and he mu
guard himself from any temptation to force the student to repr
duce a forged philosophy.

Jaspers has given his reader an overview of his concept of a
effective teacher of philosophy and the methodology he shou
follow.

> The teacher of philosophy in the service of such efforts is
> not a leader who lays down the law but an attentive and
> patient listener eager to find meaning in the broadest inter-
> relations.
>
> The teacher of philosophy reveres the individual great
> philosophers . . . but he rejects the idolization of men . . .
> for even the greatest are men and err, and no one is an
> authority who must be obeyed by right.
>
> And the teacher of philosophy has respect for each science
> whose insights are binding — but he condemns scientific
> pride. . . .
>
> His ideal is that of a rational being coexisting with other
> rational beings. He wants to doubt, he thirsts for objections
> and attacks, he strives to become capable of playing his part
> in the dialogue of ever-deepening communication, which is
> the prerequisite of all truth and without which there is no
> truth.
>
> His hope is that in the same measure as he becomes a
> rational being he may acquire the profound contents which
> can sustain man, that his will, in so far as his striving is
> honest, may become good through the direct help of the
> transcendent, without any human meditation.

As a teacher of philosophy . . . he feels that it is duty not to let his students forget the great minds of the past, to pre- serve the various philosophical methods as an object of instruction, and to see to it that the sciences influence philo- sophical thinking; to elucidate the present age and at the same time to join his students in conquering a view of the eternal.[233]

What type of education is best suited for the presentation of ᴊspers' cultural-scientific-philosophical program? He states the ᴏllowing:

A humanist education is that which exerts a selective in- fluence upon the individual. Only this education, therefore, has the wonderful quality of being able to produce good results even though the teachers are inefficient.[234]

The most important period of history for the student to master the period which lasted from about 800-200 B.C. This is the ᴀxial period" of history "in which the language of elemental sions reaches its highest point of clarity, maturity and power."[235] ᴛhe ideas man developed during this period are as a north star the individual groping for awareness of himself. In the axial ᴇriod one finds that the world had been thrown into a state turmoil and crisis which forced man to bring all his energies bear on the problems of his day. The preceding mythical age, ᴡith its peace of mind and self-evident truths, had ended. Man ᴡas uncertain of himself. It was a day of social reform; it was ᴀ era in which a struggle of all against all took place against the ᴀckground of prosperity. Out of this turmoil arose philosophers ᴡho dared to be individuals.[236] The twentieth century is ex- ᴇriencing a similar crisis; one wonders if the age is about to ᴏduce a new selection of philosophical genius.

Although this axial era is important, it is just as vital for the ᴅividual to wrestle with the Christian era and to seek to under- ᴀnd its dynamic. Our attitude toward our epoch has arisen ᴛher from or in opposition to the now abandoned Christian conception that historical process moves towards the fulfillme of a plan of salvation.[237] The individual must come to grips wit this point of view for it forms a part of his inheritance whic still influences his being in the present moment.

In higher education, Jaspers would include anthropology. Th study, which is closely allied to history, offers "one of the mea for comprehending the unique in its vitality as physique, rac character, the spirit of civilization."[238]

Since man only exists in and through society, to which h owes his life, he must study his nature by studying society. I order to accomplish this it is imperative for the young perso to be thoroughly acquainted with sociology and its allied fields.[2]

One's own language is important to master, for in the formula tion of words, concepts are created and experience is tra scended.[240] The entire field of semantics would be emphasized b Jaspers, not only so that the individual could himself express h own experiences in terms of concepts, but so that he could shar in the communication of these concepts with other individuals (his society. The elementary school would therefore emphasize curriculum built around the fundamental skills. English and a forms of oral and written communication would be stresse throughout one's education.

Jaspers also underscores the importance of fine arts and poetry. Fine arts make the visible world speak to the artist an through him to his audience. Poetry is man's initial attempt t rise towards self-consciousness and is a step towards philoso phy.[241] As a matter of fact, Jaspers captures a flavor of Gentile[2] when he advises that the outstanding teachers of the human er have been poets. As a result of their poetic teaching, the students were not only stirred but transformed into their rea selves. Art must not become merely an avenue to amusemer or pleasure, it must be an expression of the sincere desire o the part of the artists' primary will to know.[243]

Although much of the preceding sounds like an idealistic at titude towards education, Jaspers is practical. He realizes tha man must eat to live and that in order to secure food he mu work and that in order for him to work he must learn how t work.[244] He is also cognizant of the fact that the technological age is here to stay and that a person who is new to the labor market must be equipped with proper skills. He also argues that the personal needs of the individual must assume priority and therefore he would certainly, but probably a little reluctantly, admit that vocational education must have a definite place in the curriculum.

Jaspers undoubtedly would favor a program of physical fitness in the schools.

> Through bodily activities subjected to the control of the will, energy and courage are sustained, and the individual seeking contact with nature draws nearer to the elemental forces of the universe.[245]

Jaspers feels that physical exercise is an instinctive impulse toward self-preservation. Even sports would be encouraged by Jaspers, for "sport is not only play and the making of records; it is likewise a soaring and a refreshment."[246]

The Role of the Teacher in Education

Jaspers would favor creative people fulfilling their choice to be teachers as being the best teachers of children. In order to be a creative teacher, the individual must not be in the field merely for economic rewards or social prestige. Jaspers indicates that the dynamic which moves the individual towards authenticity and being a valuable teacher is that "he wants to be 'in the now' where the motive forces of history are at work."[247] According to Jaspers' own point of view, where better can this be achieved than in education?

It is essential to realize that expert knowledge alone does not make a good teacher. A teacher with expert knowledge becomes a significant educator only as a result of how he chooses to live as an individual. It is the use he will have to make of his knowledge which is critically important.[248] The teacher must show the student how to be the type of person the educational authority hopes the student to be.

> Anyone who, while carrying on an occupation . . . who acts as a teacher... can not wish to snatch the ground from under the feet of others without showing them the ground on which he himself stands.[249]

> The force of the educator is that which makes him strive his utmost, in defiance of a sense of impotence as regards the influencing of human conduct, to make man attain the highest possibilities through the utilisation of the profoundest content of what has been handed down to him.[250]

> The work of the physician, the schoolmaster, the clergyman, etc., cannot be rationalized, for here we are concerned with existential life. . . . Here, joy in work grows out of a harmony between human existence and an activity to which the doers give themselves unreservedly because what they are doing is done for a whole.[251]

The educator must be aware that he ought not impose on his students what is personally incumbent on himself. He must not force another to walk in his own pathway but rather to encourage the student to find his own way towards maturity.[252] The schoolmaster must always be aware that one can learn by rote, but that it is essential that the student learn to reason in order for him to comprehend the meaning of his existence.[253]

Jaspers' Critique of Contemporary Education

Ultimately, according to Jaspers, it is the destiny of the mind in our epoch which will determine the value of education, and what education is still possible. As the reign of reason is dwarfed so the ineffectiveness of an educational system is exposed.[254]

Education is endangered whenever the authorities rely on a false idea of an achievable total knowledge. Our day has seen many changes take place. "Changing knowledge enforces a change in life; and in turn, a changing life enforces a chang

246

the consciousness of the knower."[255] Educators are finding that they have been relying on false ideas and therefore the educational system has been set adrift without definite goals.

The disintegration of education can be seen most forcibly at the university level. The role of the university is one of research and study which is oriented towards achieving the great practical unity of the sciences and philosophy.[256] Unfortunately, the university has degenerated and has become no more than a school, almost like a diploma mill.

Furthermore, higher education is stereotyping itself to such a degree that its rigidity is becoming more pronounced with each decade. "An enforced curriculum relieves the individual from the risks attendant upon seeking a path for himself."[257] Jaspers favors a self-determined educational program for university students. The failure of the university is further signaled by the extensive departmentalization which has taken place. Particularly repugnant to Jaspers is the fact that some universities are reducing the position of philosophy as being a mere department in a broad humanities program. Another sign of the collapse of reason into mere intellectualism is the fact that "from every profession there arise complaints of the lack of effective individualities despite a continuous inrush of new aspirants. On all hands we see a swarm of mediocrities."[258]

The role of the State in Education

Jaspers definitely favors State control of education. He does not favor, however, public control of education if one defines the public as being the masses who do not really know what they want. The State is interested in education "for it is through education that the human beings are produced who will in due course have to sustain the State."[259]

The State educational authorities are confronted with two alternatives for education. They can leave education alone and permit the mass to control it on the local level, or they can come into conflict with the mass in an effort to work out an aristocratic educational system of its own.

If the state permits a multiplicity of curriculums and all sor of educational experiments to continue the school will thrive on if the personality of its local principal is forceful. The teache will continuously be at odds with each other and general co fusion will reign. "Children [will] fail to receive the sincer great, noble impressions which are able to influence charact in a way that can never be forgotten."[260] Because there is r underlying purpose in the educational system, children will I forced merely to acquire facts and to flex their ability to m morize data. "Torn hither and thither, the child finds, indee fragments of a tradition, but no world into which it can con dently enter."[261]

On the other hand, if the State acquires "control of educatic for the quiet but forcible moulding of character in accordanc with its own purposes, then we have a unified education at tl cost of paralysis of mental freedom...."[262] This would resu in turning out standardized human beings.

No simple formula can be given for an ideal education. But if education is once more to become what it was in its best days, namely the possibility, through historical continuity, of developing into a human being possessed of full selfhood, that can only ensue through a faith which amid all necessary strictness in learning and practice, indirectly conveys a spiritual value.[263]

Education will only be restored to its true level when the valuations of the masses are overridden by a distinction between teaching and discipline, between that which is comprehensible to all, and that which is attainable by an elite through a training of the inner being.[264]

Finally, Jaspers' discussion of education may be summarized b simply stating that he favors that educational system which wi show the child by what processes and what means he encounte his world.[265]

CHAPTER V

COMPARISON OF THE EXISTENTIAL CONCEPTS OF THE INDIVIDUAL AND THE EXISTENTIAL CONCEPTS OF THE PURPOSE OF EDUCATION AND SOME SPECIAL PROBLEMS WHICH CONFRONT CONTEMPORARY EDUCATIONAL AUTHORITIES

Having examined the concepts of 'the Individual' as they are developed in the writings of the existentialists under consideration, it becomes necessary to ask and answer the question of whether the men share a common viewpoint pertaining to the problems which the individual faces, the type of man he should be, and what the world situation does for or against him. The third hypothesis of this study is that "as each of the concepts of the individual is developed from the view point of the men being discussed, it will be found that the main motifs of the individual . . . will be in essential agreement."

Existential Concepts of the Individual

On succeeding pages a series of statements are made concerning situations which confront the individual. As each of the existentialists agree with a statement his initial is indicated in the appropriate column. One hundred and seventy-six statements are made, which themselves are divided into thirteen sections. All four existentialists have either directly stated or indirectly implied that they agree with 37% of the statements, and three of the four men agree on another 33% of the statements.

Very seldom does it become evident that the four men disagree about any subject. When this has occurred the following sign has been used: '-'. Sartre is the one who normally would disagree more with the other three theists, than the theists with each other. However, the theists often state that if there is no God then the conclusions which Sartre has reached would be valid. For the most part when all four are not in agreement with each other, as indicated on the chart, the reason is that they have not concerned themselves with the problem and therefore have not indicated what their position is. Although, in some cases it might have been justified to include their concurrence with a statement, this was not done unless the agreement could be verified by material discussed in this study. Certain of the statements are really stressed by one or more of the group. If this is so, then their initial has been italicized to emphasize the fact.

For purposes of comparison the 176 statements are divided into thirteen groups. A review of each of the following groups will serve by themselves to introduce one to the major emphasis of the existential writers. The topics are as follows:

I. The twentieth century's catastrophic effect on the development of the human personality.

II. The main existential goal 'Man must come to know himself.'

III. The importance of man's philosophizing.

IV. The main problems of life which confront man.

V. The importance of man's ability to decide what to do with his situation.

VI. The importance of reason to the individual.

VII. The sources of the individual's 'correct' decisions:

VIII. The individual and God.

IX. Traits of the authentic individual.

X. The individual and his relationship with others and his need for communication.

XI. The individual's relationship to the crowd.

XII. Traits of the inauthentic man.

XIII. The optimistic outlook for the individual.

It should be emphasized, before analyzing these areas of agreement, that some of these existentialists, Søren Kierkegaard most noticeably, have tried diligently to keep their authentic person from becoming a paragraph in a system. No man ought to conform to an ideal man as presented by another person. Each person must discover for himself what will make him an authentic man, and he is then responsible for choosing to fulfill his concept of authenticity.

The procedure will be to present each group of ideas individually on a chart followed by a discussion of the material. In some cases very little interpretation is needed for the chart is self-explanatory.

I. The twentieth century's catastrophic effect on the development of human personality.

A. Evidences of the Catastrophe:

1. There is a great leveling process underway, and there is a tendency to think only in abstractions or generalities. K B J

2. The age is one of mechanization, objectification of man and organizations — Man is a cog in the wheels. B J S

3. The individual is no longer held responsible for what he becomes. He is enmeshed in a feeling of helplessness. K B J S

4. There is a loss of faith, a feeling of home-

lessness; false ideologies are crumbling, everything is in question.   *K* B J

5. The crowd has infected man's sense of responsibility — he is conforming, he has lost his sense of identity.   K   J

6. God is in hiding, never was, or at least is absent from the world.   *B* J S

7. There is a lack of communication, terms are not understood.   B J

8. Man suffers from spectatoritis, he does nothing to bolster his situation.   K B J

9. There is a lack of expressed religious faith which is meaningful. There is a despiritualization of the world.   K B J S

10. There is political confusion, the rise of utilitarianism, people are dominated by propaganda.   K B J

11. There is a breakdown of the family.   B J

12. Man is arrogant.   K B

13. Man is not able to meaningfully listen.   B J

B. The problems presented to man by the catastrophes of the age:

1. Man's weltanschauung has been shattered.   K B   S

2. Man is unable to realize a new spirit, to fashion a new teaching for the age.   K B J S

3. Sin acquires a history which plagues man; man's own past influences the present.   K B J S

4. Man is not completely responsible for the absence of God.   B   S

5. How does man return to God, if even after turning he does not perceive God?   B   J

6. Because man is finite and imperfect, he has definite limitations which will hinder or prevent him from solving the crisis.   K   J

7. Man tends to avoid facing his problems by attempting to cling to the past, to fixate at a certain level of development. How can this be adequately shattered?   K   B   S

8. In some instances, it may be better to sin than to conform.   B   S

9. How does one develop a sense of responsibility in man?   K   B   *J*   S

10. Man must be made aware that he creates his own reality. He is free to work on the materials of his situation.   J   S

C. Solutions suggested to dispose of the crisis:

1. Man must fashion a teaching for his age.   B   J   S

2. Man must give all for God, and orient his life, by choice, towards transcendence.   *K*   B   J

3. Man must develop trust and faith in Being, especially transcendent being.   K   *B*   *J*

4. Man must develop a feeling of brotherhood, communication, fraternity, community.   K   *B*   J   S

5. There is no direct guidance from God.   K   B   J   S

6. There are no final solutions for finite man.   J S

7. There are very few solutions for the crisis.   K B

8. Ruin, death, stimulate man's creativity.   K   J S

9. Man must act, not merely contemplate.   K B J S

10. Philosophy-Religion will endure the crisis.   K B J

11. One must encourage the development of authenticity.   K B J S

There can be little doubt that the existentialists who are studied in this thesis believe that man is currently engaged in a world which is torn by crisis and which has suffered major catastrophes. Man has not only been confronted by the ravage of war and pestilence, he has also experienced a serious inner breakdown of his moral fiber. All of the existentialists have underscored an attitude that man is developing a feeling of helplessness and is losing his faith in his ability to solve the problems of his age. They deplore this fact, and their writings are attempting to encourage man to live courageously and assume personal responsibility for at least trying to alter the catastrophic ways of the universe. All stress that a new teaching, a new spirit, must be developed in the psyche of man to bolster him in his attempt to reconstruct experience. Furthermore, agreement is noticeable that any solutions of man's troubles will be extremely difficult to realize, because the solutions to the problems if any are few. All deplore the circumstance that God, in the traditional prophetic form, is apparently absent from the universe, and thus cannot be relied on as a source to turn man's course away from one which threatens to obliterate his basic identity. All the men studied are wrestling with the problem of how man can be made to realize that he does not live in a naturalistically or psychologically determined universe and that he is responsible for what he chooses to do and for that matter even what he happens to do. To overcome the crisis of the age man must consciously begin to work out his own destiny and in so doing become authentic. Man must become what he can become. He must integrate every possibility of his being into a force which can become active in an attempt to rise above man's pitiful condition. If man cannot succeed in rising above the threats of the age, then he is in danger of becoming a drab automaton, one who merely is a cog in the wheels of a technological age.

The major difference apparent in the writings of the men studied, in terms of how to overcome the crisis, is that the Kierkegaard-Buber-Jaspers combine generalize about man's condition, whereas Sartre deals exclusively with man's individual problems. Sartre places the single man under the microscope of creative drama and examines what that man will do under the conditions of the drama. It is for this reason that Sartre is not listed as having indicated several of the indicators of the crisis. As Ruggiero states, Sartre does not interest himself in the general problems which confront man, but he is interested in the more perverse problems which confront the individual.' In the *Flies* Sartre deals with his concept of the inevitable result of absolute freedom, namely that man will eventually find himself alone, devoid of happiness and in despair. In *No Exit* he pursues the theme that hell is to live forever in the presence of someone who is capable of seeing right through one's mask — one's persona.

Sartre is also willing to disagree with the other three over the role played by God in producing the catastrophes of the age. To the three who lean towards theism, the absence of God — or man's drift from God — is part of the catastrophe of the age, and to overcome the catastrophe man must try to find God again. To Sartre there is no God; the realization of this fact he agrees has precipitated much of the extremity of the crisis. However, now that man has realized that he cannot rely on God, so much the better. A Godless man will not try to match impossible standards of perfection, but will express more of his true potentials. Sartre goes so far as to state that no solution to the present crisis will ever be found by man, because he is much too finite to comprehend the meaning of the universe, even if there were such a meaning. This is in agreement with the three existentialists who believe in God, because these men advocate that without some orientation towards transcendence no solutions to the crisis will be found. Sartre haunts their position with an attitude of, 'So be it'.

II. The main existential goal 'Man must come to know himself'.

1. The starting point for self-knowledge is in subjectivity. Man can never divorce himself from the subjective.   K B J S

2. Man must undertake a search for stability, he must not take things for granted, his behavior must be purposive; he must be purposive; he must will himself to be, he is sustained becoming.   K B J S

3. Man must seek to know himself.   K B J S

4. Man can alter his situation, elaborate himself; man has free choice, he is not in a final situation; he is free to create.   K B J S

5. The authority for a man's action must be based on his own choice. There are no compelling external situations.   K B J S

6. Man must accept his limitations, his facticity, his ultimate situations.   K B J S

7. Man must accept the fact that life contains tragedy, that he must be anxious, that he is problematic to himself.   K B J S

8. Man is conscious that he exists. He can reflect — or is reflection — on his exis-

tence. He can transcend his physical limitations. He becomes what he is not.   K   B   J   S

9. Man is dependent upon the judgement of others for maximum self-knowledge. Others help to shape his being.   K   B   J   S

10. Unfortunately man tends to merely exist, he lives vaguely.   K   B   J   S

11. Utilitarianism must not usurp man's need to go beyond the practical, to transcend his situation.   K   B   J

12. Man must develop a faith in the transcendence, trust in the Thou, have faith in God even though His force is not immediately evident.   K   B   J

13. Man must learn about the heights and depths of man throughout the ages, the insight will provide him with a criteria for what is possible for man to achieve.   K   B   J

14. Man should learn to exist within his community, he needs love; he should avoid a crowd.   K   B   J   S

15. Man should believe in the equality of man, and that he is responsible for his fellow man.   K   B   J

16. Man must not force his convictions on other people, although he will aid them to want to know themselves.   K   B   J   S

17. Man is in the mode of not being what he is, he is in sustained becoming.   J   S

18. There is no human nature.   S

19. Man can make only an appointment with

himself for the future. He may not be
himself when the future becomes pre-
sent.   J S

20. Speech alone informs man what he
    really is.   S

21. Man's movement reveals his worth.   B

22. There can be no belief in God in a
    man who cannot meet another.   B

One of the essential tasks of the individual is to come to
know himself. The existentialists are in agreement that man
may only come to know himself subjectively, because he can
never be an object to himself. Man must not be satisfied with
any level of attainment, because his basic being changes with
each new situation. The individual must constantly be involved
in a process of reforging himself. Man is able to alter his
situation, he is capable of rising above any determinism and
actually shaping the substances which are in his situation. To
be certain man is confronted with reality. In this regard the
existentialists agree with the realists that there is a factual
situation which the individual must accept, but it is up to man
to determine how he will utilize his realistic surroundings to
make his life more meaningful. Perhaps the greatest limitation
which man must accept is the fact that he must die. To the
existentialists, the least one can do when he realizes that he is
going to die is to choose the type of person he will be at the
time of death. To the existentialists, although Buber does not
discuss the subject to any great length, most people perceive
death as a force which will strip away their persona, will deny
them their ability to determine whom they are and instead
means that others will determine who they are, and finally forces
a radical aloneness. To avoid the realization that one must die,
most people refuse to realize that they are progressing into the
future, they do not want to know their own limitations and
therefore they avoid self-knowledge, and they generally lie
to themselves.

All of these existentialists concede that others play an important role in aiding the individual to discover his true identity. For Kierkegaard, the most important 'other' is God, but even he believes that people who love one another help each other to become aware that they have worth, and encourage the acceptance of self. Buber does not stress the importance of the other as much as Jaspers and Sartre in terms of aiding in the determination of the identity of a person. To Buber the 'other' is necessary to complete the most valuable I-thou experience which is desirable, but which involves the person in a relationship which is above personal self-knowledge.

Important in man's ability to feel secure is his ability to live in a community, or in an atmosphere of love. Kierkegaard stressed this importance in his discussion of the development of the child. The child needs to be raised in a family which will give him the feeling of security and affection. As stated previously, one needs to be loved in order to feel worthy, in order to be encouraged to face one's own potentials. Sartre is the one of the four who least emphasizes the person's need for love and for a community relationship. He accepts the fact that in a loving relationship one attains an inestimable joy, but he states that one cannot sustain himself in this attitude for more than a few moments. What is significant in Sartre is his theory that individuals must cooperate with their respective minority groups in order to avoid falling prey to the majority, who will misuse them when it is economically advantageous. Sartre also accepts Jaspers' thesis that man is guilty of the activities of man in general as long as he chooses to exist in this universe. Therefore man must be interested in the development of a meaningful community.

In terms of the existential interest in man's coming to know himself, it is emphasized that what one finds in himself may not be true of his neighbor. One ought never force another person to accept the convictions which he has found valid in his own situation. This even includes demanding that the other individual comes to know himself. All an existentialist can do is to invite the other to come to know himself. He cannot force the situation.

Buber suggests that man cannot really believe in God unless he knows how to enter a sustained relationship with another person. Sartre, although stressing that man must cooperate with groups, demonstrates an agreement with Buber because he feels that it is extremely difficult for one person to meet another in the way in which Buber defines. Sartre believes there is no God.

The four men hold the joint conviction that in spite of the necessity to know oneself, and of one's need to live fully, most people live faintly and inauthentically. Only a few attain true selfhood.

III. The importance of man's philosophizing.

1. There is an emphasis on the Socratic idea 'Know thyself'.   K B J S

2. Man cannot obtain philosophical truth, he may see only dimly.   K   S

3. Man must test all his ideas, constantly correct them, and then master them.   K   J S

4. Man must learn about great philosophies.   K B J

5. Meaning is found only in action, experience is requisite for philosophical undertaking. There must be no sheer speculation.   K B J S

6. Existentialism is for specialists.   K   J S

7. Only God enables man to fully know himself.   K   J

The existentialists are positively inclined towards the need of the individual to philosophize and to learn about the great philosophies of the ages. Buber is perhaps less concerned with this endeavor than the others are; Jaspers is the most interested in fostering a philosophical attitude among the people. Kierkegaard is interested in fostering a philosophical attitude until the individual is capable of launching himself into faith, and developing the religious stage of existence. Buber would closely adhere to this emphasis on the religious obligations of man. Sartre has shown himself to be a master of previous philosophies, as has each of the existentialists who have been studied. Sartre however does not recommend that one involve himself too much in philosophy after he has become authentic because he insists that the essence of philosophy is in its application to life and that is exactly what the individual must undertake. Sartre is not as interested in a well rounded philosophy as is Jaspers because he wants to examine how philosophies of life are actually lived. How does the individual develop philosophical insight is Sartre's problem in several of his plays. Nevertheless Sartre does show how he can master philosophy by developing an ontology of man.

Two points of agreement stand out in the existential concern about philosophy. Philosophical teaching should be done by the Socratic method. The main aim of philosophy is to aid the student to come to know himself. Secondly, philosophy must not involve mere contemplation, it must speak to the needs and aspirations of the people, it must form a body of thought which will be translated into living endeavor.

Kierkegaard and Sartre emphasize that man cannot devise a philosophical system which will permit man to obtain ideal wisdom. Buber is not concerned with this problem as he is interested more in a person entering into a relationship without desiring to objectify knowledge.

It is also important to note that Kierkegaard, Jaspers and Sartre are in agreement that existentialism is for experts, and ought not be dabbled in. One must learn quite a bit about the wisdom of contemporary philosophical systems and ethical plans before one really gains existential insight at the philosophical level. Sartre puts philosophical insight into the lives of his characters but their insight remains in the rough and is undeveloped. Buber does not treat the subject at all.

IV. The main problems of life which confront man.

1. All human activities are doomed to failure, and shipwreck. Nothing is permanent. Man does not have the ability to form anything which will be enduring.   K B J S

2. Man is faced by nothingness, by nonbeing.   K B J S

3. Man suffers from guilt, dread, and anxiety; he is especially concerned about the fact that he must die.   K B J S

4. The alternative to the tragedy of life is lack of awareness, bad faith, casual living.   K B J S

5. Great men are crushed, 'Individuals' are martyred.   K B J S

6. Man is responsible, not only for himself, but for what happens in the world.   K B J S

7. Without God, man is not to be; man faces directionless chaos without God.   B

8. Without God, only man can be held accountable for what he has done and will do.   S

9. Man is anguish.   S

Little interpretation needs to be given to the content of this section. The existentialists are in agreement that man is faced by eventual annihilation and the failure of his every plan. He is haunted by guilt, dread and anxiety forces which he would like to hide from himself. Sartre states the position in the extreme when he emphasizes that man is not haunted by such feelings for he is not in the state of anything, he is identical with the state. In other words man is anguish. All of the existentialists realize that the truly noble men of the ages have been crushed by the masses, and that being authentic does not involve one in many pleasant situations. All insist that most men are not capable of handling these experiences, and therefore usually try to hide themselves in a busy surface type of living at the aesthetic level or to entertain some sort of idealism which they hold as an absolute source of comfort to themselves, even though they know that they are not being honest and are therefore existing in bad faith. Jaspers and Sartre compound man's sense of responsibility by cogently pointing out that as long as man exists he is responsible for what happens to mankind in general. Both Sartre and Jaspers accept their responsibility for the rise of the tyrannies which shook the middle of the twentieth century. This idea is not denied by the other two philosophers. As a matter of fact, Kierkegaard implies the idea when he discusses 'the Individual's' worry about whether he increases the guilt of the crowd which persecutes him because he will not conform to mediocrity.

Buber argues that without God man is directionless and is not to be. Sartre takes issue with Buber's concept that such a man will not be. The individual chooses to make himself and in the act of making himself comes into being. Of course Sartre's individual must realize that he faces nothingness when he dies. At death his meaning becomes the property of others, and he is nothing. Sartre agrees that in death, man without God faces total annihilation. However, because man is not told which way he ought to travel, he becomes absolutely responsible for the way he goes. The responsibility is not that of the individual's responsibility to do God's will, but rather that man must be responsible to himself in terms of the man he is going to be.

V. The importance of man's ability to decide what to do with his situation.

1. Man has free will.   K   B   J   S

2. Man was created to be free by God.   K   B   J

3. The divine force demands human decisions.   K   B   J

4. Man works in freedom upon his own existence. He determines who he will be.   B   J   S

5. Man's freedom permits him to manipulate the factual existence of the world.   B   J   S

6. Man can choose to alter his choice; effects of previous decisions influence him, but he may choose new directions.   K   B   J   S

7. Freedom does not mean that man always receives what he wants, or is capable of altering his situation.   K   B   J   S

8. Man's freedom to organize his environment permits cause-effect to operate.   K   B   J   S

9. Decision is the only criterion for human action.   K   J   S

10. Man chooses to interpret what happens to him.   J   S

11. Indecision is itself evil.   K   J

12. Meaning comes into being with man's choice which has been put into effect.   S

It has already been noted that the existentialists are in agreement that man has freedom of choice, he is not determined psychologically, nor by the pressure of an unconscious force. Not only is man capable of freedom of choice but he can also act upon his decisions. To all but Sartre, God created man with the possibility of freedom. After man has made his decision, the existentialists insist that he must continue to choose, not only in relation to his new experiences, but also to re-choose previous ideas which are still relevant to the situation. This latter emphasis is of vital importance, because according to these writers too many feel that once they have chosen to be good, or have failed to choose the good, no more choices are open in that area. They are therefore lulled into irresponsibility and inappropriate behavior. Of course these men agree that merely because one has freedom one cannot will something alien to the factual limitations of existence. The existentialists do not advocate a mind over matter philosophy per se. It is true that the mind will interpret matter, but matter itself is a vital and real force impinging upon the freedom of the individual. Man must work with his existence. His existence provides him with his raw materials. It is what man does with the real substance that makes the difference in his life. Once man has decided, and acted upon his decision, by hindsight he can perceive certain cause-effect principles at work, because that was the way the situation unfolded. But the individual chooses to set the cause and effect principle to work, and he ought to control the principle so that it will work for him rather than enslave him. The choice of an individual is the only thing which is valid for that individual in the moment of decision. 'Moment', of course, does not mean sixty seconds, but rather the time involved in being confronted by a problem, making the decision, and acting upon the decision. The making of the decision involves an evaluation of one's past knowledge and of his future expectancies.

Apparently all the existentialists believe that the only things that can happen in the world at this historical hour are the result of man's decision. Buber stresses that God is eclipsed from the world but still entertains the idea that he may re-enter the historical hour. Kierkegaard advises one to listen to the command of God, but tends to believe that God's essential message is revealed in the Bible or more specifically in the teachings of Jesus.

To Kierkegaard and Buber, the revelations of the Bible are extraordinarily significant, and should at least be studied by the individual. Jaspers believes that the Judaic-Christian culture has been influential on the development of man today and ought to be studied for that reason. He does not stress this as much as Kierkegaard or Buber because Jaspers is more interested in the Axial period (800-200 B.C.). One must familiarize himself with the attainments of the Biblical prophets and Apostles. As one studies what these men sought to do, one gains an idea of what it is possible for man to do at any time of man's history. It is the task of man today to reconstruct the Biblical experience for the twentieth century. Man must reforge the insights of these men so that they are relevant to this day and time. For Sartre, man learns that his world has been possessed by others and that others have left signs to be interpreted by man. As indicated, Sartre holds that the individual creates meaning by what he chooses to have meaning. He never encounters meaning in any other way. Thus a study of the Biblical prophets would not be as important to him save as the person might be inspired to grant meaning to the study of the Biblical personalities.

VI. The importance of reason to the individual.

1. Intuitive knowledge is the basis of all learning, subjective knowledge and objective knowledge cannot be separated.   K B J S

2. To realize man's full potentials he must think and reason. What man becomes will be the result of his reason.   B J S

3. Man must choose to be reasonable.   K B J S

4. Reason in the authentic person utilizes past experiences as well as future speculation.   K B J S

5. The individual must go beyond reason and develop trust and faith.   K B J

6. Man selectively inattends because of bad faith; the aesthetic does not reason, no

anti-rationalism is to be condoned.   K   B   J   S

7. Reason is attainable only because of God.   K   J

8. Reason sometimes usurps more importance than it should, or narrows its base to leave out emotional understanding.   K   B

9. Reason is meaningful only when action is involved.   K   B   J   S

10. Thinking requires social binding.   B   J

11. Intellect must liberate itself from the philosophy of utilitarianism.   K   B

All four of the existentialists emphasize that reason plays an important role in the development of an authentic person. However, reason must be supported by intuitive knowledge and must never usurp control of the person's life without reference to what might be termed the wisdom of the body. Inauthentic living involves irregularities of thinking and outright lying to oneself. The use of the tool of reason or logic is very explicitly demonstrated in the writing of Jean-Paul Sartre's, *Being and Nothingness*. In use of reason, the individual must never be permitted to retreat into an ivory tower of thought, or become an arm chair logician. Reason must work for a decision, and with the decision one must become active.

Buber and Jaspers allege that reason will be valid only if it produces a social binding, which is to say aids in the development of a community. The more rugged existentialists, Kierkegaard and Sartre, do not share this emphasis. In Kierkegaard's case, one must love God, one's neighbor who is loved by God and one's enemy who is also loved by God. If one fully understands himself, he knows himself to be loved by God, and he feels love for his fellow man. Sartre argues that a member of a social minority must identify himself with his group so as to achieve some measure of security against the majority who will persecute him if the economic situation is favorable for persecution and if he, as the minority member, does not have a strong organized group. Indirectly Sartre and Kierkegaard would also argue that a community interest would be developed by the individual who rationally evaluates his situation.

Kierkegaard and Jaspers believe, and probably Buber would not disagree, that one's reason is attainable only because God wills that one should be reasonable. Sartre agrees via the negative: since God does not exist, He has no power to control man and therefore man must be free.

VII. The sources of the individual's 'correct' decisions.

1. There are no sources which guarantee correct decisions; man can never evaluate what he has done in terms of right and wrong.   K B J S

2. If man knows how to evaluate himself, his past and his future, and then decides by using his intelligence and his emotional understanding — this is all that can be required of man. This is the best he can do.   K B J S

3. No decision is binding, one always can choose anew.   K B J S

4. Decisions may be sustained by God, individuals can only hope and trust and have faith.   K B J

5. Man must risk himself in sustained choice if he is to meaningfully remold his world.   K J S

6. In that man creates reality, great trust is placed in the ability of man to decide and that decision will be as good as possible.   B J S

7. Love gives man the clue as to whether or not his decision is valid.   **K B J**

8. God gives ciphers, clues, the Bible, which correctly interpreted will aid man when he makes a decision.   **K B J**

9. The judgement of others is important when man seeks to arrive at a decision.   **B J S**

10. Whatever man affirms is valuable by definition.   **S**

11. There is the possibility of divine commission.   **K B**

Existentialists are constantly challenged as to how they know that their decisions will lead to correct behavior. Even Buber raises the question of how Kierkegaard's 'Single Individual' would arrive at valid decisions. In the first place the existentialists are the first to admit that there is no certainty that one's decisions will be correct or appropriate, or even that there are 'correct' and 'appropriate' decisions which the individual is able to make. The best man can do is to be wholly cognizant of the present situation and to permit his evaluations of his past experiences and his anticipations of future experiences to weigh together in his attempt to arrive at a decision. If the decision is arrived at enthusiastically in the moment of decision, if it has been considered on the basis of previous experience and future speculations and if the decision is grounded in love (Sartre excepted), then it must be as correct a decision as man can possibly attain. Should man make an error in judgement due either to his finite limitations or to being deceived by his bad faith, then he may always choose to go in another direction, even as he must again choose to go in the direction that he is traveling. The new choice will not undo the past, but it will certainly influence the future development of man and all that he influences. Kierkegaard and Buber especially, but also Jaspers, hope that the Transcendence will sustain the decisions of man and, if necessary, supplement them if man has bungled his freedom. Kierkegaard insists that when man decides he has heard God's command, he should obey without question. Even here Kierkegaard insists that man must choose to believe that he has received the command of God and he is responsible for the decision.

Merely because man does not know how sound his choices are, he must not permit himself to be reduced to a state of inactivity. Man must be willing to dare to act on the assumption that he has made the best decision and that the course he has chosen will prove satisfactory. He must risk failure. As stated previously, indecision may be the only incorrect decision which the person can make. All but Kierkegaard point out that man can partially validate his decisions by seeking the counsel of other people. This counsel he should consider and weigh, however, when he makes his decision it is his, and the results are his responsibility.

VIII. The Individual and his God.

1. The authentic man is derived from God. K B J

2. God helps man to differentiate himself from animal existence. K B J

3. God wills to operate in human affairs, but is not as evident in recent years. K B J

4. It is very difficult for man to encounter God in this historical period. K B J S

5. There must be no absorption into God; man is always independent of God. K B J S

6. One may only enter into the way of God; there are no prescriptions for behavior. K B J

7. Man's way of worshipping God has lost its power in the present moment. K B J S

8. God may encounter man in special ways — Spokesmen for God = the Nabi, the Apostle. K B

9. Speaking for God means to spell out the
   implications of man's conduct for his future existence. (By future is meant the
   tomorrow's existence, not the afterlife.)   K   B

10. It is God who enables man to love and
    who thereby creates the possibility for
    community.   K   B

11. God is still in the process of creating.   B   J

The most noticeable difference between the existentialists comes
as a result of their concepts of God. Sartre denies that there is
a God. Jaspers denies the Judaic-Christian God and posits a
Transcendence which man must not think too much about because
any thinking about the Transcendence would involve man in
idolization of the force. Buber and Kierkegaard disagree over the
divinity of Jesus. Buber's God is more socially toned than is Kierkegaard's God, who still retains much of the God of judgment.
In actuality, all four men are in agreement that God must not
affect man's ability to make free choices and, for that matter,
all more or less remove God from directly participating in this
historical hour. All of their approaches to God would decry any
attempt to think that man must be reabsorbed by the divine. All
have also agreed that the modern church has lost much of its
vitality and spiritual impact. Kierkegaard, Buber and Jaspers are
in agreement that man has derived his existence from God, and
that the authentic man is aware of this fact. They also believe
that the fact that man has a positive relationship with transcendence differentiates him from the animal stage which, scientifically, he is classified with. They are also in agreement that
belief in God does not imply that there are a group of rules which
man must follow. One must step into the way of God and be
religious, if one is to be authentic.

Kierkegaard and Buber both consider it possible that God may
actively intervene in history and appoint either an apostle or
nabi to challenge men to reform. Even if this occurs, the role
of the nabi is only to warn people of the consequences if they

persist in godless ways. The choice is still left in the individual's hands. Buber and Jaspers are not unfriendly to the idea that God is still creating. Of course Sartre insists that with each decision of the individual, the world is being created.

IX. Traits of the authentic individual.

1. He accepts responsibility for everything which he does; everything he does is based on his power of decision.   K   B   J   S

2. The authentic person is a man of action.   K   B   J   S

3. He is faithful to God, his life is lived by faith or in trust.   K   B   J

4. The essence of the authentic man involves his ability to love others, and be in a community.   K   B   J

5. He is oriented to the present, but knows of the influence of the past and the draw of the future. His choice integrates the three.   K   B   J   S

6. His life is fulfilled by personal choice. He is not dominated by others, nor by cause and effect.   K   B   J   S

7. The authentic person is living to the fullest possible degree in this existence. He is 'this world' centered. He works with his life.   K   B   J   S

8. The authentic person feels that he must first fulfill his immediate responsibilities of life tasks.   K   B   J

9. He seeks to BE that which he is; to choose to work with his real situation is his main interest.   K   B   J   S

10. He is a unified person who actively seeks
to be what he can be. He seeks the most
from life.   B   J   S

11. He does not lie to himself.   K   B   J   S

12. The authentic person is decisive for the
success or failure of this era.   K   J

The existentialists are all concerned with the formation of a
person who is capable of being an authentic person. To be authentic one must accept personal responsibility for everything
which one does. Every choice must be responsibly made. To
whom is one responsible, as discussed previously, depends on
which existentialist is speaking. For all of the men, what one
does influences him later on, so minimumly he must be responsible to himself. For Buber and Kierkegaard as well as Jaspers
one must be responsible to the transcendent force.

Under any condition the authentic person is a man of action.
He is not a spectator of the life process, he does not live faintly.
He is involved with the contemporary situation which life involves him in and which he chooses to be involved in. The
authentic person, while becoming something other than he is
by each of his decisions, while he reconstructs himself and his
environment, must none the less accept himself as an existent and
as a person with certain definite finite characteristics. It is what
the person chooses to make of these characteristics that will be
important, but first he must acknowledge that he has the traits,
that he is the traits. He must be the traits before he is capable
of altering them. This requires an act of choice.

Kierkegaard, Buber and Jaspers emphasize that the authentic
person is oriented towards transcendence, and bases his life on
trust of faith that all of this is not in vain. The implication of
using the word 'trust' instead of 'know' indicates that life might
be in vain. Sartre is perfectly willing to accept the idea that life
in vain, but in that man is here he might as well make the
best out of the situation if for no other reason than to make his
existence more stimulating. It has also been stated that the

authentic person, according to the trilogy of theists, believes that love characterizes the authentic man. For Sartre, man can only attempt to realize this plateau of existence, but usually fall short of it.

Buber, Jaspers and Sartre tend to agree that the authentic person is fully involved in working with that which is at hand. He is attempting to develop to the fullest the possibilities which lie in his existence. To Kierkegaard, the person may be a little more other-world centered but not to the exclusion of fulfilling his finite obligations. Kierkegaard, Buber and Jaspers insist that immediate obligations should be fulfilled before the individual focuses on distant concerns. Sartre does not go into the subject but would probably agree.

The importance of the authentic person to the age of crisis is testified to by Kierkegaard and Jaspers who believe that only if these types of persons can bring their influence to bear in the crisis, the crisis might be resolved.

X. The individual and his relationship with others and his need for communication

1. Everyone is responsible for himself and for the well-being of every other person.	K	B	J	S
2. The 'Other's' existence is a contingent, an irreducible fact.	K	B	J	S
3. Each individual needs to work with and to help develop his community.		B	J	S
4. One's knowledge of oneself is influenced by other people. The other person is needed for maximum self-appraisal or knowing of the self.	K		J	S
5. Love permits man to know joy and feel free.		B	J	S
6. Communication, while a necessary experience, is difficult to maintain over an extended period of time.	K	B	J	S

7. All men are equal because God is either in all men, or loves all men equally.   K   B

8. One's neighbor is important to the individual, he is the nearest person.   K   B

9. Alone man is absolutely nothing.   K   J

10. In communication or in love there are no generalized situations, all is specific.   K   J

11. After death, 'the Other' controls my existence and my meaning for life.   J   S

12. There is a need for social binding, fraternity and dialogue.   B   J

13. The richness of a man is the amount of love he possesses.   K

14. When one is loved he is threatened with the loss of his being.   S

15. The fall of man occurs when he is aware that another person is watching him.   S

It has already been mentioned that all four existentialists concur that the authentic man must involve himself in community living, and that he must seek to establish close mutual relations with other people. Mutual relationships must be established for no other reason than that all men are responsible for what any other group of people does. Man is co-responsible for the activities of others. Furthermore the existence of the person is a irreducible fact which the authentic man must react to. Nevertheless, all four of the men indicate that communication at the highest level with this other person is very difficult to maintain, and it will tax the ability of the individual to do so.

Kierkegaard is the only one who comes close to permitting his individual to completely defy the community in which he lives.

The other three existentialists encourage the authentic person to develop solidarity with the community even if compromise is involved. Kierkegaard permits no compromise on principles.

As stated previously, the Other is an important person because he has the effect of organizing man's experience and plays an important role of showing a person how he appears to another. This fosters the development of the self-system which may or may not be authentic.

Kierkegaard and Buber accept the complete equality of man because of man's relationship to God. Sartre, although an active socialist, has not addressed himself to the problem.

XI. The individual's relationship to the crowd.

1. One may participate in the group, but must not be identical with it. K B J S

2. One is responsible for any of the decisions of the group, there are no fractional responsibilities. K B J S

3. The crowd is not responsible for its behavior, it shifts its position too readily, and is oriented towards immediate hedonistic satisfactions. K B J

4. The rise of technology creates the horror of the crowd and its demand for conformity. B J

5. The crowd demands conformity. K B J

6. Collectivism and conformity are not good for the individual. They are a threat to him. K B J S

7. The factual reality that the individual must live within groups must be accepted. B J S

8. Real potential may develop from the

mass.   **B   J**

9. God is capable of transforming the crowd
   into a community.   **B**

All of the existentialists would preserve the individual from being absorbed into the masses, the crowd, or an unstructured group. When someone does choose to become a part of the group, he assumes complete responsibility for what the group does. He ought not to think that he is only a fraction of the group and is thus only partially responsible for the group's decision. All of the existentialists studied here take a stand against collectivism and conformity. All but Kierkegaard realize that the existence of the crowd is a fact which must be worked with by the authentic person.

Sartre, at this point, drops out of the discussion because the crowd has not interested him very much. It is again another example of generalization versus his individualistic interest. For the remaining three existentialists, the crowd is unreliable and constantly shifting its position. It reacts without a conscience, or an awareness of any responsibility. It is completely dominated by hedonist interests. The crowd inevitably oppresses the individual by a demand that the individual conform.

Buber and Jaspers, and perhaps Kierkegaard too, accept the thesis that the rise of the crowd is directly correlated with the rise of technology. It is an inevitable and a real threat to man's becoming authentic. Fortunately at least Buber and Jaspers think that something favorable can come from the crowd. Jaspers goes so far as to indicate that the crowd occasionally may even be wiser than the individual person. For Buber, it is always possible that God may transform the crowd into a community.

XII. Traits of the inauthentic man.

1. He postpones decisions which should be
   made.   **K   B   J   S**

2. He over-generalizes, thinks too categorically and abides by his concept of uni-

	K	B		S
versal principles.	K	B		S
3. He accepts no personal responsibility, he lives at an aesthetic level. His life is oriented only in the present. Pleasure is his chief goal.	K	B	J	S
4. He hides displeasing truths from himself.	K		J	S
5. He has no critical awareness of reality.	K		J	S
6. He excuses his behavior by saying that everything is determined by either cause-effect principles or by some psychological influence beyond his ability to control.	K		J	S
7. He tends to be inauthentic because of his fear of death, doom and shipwreck.	K		J	S
8. Most people are in bad faith, few attain the authentic stage.	K	B	J	S
9. He has no appreciation of how he can use the past in free decision so as to alter his future possibilities.	K		J	S
10. He fears being alone and dying alone.	K		J	
11. He develops a persona to hide from himself.	K			S
12. He is one who tries to live without faith, or orientation to God.	K	B	J	
13. It is easier to be inauthentic during times of plenty, than when crises are present.	K	B	J	S
14. He is a complete conformist or at least he tries to please the crowd.	K			
15. He treats other people as instruments, he uses others for his selfish ends.	K	B	J	

It is sometimes well to study a positive concept by studying its negative. The attempt of this study is to see what goes into being an authentic person. All of the existentialists agree that this type of person rarely exists for most people do not live fully, do not participate in the moment, postpone choice and tend to lull themselves into a false security. The inauthentic person accepts no personal responsibility for his behavior, he seldom understands that the past is influencing his present condition, nor does he plan very adequately for the future.

Buber does not discuss the inauthentic man in any great detail and thus he is not indicated as agreeing with some of the statements on the chart. The remaining three agree that the inauthentic man hides truth from himself, and exists in bad faith. All three oppose the psychoanalytical idea of the unconscious influence over the person or of the dynamics of repression. The person always knows when he is not living up to his best potentials. An unauthentic man does not permit himself the luxury of critically evaluating even the present moment.

The motivation behind the inauthentic person is his fear of death, and his disliking of the experience of being completely responsible for his behavior. Because of anxiety about ultimate life situations, few people will permit themselves to become authentic; most people want to tranquilize themselves with dreams and wishes, but very seldom work to achieve their dreams. Man usually is capable of lulling himself into a false sense of security if he is confronted with no major crisis. Tragedy proves itself to be beneficial to the awakening of a person to his full potentials.

The inauthentic person tends towards generalizations, conformity to a hierarchy of preconceived ethical standards, and otherwise jumps to conclusions very rapidly. Only Jaspers does not discuss this trait. Kierkegaard, Buber and Jaspers emphasize that inauthentic persons treat other people as objects to be manipulated. They use other people. Sartre states that this is inevitable.

XIII. The optimistic outlook of existentialists.

1. Man can always turn, reform or re-

choose.   **K B J S**

2. Man has worth — his worth is either derived from God, *or* he makes his own value.   **K B J S**

3. Each new person plays a decisive role in history.   **K B J S**

4. Man is never permanently degraded.   **K B J S**

5. Man can create meaning out of his existence.   **B J S**

6. Man is under divine destiny, he is not at the mercy of divine sport. The universe is trustworthy.   **K B J**

7. If one's preaching is ignored, God listens.   **K B**

8. Man has everything to gain and nothing to lose by risking himself in life.   **K   J S**

Some critics have accused existentialism of purveying pessimism and dread. Actually the position is reasonably optimistic. All the existentialists examined here agree that man has worth, and that worth is either derived from God, or it is self made. All agree that if man makes a wrong decision he can remake his choice, and veer off onto a new road of existence. All view man with the highest regard and emphasize that he is not totally depraved, nor sinful at all before he chooses to be sinful. Even when he chooses to degrade himself, man is never permanently evil, because man is in the process of not being what he is. All but Kierkegaard feel that man can carve meaning out of life situations, and even he does not deny the possibility. Of course, man's work will not stand the test of time unless what man has done is reduplicated by someone in the future.

Kierkegaard, Buber and Jaspers also reassure man that the

universe is trustworthy, and that man exists under divine destiny. Should the individual ever become lonely as he encourages others to accept their real being but finds himself to be ridiculed, Kierkegaard and Buber hold out the hope that a personal God is potentially interested in him, loves him, and is aware of his efforts.

Finally, all but Buber, who emphasizes trust, agree that man has everything to gain in this life and absolutely nothing to lose, and thus one might as well be involved in the life process actively.

An Integration of the Existential Discussion of Education

One might expect to find less agreement, among the existentialists studied here, on the development of a meaningful educational program which will aid the individual to become authentic, than on who the authentic individual is. The reason for this is that none of the existentialists has concerned himself to any great extent about the educational problem of fostering the type of individual he seeks to challenge men to be. In that the existentialists insist that one must choose to become authentic, it might seem incongruous to suggest that a specific educational curriculum might encourage one to become authentic. Furthermore, the existentialists do not believe that the authentic individual can be stereotyped to the degree that one might recommend an educational program for the cultivation of such a person. The third hypothesis of the study, however, posits that there is an implied existential philosophy of education and that the four men would agree about the development of an educational program.

The second hypothesis, that each existentialist presents material which has definite implications for the development of an educational philosophy which will make a difference in the educational endeavor was accepted in the fourth chapter. Each man did have definite opinions about the nature of education, what its curriculum should include, how teachers ought to approach the child in order to foster in him a spirit which

281

will be conducive to the development of an authentic person and what type of person a teacher ought to be when he does teach.

In the following charts, which attempt to compare the educational outlook of the existential thinkers, one hundred nineteen statements are made. The four existentialists are in unanimous agreement, explicitly or implicitly, on thirty-one percent of the concepts, and three out of four of the group agree on another thirty-six percent of the statements. Thus, sixty-seven percent of the statements are acceded to by a majority of the existentialists. The fact that some men are not listed as agreeing with a viewpoint ought not be judged to mean that they are in disagreement with the statement but rather that they have not discussed the problem. Actually, very few of the statements are disagreed with by any one of the existentialists. What disagreement there is, is usually related to the atheistic-theistic differences between the men.

As a matter of convenience the one hundred nineteen statements were divided into seven major topics which express the existential positions pertaining to education. These topics are as follows:

I. An examination of the existential understanding of the child as he exists and matures.

II. The purposes of education.

III. Educational practices condemned by the existentialists.

IV. The existential emphasis on the use of reason in the educational endeavor.

V. The type of curriculum which would aid the development of an authentic person.

VI. The qualifications of the teacher — a major existential concern.

VII. An examination of good teaching techniques.

The procedure for the examination of the existential ideas pertaining to education is the same as employed in the first part of this chapter.

I. An examination of the existential understanding of the child as he exists and as he matures.

A. Permit children to mature at their own speed.

1. Encourage children to enjoy life, to not grow up too fast.   K   J   S

2. Permit the child to develop affective behavior — especially joy, play and passion.   K   B   J   S

3. Give the child no artificial problems to solve, nor problems beyond his capacity, but do encourage him to solve problems.   K   S

4. The main emphasis: Remember the smile of the child.   K   B   J   S

B. Encourage intellectual growth of the child.

1. Children have an inquiring spirit, it is good that they do.   K   B   J   S

2. The teacher must encourage children to implement their decisions.   S

3. The child needs the aid of education to fully mature and master his world.   K   B   J   S

4. It is good that the child has little tragic awareness of the real world.   K   B   S

5. Dispassionate learning should be discouraged.   K   J   S

6. Existentialism is not for children.   K   J   S

283

C. The child as a human being.

1. The child must not be manipulated as an object.   K   B   S

2. Others help form the child's personality.   K   B   J   S

3. Young people are being spoiled and tarnished.   K   B   J   S

4. Childhood is a reality.   K   B   J   S

5. The child is a trust.   K   B   J   S

D. Evaluation of the moral caliber of the child.

1. There is no total depravity, or sinful condition inherent in the child's nature.   K   B   J   S

2. The child is born innocent.   K   J

3. Never believe badly of the child.   K   B   J   S

E. Miscellaneous important emphases about the child.

1. The child must be loved.   K   B   J

2. The child is dependent upon the parent.   K   B   S

3. Children worry about finding themselves when they grow up.   B   S

4. Adolescence is an age of storm and stress.   B

5. I-Thou developed before birth, present in infancy.   B

6. The child is actually good.   B

The existentialists agree that existential attitudes are for the adult mind and ought not be stimulated in the immature mind. Children should not be exposed to problems which they can not solve, nor should children become aware of the consequences of their actions when they are still dependent on their parents. Buber is the least concerned about this problem because he emphasizes the more positive aspects of existentialism. He is concerned with the forming of a relationship which lifts the person out of the time-space dichotomy of life. Buber wants the child to be encouraged in his natural wholehearted approach to life and nothing should be presented to the child which would devastate his reverence for life.

All of the existentialists are impressed with the pre-existential awareness which most children have. They comment about their inquisitive spirit, their wholehearted commitment to what they are doing, and about their feelings of spontaneity. They are also impressed by the penetration of a child into the nature of critical problems. Still, they are aware that the child will be tarnished by his experiences as he becomes more aware of the crisis of the age and is made to develop in the socially approved ways in the public school. As the child's awareness of reality develops, all of the men studied express their conviction that the child must have a guide — a teacher — who will help him to gain an understanding of his age and who will penetrate any irregular thoughts he might harbor in himself.

The existentialists insist that the child is a reality and that he has not only the right, but the obligation to live his situation to the maximum. The child must not be encouraged to be old before his time. Adult-like standards must not be imposed on the child. At the same time the child must not be deliberately kept immature by some doting parent, but rather be permitted to develop naturally. Existential educational plans would be guided by the children's maturational ability.

The existentialists are not opposed to the child's nature. Not only is that nature spontaneous and refreshingly honest, but it is unsullied by any form of total depravity. The child is not conceived in sin, nor has the child inherited a sinful condition. The child may have chosen to be sinful by someone else's standard, but even this is a temporary state because the child is always becoming what he is not. For instance, if the adolescent is a juvenile delinquent the existential counselor would not be too distressed because he knows that the adolescent must constantly change for he is in the mode of not being what he is, or he is becoming what he is not. Therefore the wayward youth offers considerable material for a skilled teacher or counselor to work with and to help mold the child into someone of value.

Despite some discussions of existential implications for education to the contrary, the existentialists would not present materials prematurely to the child which would precipitate feelings of dread and uncertainty. They would not enthusiastically launch a discussion in school about the fact that all men must die, or that the child's existence is limited and that he must desperately seek to fulfill himself at that moment. For the adult, in an adult education program this probably would be done, but it certainly would not be premeditated for children. One might ask when the child is ready for such a discussion, and at what stage of development the child needs a guide to help him explore the tragedies of life. The proper time is when the child becomes aware of and is interested in these problems as a result of the maturation of his own experience and powers of observation. It is when he asks questions because he wants to know about these subjects. At this time it is important that the teacher does not just gloss over the questions but is prepared to answer the child's questions honestly.

All these existentialists are in agreement that the child is highly impressionable and that the adult must be very careful not to tarnish him, nor warp his personality. Sartre states that the child's interpretation of himself will come directly from others, while Kierkegaard writes that the parents in particular can warp the child's personality before the age of ten to such a degree that he may be unhappy for the rest of his life. Here there is an area of slight disagreement. Kierkegaard suggests that permanent unhappiness may result from an unhappy childhood, while Sartre insists that one must continually reaffirm the experience of unhappiness to retain oneself in that mode of existence. The disagreement is more apparent than real because Kierkegaard certainly admits that the individual can change and definitely will be changed if, for example, he encounters God.

All but Sartre stress that for maximum development, the child must receive an abundance of tender loving care. All agree that the raising of the child places great responsibility on the parents and the teachers who are guiding the child's growth.

II. The purposes of education.

1. To develop the child's ability to reason and to solve problems. **K B J S**

2. To transmit the culture — to explain what humans have already done with their lives. **K B J S**

3. To aid the child in social reconstruction. **B J S**

4. To increase the child's critical awareness of the present age (how much awareness will depend on maturation and interest of the child). **K B J S**

5. The purposes of education would vary with the age level of the child. The adult too. **K B J S**

6. To teach the child how to carry on meaningful conversations as well as how to listen. **B J**

7. To encourage the child to know himself, to penetrate any irregularities in his thinking. **K B J**

8. To encourage the philosophical inclinations of the child. **K B J**

9. To help the child learn to control his world — develop science education.   J S

10. The state has a need to educate her citizens for patriotism and how to be a citizen.   K   J

11. Children should be schooled in trust and experience honesty.   K   B

12. The child should be encouraged to develop a community within his school to participate in a program of living together.   B

13. To teach the child to be responsible for what he does.   K   B   J   S

14. To give the child an appreciation of the hallowedness of life.   K   B

All of the existentialists agree that one of the main purposes of education is to aid the immature child to grow into an awareness of his cultural environment. This corresponds to the fundamental factors of education suggested by John Dewey.[2] To foster the growth and development of the child, it is necessary to bring to him the cultural wisdom of mankind, so that he can at least see the heights of existence which are attainable by man and, during secondary school at least, can see the misery that man brings to himself by his erroneous choices. The purpose of this education will not be to encourage the child to meditate on the past, nor to duplicate the lives of successful men, but to translate the teachings of the past so that the values of the past may be fed into the actual life of the child as he grows and matures. Education, according to this position, must involve the reconstruction of experience, not only of the child's experiences in the present, but the experience of mankind through history. The teacher also must be engaged in the process of reconstruction, not only of the historical knowledge he may have to bring to the child, but also of his own personal life. Under all conditions the goal of education will encompass the development of the child's critical faculties to reason, to be sincere with himself, and to solve problems which he is able to master.

As already implied, the educational curriculum, as well as the educational methodology which existentialists would recommend, varies with the age and maturity of the child. The teacher of the young child must radiate more love for the child, in order to foster in him the realization that he is worthy of love, than the teacher of the adults who, quite the reverse, often will be trying to shake the security of the adult personality and to precipitate some type of crisis in him.

Most of the remaining discussion in this section is the educational point of view of one or two of the existentialists. Buber and Jaspers stress that the educational authorities ought to be responsible for helping the child to develop a meaningful ability to carry on real, sharing conversations with each other. This also includes the ability to listen to what others are saying. Kierkegaard was certainly interested in listening to his father when he was a boy, but does not concern himself with conversation as such. Sartre would certainly not argue against the idea because an individual becomes what he discerns to be the interpretation of himself by other people. Sartre has proven his listening ability by his successful counseling and is known to be an attentive listener. Nevertheless, he still assumed that a person has the solution to his problem within himself and that he is not interested in conversation as much as he is interested in verification and support when talking with another person.

Against a common opinion that existentialists are opposed to a scientific curriculum, Jaspers and Sartre offer a direct contradiction. Both men favor the development of science education because through it man learns more and more how to control his realistic situation. In science man has a tool which aids him to become more free of his factual situation than ever before. Buber is primarily interested in fostering communication between people, and furthering the re-establishment of the feeling of community and thus does not discuss science at length. He has stated, however, that technology and science are a part of culture and although they may be responsible for preventing man from obtaining great heights are nevertheless factors in man's existence which he will not choose to do without. They must be taken into consideration and man must learn to master them, rather than be mastered by them. Kierkegaard stands opposed to science because it tends to reduce everything to calm and objective observation. Yet as one examines his writings, one discerns a stereotype of science which Jaspers and Sartre do not accept.

Although the child should not be burdened with responsibilities he could not possibly carry out, nor with responsibilities which are artificially contrived, all the existentialists agree that the child should be made aware that he is responsible for what he is doing, that he is responsible for activities which he initiates. Under no circumstances should he be permitted to alibi his actions except when he is really under the direction of a parent or significant adult.

Buber and Kierkegaard are also interested in fostering a reverence for life which will aid the child develop trust in his world. Sartre, who finds no religious atmosphere in life at all, would not agree with this direction of education.

III. Educational practices condemned by the existentialists.

1. Denying the child spontaneity and freedom of expression.   K B J S

2. Encouraging the child to learn dispassionately; he must participate fully in the learning situation.   K B J S

3. Permitting the child to only think instead of putting his thoughts into action. The school must avoid the students being absorbed into the past or abstracted into the future completely. Subjects must not be treated as ends in themselves.   K B J S

290

4. Ever believing badly of the child; give him the benefit of the doubt. Don't be tempted to view the child as being permanently evil.   K B   S

5. Treating the child as an object to be manipulated so as to gain some goal which is exterior to the child's being.   K B   S

6. Foisting adult-like roles on the child, or breaking him with too much responsibility.   K   S

7. Infecting the child with too much doubt, and uncertainty about life.   K B J S

8. Exposing the child to too much Christian theology.   K B J S

9. Evading frank explanations whenever the child sincerely seeks an answer to a question. Don't introduce problems prematurely.   K   S

10. Permitting the child to be smugly complacent or satisfied with his role in life.   K   J S

11. Suggesting to the child that what he does is automatically determined by cause-effect.   J S

12. Tolerating a completely irrational education.   K   J S

It is sometimes useful to examine what philosophers advise against doing in the educational endeavor to realize more fully the positions that they favor. There are certain practices which all four men agree that the educational authorities must not do, besides introducing a theological education, when attempting to pass the cultural heritage on to children. The child's experience in school must not be structured so as to deny him freedom of expression or that which will suppress his spontaneous nature. Related to the avoidance of suppressing the child's spontaneous nature is the concept that the schools must not be places in which only the intellectual side of the child develops. The educational authorities must seek to aid the child to develop his full potentials, not merely his intellectual ability. Under no condition should the child be permitted to learn dispassionately. The learning experience must be one which involves meaningful action or doing. The existentialists accept Dewey's dictum that one learns by doing. Finally, the educational authorities must never bring discouragement to the door of the rather impressionable child. The child must not become dismayed at his inability to solve problems, which means careful grade placement is required as well as much individual attention for each student. The student must not be allowed to become disheartened as a result of studying the failures of man through history, and he must be shielded from the dispiriting (or depressing) experience of being taught by a person with a negative personality.

All but Buber emphasize that the teacher must not permit the child to become content with life as he is living it. The process of life ought to be one of growth. The maturation of the child must not be allowed to freeze because of the child's fear of growing up nor because of the happiness he knows as a child.

Finally, it is to be noted that this group of philosophers also take a position against a completely permissive education which aims at the development of an emotionally uninhibited child. There is a definite place in the school structure for the rational ordering of learned sequences.

IV. The existential emphasis on the use of reason
in the educational endeavor.

1. The child must be encouraged to be
critical about what he experiences.   K B J S

2. Education must encourage the child's reason.　　　　K　　J　S

3. It must be recognized that it is impossible to ever gain absolute knowledge.　　K　B　J　S

4. The child should be encouraged to seek after ordered knowledge.　　K　　J

5. One knows oneself only by encountering the 'other's' interpretation of oneself.　　K　　　S

6. Education develops the child's subjective ability.　　K　　J　S

7. All ages are educable.　　K　B　　S

8. Ethics cannot be logically taught.　　K　B

9. Everything must be refashioned and reconstructed to meet the needs of the age.　　　B　　S

10. The student always knows something. The teacher must find out what and begin there.　　K　B

11. The child must not be forced to make premature closures.　　K　　J　S

12. One chooses to permit himself to learn.　　　　　S

It has been brought out in several places that the existentialists insist that man must utilize his vitally important ability to reason in order to solve problems which confront him. The development of reason is one of the prime responsibilities of the teacher. The child's critical powers must be encouraged and nourished under the direction of the Socratic educator. While it is true that the child may never possess absolute knowledge, or anything that approaches it, he still benefits when he employs his reason to gain knowledge of the universe.

The Socratic method is very important for bringing into fruition the person's ability to evaluate his situation, for only the person knows what his situation actually is. Kierkegaard and Buber affirm that ethics can not be taught in terms of a content method. One can only hope to bring to birth the ethical interest which is latent in the person. For Sartre, nothing is latent, everything must be chosen by the individual. Ethics must be ratified by him at the time of decision.

V. The type of curriculum which would aid the development of an authentic person.

1. The curriculum would depend on the age level of the child with probably four main subdivisions — elementary, junior high, high school and adult education.   K B J S

2. The existentialists favor a humanistic educational system.   K B J S

3. History should be given a major role.   K B J S

   a. The student must reinterpret history to meet his present situation.   K B J S

   b. The student needs history to understand how his world situation developed.   K   J S

   c. History must be re-interpreted, facts are not merely recorded.   K B J S

4. Philosophy should be emphasized.   B J S

   a. One can't teach ethics, but merely point the way.   K B

5. Science education must be fostered.   - B J S

   a. Science is necessary for understanding and gaining control of nature. Man is

freed of nature by science.		B J	S

b. Science must not be cold, it should be passionately studied.   K B J

c. Science is dangerous because it may seduce the minds of children, create doubt in them, or over-emphasize only one facet of man's existence.   K B J

6. Religion

   a. The child should be introduced to the prophets, possibly in high school.   K B J

   b. The elementary school child should have no formal introduction to theology or the fate of the prophetic voice.   K   S

7. Literature is an important subject.   K   S

8. It is beneficial to develop an appreciation of poetry.   K   J S

9. Anthropology is necessary for understanding man's civilization.   J

10. The national language is important to learn, semantics would be emphasized.   J S

11. Fine arts should be studied.   J S

12. In the high school and adult school curriculum the events of the Axial period would be stressed — 800 B.C.-200 B.C.   J

13. Classical education is inadequate.   K

14. The student must be involved with the curriculum.   B   S

15. Physical fitness is important.   J

The curriculum that the existentialists favor depends entirely upon the maturation of the student. Generally speaking, the existentialists appear to break down human growth and development into four stages. The older one is, the more he will be challenged to assume responsibility, not only for what he is doing, but the influence his actions have on others. The older the person is the more the existentialists will guide him into an awareness of ultimate situations, especially that of death. The older one is, the more deeply he will be encouraged to delve into philosophical considerations about the meaning of life. The basic characteristics of the existential curriculum are attuned with those recommended by humanistic philosophers. Jaspers states forthrightly that the humanities provide an educational curriculum which will not permit poor teachers to do too much damage to the child's developing abilities. Spier has also noted that the existential concept of personality is in attunement with the humanistic approach.

The existentialists are in agreement that history should be a basic subject in the curriculum. The important task in teaching history is not to allow a student merely to analyze a past situation. The historical situation must be brought to bear on the immediate situation of the student. The teacher must make it clear to the student how the present situation has been influenced by past situations. The teacher must also help the child to realize that the past situation itself is constantly re-interpreted according to the needs of the present moment. Therefore there is no absolute historical knowledge or for that matter, any other type of knowledge. Historical knowledge must continually be reconstructed to meet the present needs.

All but Kierkegaard stress the need for developing the child's philosophical outlook throughout his education. Children are natural philosophers according to these men and their natural ability ought to be encouraged. Buber especially emphasizes how the thought systems of Nietzsche and Kierkegaard helped him to bridge an important crisis during his adolescence.

All but Kierkegaard are in favor of teaching science so that children will learn how the universe may be manipulated. All but Sartre express their concern that science might seduce the child's mind and cause him to be too analytical, or too imbued with doubt. Under no circumstance should science be taught in a cold, dispassionate way. It must never be divorced from the subjective ability of the person.

Buber and Jaspers would make the more mature person aware of the Biblical prophets as would Kierkegaard. Kierkegaard and Sartre would not introduce any theological education to young children. One definitely gains the impression that all four men are opposed to the introduction of doctrinaire theology at any age level of the person. The main place that religion has in the curriculum is in the context of history courses. The Judaic-Christian heritage especially must be presented to the student because so much of the present day social structure is related to this heritage. The Bible ought to be introduced through literature courses to the adolescent.

Kierkegaard and Sartre especially stress the importance of a person being introduced to literature. All four men have obviously studied world literature with great diligence. In order to understand their writings alone, a knowledge of literature is most vital. In literature one might examine what men dream they might be capable of doing. In a way literature provides man with a test-tube situation. He can analyze a fraction of man's problems while not actually becoming engrossed in the real situation. In the great novels and plays can be studied the authentic type of men and women as well as those who do not realize their full potentials. Furthermore the general public is more interested in literature than philosophy. As a result three of the four men have utilized novels or plays to bring to the general public their philosophical points of view.

Poetry as well as literature is drawn upon extensively by Kierkegaard, Jaspers and Sartre. Jaspers suggests that the teacher ought to be poetic himself. Certainly poetry provides an incalculable tool for introducing the child to his subjective self.

Jaspers and Sartre agree that fine arts help the maturing mind to realize a stage of integration and harmony. Sartre cogently points out that one's interest in aesthetics is directly correlated with each maturational period. Jaspers would encourage the student to study the art forms of the axial period, especially as they are found in ancient Greece.

The effective use of language is especially important to man as he attempts to come to terms with his universe. It is through language that one gains an idea of what man is capable of being. It is through language that a person learns about himself through the concepts others have of himself. In order to express oneself fluently and accurately, one must have mastered language. When one reads the philosophy of an existentialist, or hears him present his material, much will be unintelligible without an understanding of his basic vocabulary. Much of his effort will be to define the terms which he is utilizing. For example, terms such as I-Thou, being-in-itself and being-for-itself, the transcendence, the individual, the authentic man, the I-it have specialized meanings which must be learned. Semantics and much attention to the meaning of language would be included in the curriculum at every level.

Jaspers even insists that the physical body must be fit for one to develop into authenticity. Kierkegaard complains that he was physically weak and that this detracted from his creative ability. One might expect therefore some support for a comprehensive physical education program throughout the school system.

Whatever the curriculum includes, the educational authority must not merely bring the subject matter before the mind of the student and permit him to be a spectator of the learning process. The student must be challenged to become active and an interested participant in the educational endeavor.

VI. The qualifications of the teacher — a major
existential concern.

1. The teacher should be a leader, and one who will guide the student as far as possible. He will then point the way to new heights. K B J S

2. The teacher should be an individual who is honest, intelligent and has integrity. K B J S

3. It is necessary to carefully select teachers.

K B J S

4. The teacher should be treated with respect by the students. Some tension should exist between the teacher and student.

K B J

5. There should be no melancholy teachers.

K B J

6. The teacher should be prepared to do more than teach — she should be interested in the whole student. She is to be a friend.

K B J

7. The teacher should help the student escape from bad faith.

K   J S

8. The teacher's disposition should be loving.

K B J

9. The teacher has tremendous influence on the student.

K B J S

10. Because the teacher chose to influence children she has a greater responsibility than do the parents of the children.

K   S

11. The teacher must be capable of learning, self-improvement and actively engaging in social reconstruction.

K B J

12. The teacher must be able to withstand critical examinations of himself by his students.

K B J

13. The teaching process requires the entire being of the teacher; he must launch himself fully and without reserve into the moment of teaching.

K B J

14. The teacher does not seek disciples.

K B   S

299

15. The teacher must choose to be a teacher. She must not become a teacher merely because it is a path of least resistance or because of external inducements such as parental pressure or salary expectations.   K B   S

16. The teacher must not descend permanently to the students' level. He must not always be a 'pal' to the students.   K   S

17. The teacher must avoid permitting the students to objectify him or to define him solely as a teacher; likewise he must resist the temptation to consider himself nothing but a teacher.   B   S

18. The teacher should invite a close relationship between the student and himself, but not demand it. He should have the capacity for intimacy.   B

19. The teacher should not be burdened with administrative details.   K

20. How authentic the teacher must be is qualified only by the grade level he is teaching.   K B J S

21. The humanist curriculum guards against poor teachers.   J

Much of the existential emphasis and influence in education will be in the direction of determining who should be a teacher. Perhaps no other philosophical point of view would stress more the influence of the teacher upon the maturation of the child than the existentialists. In proclaiming the importance of the teacher this group would be allied with current emphases in psychology.

In the first place, existentialists would want the teacher to be selected with great care and responsibility. One must select omeone not merely because he is well equipped in terms of his subject. Only those who have chosen the teaching profession for sound reasons should be considered. One must seek the person who will be willing to assume personal responsibility for what he does to his children. He must realize that, more than what he teaches, his personality impact will shape much of the child's way of responding to his life situation. While it is true that the child bears ultimate responsibility for what he does, he is dependent upon his parents and teachers. His teachers bring to him selected culture. What the teacher fails to present to the student, the student may never become aware of. The teacher must realize that he is not merely a repeater of his subject specialty but that he is a leader of children; he is their guide into an unknown existence. The children are in the process of becoming which means minimally that they become acquainted with their culture. The guide must know how to present the material interestingly. He must know what is important to point out. What possibly is more consequential, he must teach the children to become independent of him so that as they mature they will need his services less and less. The teacher must often only point the way to the child, and then encourage the child to assume personal responsibility for what happens to him beyond the guidance of the teacher. As a teacher, however, it is his task to see that the students do not become discouraged, that they do not have to face the trials of life before they are ready.

In the personality of the teacher, one must search for sincerity, responsibility, honesty and intelligence for the teacher's personality will have an impact on the children. The teacher must at least approach authenticity to qualify for the profession. Kierkegaard might permit a teacher who is matured ethically to guide elementary school children who exist on the aesthetic level, but by the time the student has reached high school he will require a more authentic person. Kierkegaard, Buber and Jaspers emphasize that at no grade level ought one be allowed to teach who is caught in the throes of melancholy. The elementary teacher especially must be a cheerful soul. This light-hearted attitude must not be confused with irresponsibility. It has already been indicated that the teacher is not hired merely to transfer subject matter to the brains of children. He is responsible for the molding of their situation. He is to penetrate every irregularity of their thinking which he suspects, and expose same to the student. Great value is placed on the teacher encouraging honesty in the child. Underneath his sense of responsibility, the teacher must have a loving disposition. Kierkegaard, Jaspers and Buber emphasize that only when a person feels himself loved does he recognize his potential worth as a real person, and thus is capable of discarding any cloaks he may have thrown over his personality to impress others, as well as himself.

The teacher must not be a stern personality who weights his class down with much authority. He must have the knack that encourages young people to think, to become critical. As his young people develop a critical nature, as they become more and more aware of reality, the teacher can expect them to ask him more and more penetrating questions which he must be equipped to answer. The teacher must relish this form of challenge. He must also have ego-integrity so as to permit critical examination of himself by his students. Kierkegaard and Sartre both advise against the teacher's becoming an equal with the students — a 'pal'. Kierkegaard suggests that there must be some creative tension between the student and the teacher in order for the student to do his best in the learning situation. Along this line of thought, all but Jaspers emphasize that the teacher must not seek disciples who will replicate her thought. Even Jaspers has avoided too much systematization so that others will be unable to copy his thought.

If the teacher must penetrate the child's irregular thinking, withstand his critical examinations, foster the child's worth by his loving disposition, present material in order to bring culture to the child, guide him in the interpretation of the learning process and then point the way for him, it becomes obvious that the teacher must be wholly committed to the teaching profession, and be fully engaged in the teaching situation. He cannot be mouthing his lessons thinking about what he will do when he returns home, about a salary raise, or about the development of his own research interests. Only Sartre, who does not concern himself at all with the personality of the teacher, fails to make this point strongly.

Buber clearly states the importance of the teacher fostering an intimate relationship with his pupil. While the others have not expressed this view per se, it becomes obvious that for the teacher to come to know the students and to penetrate irregularities in their thinking, he must have a close relationship with them. Kierkegaard adds that the teacher must also have a private sanctuary where he can retreat and recoup his strength in quiet meditation.

Finally, one hundred years ago Kierkegaard stated explicitly that one can not be an effective teacher if he is burdened by too many administrative responsibilities.

VII. An examination of good teaching techniques.

1. The teaching techniques should conform to the child's level of ability to learn.   K   B   J   S

2. The teacher is the guide, the one whose attitude is that of, "Follow-me as far as I can take you," and who will then point the way.   K   B   J   S

3. Teaching requires considerable flexibility and spontaneity. No single techniques.   K   B   J   S

4. The teacher should encourage the child's spontaneity and enjoyment of life.   K   B   J   S

5. Learning requires much more than memorization; the teacher must stress the 'how' in the learning situation.   K   B   J

6. Learning is accomplished by doing, action, and applying the lesson material.   K   B   J   S

7. The teaching technique must exclude presenting artificial problems to the child.   K   J   S

8. The teacher should be non-authoritarian.   K   J   S

9. The Socratic approach is desirable in those situations where the student already possesses the needed knowledge.   K   J   S

10. The child must not be permitted to be too smug and self-satisfied for effective learning to take place.   K   J   S

11. There must be no artificial conformity in the class room, only that which is necessary for community spirit.   B   J   S

12. Audio-visual aids are useful.   K   B

13. The child must never be an object to be manipulated, nor is he the end of the education goal.   K   S

14. The child must be encouraged to assume responsibility for what he does whenever possible.   K   B   J   S

15. The child must be stimulated to participate fully in the learning situation. If he has needs which distract his attention they must be taken care of (for instance diet deficiency or medical problem).   K   B   S

16. The child must always be treated with respect and honesty.   K   B.

Not only have the existentialists been concerned about the personality of the teacher, but they have also taken time to indicate what some of the actual teaching techniques ought to be. In fact, these men may be in more agreement over the teaching techniques than any other aspect of the educational endeavor.

The teacher must act as a guide, but the implications of being a guide are manifold. In the first place one must be willing to travel at the speed of the initiate. The teacher must not demand more of the student than he can perform. The teacher must study the child with whatever techniques are at his disposal to learn how well equipped the child is for the learning voyage. A good guide does not fill the neophyte with tales of horror about what he might encounter on his trip, but rather helps him surmount problems as they arise. Of course, the good guide will not lead his charge into inescapable situations.

The teacher must be an individual who is the polar opposite of a rigid personality. Or to use Carl Rogers' suggestion, he must be a well-integrated person. He will take advantage of any situation to clarify the situation or to foster the child's acculturation. He will be very flexible and know how to utilize many methods of instruction. He will not unyieldingly adhere to an approach merely because it has worked with another group at another time. He, himself, is constantly in search of new techniques which will aid the students not only to learn more about the subject matter, but also to become better acquainted with themselves.

The teacher will use those techniques of teaching which stimulate the child to solve problems for himself, and to become actively interested in the curriculum. As previously stated, the existentialists are interested in commitment and action more than merely sopping up memorizable material. The teacher will also constantly be challenging the student to re-interpret what he is learning, and to apply what he is learning to his own situation. Under no circumstance will the teacher present materials which cannot in some way or other be tied into an interpretation of how the event influences the present situation. The teacher will continually be fostering a reconstruction of experience in the student, and will also be in the process of reconstructing his own experience.

The teacher will structure the school community experience

in such a way as to bring to bear as much awareness as possible that the classroom atmosphere is the responsibility of each child. Children will be encouraged to assume definite responsibility for the functioning of their class. As a matter of emphasis the teacher will show the student how a decision he arrived at and acted upon yesterday has furthered or hindered his cause today. However the teacher will not moralize, nor will he foster this feeling of responsibility in the child who is young enough to be in reality dependent on others.

The child will never be made to feel the brunt of responsibilities when he can not handle the tasks. Nor will the child be encouraged to tackle problems in the classroom which he cannot hope to solve. Nothing will be done to discourage the child when he truly is attempting to master his situation. If, on the other hand, the child is self-satisfied, complacent or smug, if he appears 'fixated' at a certain level and is refusing to grow up, then it is the teacher's responsibility to blast him from his lethargy, and to shame him from passively accepting the status quo. While the teacher will never press the child into responsibilities which are grown-up in nature, he will also not tolerate a clinging to the past. The child will always be encouraged to grow and mature, both physiologically and psychologically.

Any methodology approved of by these existentialists will involve permissiveness. The teacher should not be a stern authoritarian handing down material to a group of children who are to obey instantly or to memorize it promptly. He is not a demanding person except in the situation described in the preceding paragraph. He has confidence in the child's desire to grow, and to become spontaneously. He has faith and trust in the child's willingness to learn if he structures the learning situation in such a way that his 'look' is of an encouraging, positive nature.

The one thing which the teacher will seek to avoid is conformity. He will utilize no technique which involves the student merely applying a rubber stamp. He does not strive to produce assembly-line uniformity. He wants his students to be what they can be, to learn what they can learn, to express what they can express.

The student is never an end in himself. He is not an object to be manipulated by the teacher, but is a real person who desires to encounter a teacher, and to cooperate with that teacher. Basically, the child is an ally of the teacher because he wants to go beyond himself; he wants to be that which he is not, and he knows that by being educated he will become what he is not.

Chapter VI

SUMMARY AND CONCLUSIONS

> Granted that we cannot do anything
> with philosophy, might not philosophy,
> if we concern ourselves with it, do
> something with us?

> Martin Heidegger[1]

Re-statement of the Problem of This Study

John Dewey, as previously cited, has written that "if a theory makes no difference in educational endeavor, it must be artificial." Essentially, the problem of this thesis was to discern in what ways existentialism might make a difference in educational endeavor so as to aid man to overcome the crisis of the twentieth century.

The hypotheses of the study were threefold:

1. Each existential writer being considered has a concept of the individual, the nature of his existence and the purpose of his existence. This concept is expressed with some consistency in his basic writings.

2. The concept of the individual has definite implications for developing an educational philosophy which could make a difference in the educational endeavor.

3. As each of the concepts of the individual is developed from the viewpoint of the men under study, it will be found

that they and the educational implications derived from
them are in essential agreement. This essential agreement
provides a framework for the development of an existential
philosophy of education.

The Findings of the Study

The result of the collation, analysis and evaluation of the pre
ceding material confirms the first hypothesis of this study. Each
of the existentialists who was discussed does have a concept of
the individual, the nature of his existence and the purpose of his
existence. Although they are not always specific about their
concepts of the authentic individual, they present enough ma
terial for one to build an adequate concept of authenticity.
Furthermore, no major inconsistencies were discerned in their
individual writings, even though they, as individuals, have writ
ten over an extended period of years.

As reported in the fourth chapter, the second hypothesis was
also confirmed. From the concepts of the individual as well as
from the general discussions of each of these existentialists de
finite implications for the building of a framework for an exis
tential educational philosophy were discerned. It was, however
noted throughout the study, that the authentic existence which
existentialists demand for adults is not as rigorously sought after
for children.

The third hypothesis is also acceptable on the basis of the
evidence provided in chapter five. In this chapter a series of one
hundred and seventy-six statements were made all of which
related to the existentialists' concept of the individual, the nature
of his existence and the purpose of his existence. All four of the
existentialists have either directly stated or indirectly implied
that they agree with thirty-seven percent of the statements, and
three of the four men agree with another thirty-three percent
of the statements. Very seldom does it become evident that the
four men disagree about any of the listed subjects. When dis
agreement is registered it usually pertains to the theological dif
ference among the four men as three of the group are theistically

nclined while the fourth tends towards an atheistic position.

The educational outlook of the existential thinkers was compared on the basis of one hundred nineteen statements which
pertain to the educational endeavor. The four existentialists
adhere to thirty-one percent of the statements and three out of
four agree with another forty-three percent of the statements.
There is practically no statement upon which any one of the
existentialists vehemently disagrees. When the existentialist is
not listed as agreeing with a statement it usually means that he
has not been interested in that idea and has not expressed himself about the subject in such a way that his position can be
objectively stated.

The Conclusions of the Study.
Authentic existence

The first conclusion of this study is that there are traits of
authentic becoming which are inherent in existential thinking.
The word 'becoming' is very important, for the existentialists
agree that an individual does not attain the authentic stage in
gigantic, once and forever, leap. No one is permanently authentic; everyone tends to hide himself in bad faith even as he
tries to obtain authenticity. While authenticity may be achieved
by everyone for a limited period of time, he soon finds himself
slipping out of the stage. However, the more one makes the
effort to be authentic the more one finds it possible to choose
continually the authentic existence in a series of definite choices.

The primary requisite of authentic becoming is the full realization on the part of the person that he is a free agent capable of
choosing the path in life he is to trod. Although existentialists
admit that man finds himself limited, not only by his finite condition, but also by the factual world which surrounds him, the
authentic man realizes that the factual world provides the raw
materials from which he is to create for himself his situation in
the present moment. Man molds the materials which are at his
disposal. He chooses what to do with the world which encompasses him. Not only must the person realize that it is up

to him to take the materials of his environment and his life an
mold them into something which is significant, but he mus
realize that he will be nothing more than what he does with h
environment. Man must develop a sense of responsibility if h
is to obtain authenticity. Man is responsible to himself — or pe
haps better — man is responsible to the man he shall be as h
molds the materials at hand into a future situation.

In that man's factual existence also includes the existence c
others, man soon realizes that he must become responsible fc
them too if he is to be authentic. What he chooses to do with h
life influences what facticity these other people will be co
fronted with, for in truth he is a fact to them. They then tak
this fact and react to it, and mold it into something which
meaningful to them. What they become as a result of the
efforts in their situation then becomes an additional ingredie
in the authentic man's environment, and thus he is again respo
sible to himself for how he has presented himself in the ey
of others so as to influence them, which in turn enables them t
influence him. Man is concerned about others, not necessaril
for altruistic reasons, but because his existence is involved in th
existence of others.

The authentic man, who is aware of his freedom of choice, an
his responsibility to himself and for his behavior towards other
is a man of action. No one who is responsible can merely perm
things to happen. He wants to be at the heart of precipitatin
events. The authentic man is continually active, not only as h
structures his environment, but also as he reconstructs his pa
situations in the light of his present awareness and his futur
expectations.

The authentic man must function as a coherent unity. H
must know himself, he must penetrate every irregularity in h
life with the desire to understand how this force operates o
him so that he can choose to use the force himself. In the effo
to understand himself the authentic man is not opposed to see
ing the counsel and the wisdom of other people — both his frienc
as well as his enemies — so that he can obtain their reactions t
him. It is difficult for man to be an object to himself, for ma

is subjectivity. However, he can see the objectivity of others, and he can discern how others interpret him and thus he gains valuable insight into himself as he is seen by others.

The authentic man is never satisfied with his present situation. He is constantly transcending his present and passing over into the future moment. He is constantly in the process of not being what he is and of becoming what he is not. This transcendence according to Kierkegaard, Buber and Jaspers will eventually lead the individual into the presence of God. However, once the idea of a transcendent force is accepted, this does not mean that the individual ought to surrender his authority to God. As a matter of fact, God is not a particularly active force in man's affairs in the twentieth century. To Sartre, God does not exist and the transcending ability of man leads only to nothingness.

The main attributes of authenticity are thus defined:

1. Man has the freedom to influence his situation. He does exist in a factual world, but he is capable of molding the real objects of his situation into a new constellation of being.

2. In that man is always in the process of becoming, and in that he can influence what he is becoming, man is able to develop a feeling of responsibility. The authentic man assumes responsibility for what he does. The responsibility of the authentic man is to himself.

3. Man must actively engage his universe. He is in the process of sustained becoming. He must constantly involve himself in reconstructing his being in accord with his factual situation and his future anticipations.

4. The authentic person who accepts his responsibility for altering the universe, knows that he must know himself. He must not permit any avenue of his talent to lie unused in the process of self-actualization. He furthermore must

not permit any irregularity in his thinking to blind his perception of reality.

5. The authentic man realizes that he can never continue to be what he is; he is in the process of becoming. He knows that he will be what he is not. At least three of the existentialists insist that as man transcends himself he must eventually become aware that a force superior to himself makes the transcendence possible. Man cannot be an unmotivated transcending force.

From the main attributes of the authentic person other characteristics may be derived. These secondary attributes are in no way of less importance than the five primary ones in terms of their influence in the life of the person. To a degree they assume a functional autonomy once they have come into being.

Because man is never sure of his future, he lives in an existential anxiety. The existential anxiety is not a form of neurosis, and has been best described by Paul Tillich in his book, *The Courage to Be.*[2] The authentic person is aware that he is molding his situation so as to be someone new in the future. He realizes that he is to be what he is not now. What he does not know is just how meaningful his work in the present will be for the self he will become in the future. In the first place he may find that he will not like the self he will be. He may make wrong appraisals of his current situation which will leave him in a crisis on the next day. The term 'wrong' applies to how the person views his situation at the time. Actually, in an ethical sense there is no 'wrong' for the individual, because he cannot know what different decisions might have precipitated. As stated before, he knows that he is responsible for what he is going to be, unless, death cuts off his life. At the point of death man becomes responsible for how he chooses to die. After death the meaning of man's life becomes the responsibility of his survivors. Yet, many men do not like responsibility. They prefer to pass the buck, to blame someone else and not to recognize the existential quality of their lives. Many prefer to surrender their responsibility to some political or religious authority, to some

314

psychical determinism or other cause-effect explanation. Still others search for inherent truth in the universe and seek to find an ordered hierarchy of value by which their decisions might be made. Man is on edge because he knows he is responsible for what he will make of himself. Furthermore, man is aware that he is finite, that he cannot truly evaluate the situation as well as he would like. He knows that actually he cannot develop a safe criteria for action, and as a result is thrown on his own personal resources to make a decision which shall direct his activity. He must advance into the unknown, into an uncertain future. His decisions will be untried and without real authority until they have been put into action and man has committed himself. Man's experience with the unknown has too often produced pain for his organism for him to be relaxed as he faces the ordeal. Nevertheless man must not cling to the known; he must meet the unknown. This he does in anguish. Thus one might describe the authentic individual as being one who is not cool, calm, and collected. He is anguished. This anguish, man must learn to master and he must choose to live with it. Anguish must be a part of man's facticity which he will utilize as he constructs for himself a new moment — his next situation.

Throughout the discussion of authenticity the theme that man is oriented towards his present situation is constantly implied. Man participates fully in the present. However, man does not live exclusively in the present. He realizes if he is authentic, that his past, as a factual part of his being-in-itself, abides as an influential force which must be reckoned with. He also knows that the future is waiting for him. The nearer the future, the more capable man is of determining its influence on his decision. The authentic man blends the past, the future, and the present into a real moment which transcends normative time.

As a person becomes authentic, he realizes that he has worth. His choices alone are helping to shape the destiny of mankind. As the authentic person becomes aware of the transcendent he comes to know the love and acceptance of God, and if God loves and accepts man, it follows that man must have worth. The person is also shown that he has worth as he experiences the

315

loving-tender-care of his parents and of his teachers. Once man is able to perceive himself as having worth, and as being lovable, he becomes capable of loving others. Love is the polar opposite of defensiveness and insecurity. As the authentic person becomes aware of the factual existence of others, he comes to be concerned about them and because he knows they also share in the Transcendence he knows that they are worthy of his love. The authentic man is open to the needs of his fellowman and he seeks a positive relationship with him. Although Sartre rejects the concept of God, and discerns the other person as being much too threatening to the individual for him to be relaxed, he also insists that there must be a positive relationship among people. To Sartre, man needs the collective security of a community in order to realize his freedom maximumly. He also needs the other to come and to define who he is, so that subjective man may evaluate his objectivity through the other's eyes.

As a result of man's coming to know himself as being derived from God (Jaspers, Kierkegaard and Buber), or merely as coming into being for some unexplained reason (Sartre), there arises the concept that he shares equality with all men. There is not even a natural aristocracy among the existentialists (save possibly Kierkegaard's political outlook) which would suggest that the authentic man is a superior person. Authenticity by no means implies that the individual is superior, nor has he been selected by God to obtain his exalted position. As a matter of fact, all men are capable of becoming authentic even though only a few will realize authentic existence. Authenticity involves no authoritarianism. While it is the choice of the authentic person to challenge other men to rise from their lethargy, while the existentialists attempt to shake men and use the tragedies of the age to show mankind that there are no secure havens of thought, they do not demand that all mankind become authentic. They cherish the hope that all mankind will someday become authentic, but they will not attempt to force the decision. Each individual must decide for himself to become authentic — all the existentialist can do is to challenge the person and to stimulate his thinking.

The derived implications of existential thought for the development of an authentic person are listed as follows:

1. Man is anguish. He must accept the anguish and not try to hide from it.

2. Authentic man is above a time dichotomy for he abides in a combination of the present, past and future. His orientation, however, tends to be in the immediate present which as yet has not become past.

3. The authentic personality radiates love. Persons who meet an authentic man may know his presence by his ability to open himself to his neighbor, to be concerned about his enemy, and to be fully interested in the situation which involves meeting another person.

4. The authentic person believes in the equality of all men. There is no disposition to lord it over one's fellow beings. It may be that their integrity forces them into the role of leadership, but they do not seek leadership per se. Their integrity also may earn for them a martyr's role because they will not conform to the will of the mass, nor of individuals who have authority unless they choose to assume the responsibility for the act by their conforming.

5. The authentic personality does not demand that others duplicate his type of existence for each man is confronted by a different combination of circumstances. The authentic man realizes that he must first be concerned about the beam that is in his own eye before he becomes too concerned about the mote that is in another's eye. Yet, because the authentic man is concerned about his fellowman, he does seek to challenge him to penetrate his personal existence a little more thoughtfully.

As Rollo May states, the existentialists agree that man is in a state of crisis.[3] It is undoubtedly true, as some have alleged, that existentialists have used the catastrophes of the twentieth century to further their point of view. They would be the first to agree with their adversary D.J.B. Hawkins that as the crises of the twentieth century fade away, the existential doctrines will become more obscure.[4] However, where they disagree with Hawkins is on the reason for the potential demise of existentialism. Will it be because man will have found his authentic self, or because he will have tranquillized himself into a state of repose and is unable to realize authentic existence? The existentialists would answer the latter, and as a result, they will try to make the most of the catastrophic twentieth century to encourage man to taste of authenticity — to choose to take command of himself. If it were possible they would even be willing to keep the wounds of the century opened so that they would not prematurely close. However, even though they stress the meaning of crisis for the production of authenticity, they are thinking only of the mature person. It is the farthest thing from their minds to foster crisis in the life of children.

Kierkegaard and Jaspers have explicitly emphasized, and Buber implicitly, that the authentic person is necessary for humanity to survive as such. It is interesting to note that Carl Rogers, as a result of clinical experience and with no preknowledge of the existentialists, has come to the same opinion. Rogers advocates the need of creative people in our age. His description of the creative person summarizes quite effectively the qualities of the authentic person. To Rogers, a creative person is one who may be characterized as follows:

1. He is open to his experience. "In a person who is open to experience each stimulus is freely relayed through the nervous system, without being distorted by any process of defensiveness. ... The individual is aware of this existential moment as it *is*, thus being alive to many experiences which fall outside the usual categories. ... It means lack of rigidity and permeability of boundaries in concepts, beliefs, perceptions and hypotheses. It means a tolerance for ambiguity where ambiguity exists. It means the ability to receive

much conflicting information without forcing closure upon the situation.

"... The more the individual has available to himself a sensitive awareness of all phases of his experience the more sure we can be that his creativity will be personally and socially constructive."

2. He has an internal locus of evaluation.

"It is simply that the basis of evaluation lies within himself. If to the person it has 'feel' of being 'me in action', or being an actualization of potentialities in himself which hithertofore have not existed and are now emerging into existence, then it is satisfying and creative, and no outside evaluation can change that fundamental fact."[5]

Thus the authentic person is given a comprehensive basis for making decisions which assumes that everything which the individual is aware of is taken into consideration. Assuming the decisions are made from this orientation, then little more can be expected of the individual as he attempts to wrestle with his own situation and the situation of his world.

If authentic individuals are able to stimulate humanity to rise to a new height of honest existence, it becomes challenging to search for the type of educational program which will at least not tarnish man to the point that his encrustment seriously interferes with his choosing to be authentic. The educational system which will aid man in his attempt to be authentic is the educational system which must be fostered by a society of persons who would like to be authentic.

It is difficult to develop the educational position of the existentialists, not only because they have not concerned themselves specifically with this problem, but also because when they do express an opinion on education it often seemingly is diametrically opposed to their philosophical writing. The education of children is not an education of crisis or for crisis. In fact, the major goal of the education of children is to not burden their young hearts with an awareness of the tragic situation in which the

319

twentieth century is enmeshed. Although the existentialists do not so state explicitly, there is an implicit assumption on their part that if the experiences of the child are pleasant, yet stimulating, his growth towards authenticity will at least not be impeded.

The Educational Program for Children

The elementary school atmosphere must be one which develops in the child a feeling of confidence and trust in the learning experience. At all times the child should be treated with the utmost honesty by the teachers and the school administrators. His personality should be respected and his questions should be honored with answers which penetrate to the point of the child's problem. The countenance of the educational situation must be one of loving concern. The student must feel that his teachers are interested in him and that they consider him to be a person of worth. It is important that the school atmosphere be one which maximumly stimulates the spontaneity of the child, and encourages him to express himself openly and without fear of intimidation. The entire orientation of the educational program should permit the child to enjoy himself while he is at school. No artificial problems or tensions should be introduced into the child's life which would diminish the joys that are rightfully his during the innocency of childhood. This would include not only the way the teachers respond to the student, it also would include the services of the school, for example, a hot lunch program to guarantee that no child is hungry, and a medical program.

Nevertheless the school situation is factually an educational one. The child is not in school merely to play, nor do the existentialists assume that the child wants to play in school. One of the main purposes of the school is to transmit culture. The school provides an atmosphere for the child's inquiring spirit to grow and to find some answers to the problems he is pondering. The atmosphere of the school must maximize the child's critical abilities and stimulate the development of his reasoning capabilities. The school definitely should foster a program of rational learning.

The teacher on the elementary level is a very important person for the development of the child's outlook on life. The child, who is entirely a subject to himself, is able to gain an impression of himself by observing the reactions of others towards him. Children come to school primarily with an interpretation of themselves which has been given to them by their parents. The teacher is one of the first persons who is capable of fostering in the child a feeling of worth, if that feeling has not already been established by the parents. In that the teacher's way of reacting to the child helps to mold the child's character, the personality of the teacher is of prime consideration in the recruitment for teaching assignments. The teacher must be a person who has a positive orientation towards the child. The teacher must not be steeped in the religious notion that the child is a sinner or is hopelessly inclined to be bad. He must never believe badly of a child, and even if the child proves himself to be bad the teacher must carry the conviction within him that the child is bad only temporarily, and that new decisions will transform the child's personality. It is preferable that the teacher be an authentic person although, as previously discussed, he may qualify if he has considerable ethical integrity and a warm personality. Under any condition the teacher must be a person who is willing to assume complete responsibility for what he does in the educational situation. He must not explain that what he does is precipitated by an educational administration, nor must he conform to the will of a parent-teachers organization nor routinely apply some memorized techniques designed to foster learning in children. The teacher is responsible himself for what he does in his classroom as long as he chooses to remain there. It is also necessary that the teacher have a sound knowledge of human growth and development as much of the teaching technique will depend on the maturational level of the child. The teacher must have an idea of where he is going to begin in the teaching situation, and where he is to begin is where the child currently is in the learning process. The existentialists would advise strongly against employing any teacher who has a melancholy nature or any related negative personality trait. The existentialists emphasize that the child's attitude reflects the teacher's personality.

The existentialists favor instilling in the child a thorough command of the fundamental processes. The existentialists are most aware that one cannot achieve maximum efficiency without acquiring the basic academic skills. The presentation of the fundamental skills must be geared to the child's level of maturation. They do not want the spontaneity of the child spoiled by a series of failures nor do they want the joys of childhood transformed into experiences of discouragement. The existentialists are in complete harmony over this point with Alfred Adler.[6]

The existential curriculum would be child-centered to the degree that it is the responsibility of the teacher to discern the level of the child's ability, and then begin to aid him to reconstruct his experiences from that point. Furthermore, children are to be encouraged to be spontaneous, and to foist upon them a curriculum which is not interesting to them would certainly dampen any feeling of spontaneity.

The existentialists leave the impression that much of the elementary school curriculum would definitely be problem-centered. All of life involves problem solving. The greatest challenge which man faces continuously is to become what he is not. While the existentialists argue that the child should not be presented with problems beyond his level of maturation and should not be given artificial problems which he has no interest in considering, they still insist that the child must be encouraged to develop a methodology for solving problems. By encouraging them to find answers to questions which they are capable of handling, the teacher can also nourish an attitude of responsibility in children. The child becomes responsible for the solutions of his problems. If the child's solutions are normally satisfactory, he builds confidence in his ability to solve problems, to come to definite conclusions, and to act on the basis of his decisions.

The existentialists are markedly opposed to a program which involves spectatoritis. Thus, to an extent one may describe the existentialist curriculum as activity-centered. Learning must not merely involve cortical functioning. Learning experiences must be translated into action — into doing. The student must see how what he is learning is applicable to his life. The equipment of the school, including room space and the teacher load, must be arranged so as to encourage a maximum expression of the child's abilities as he applies his new knowledge. In agreement with John Dewey, the existentialists stand ready to defend their belief that the learning situation involves the active reconstruction of one's own experiences and the society in which one's existence is engaged.[7]

In spite of the tendency of the curriculum which is presented to the student according to his level of maturation, to be child-centered, problem centered and activity-centered the teacher is still responsible for what he teaches and how the material is presented to the child. There is no abdication of teacher responsibility according to the existentialists. The existentialists are not irrationalists, as has been suggested, nor do they favor an irrational curriculum based merely on the whims of the students. The existentialist teacher will constantly use his expertness in helping the child to order his knowledge — to fit his knowledge into an understandable and explainable frame of reference. The application of the child's knowledge to his life situation will not be done in a random way, but will be planned by the teacher with the student's participation so that the relationship between that which is learned and that which is applied is clearly understood.

There is one other point with reference to the curriculum which ought to be stressed. While the existentialists are not in favor of the child's ever becoming discouraged in the educational process they are not opposed to permitting the child to risk himself in problem solving attempts to the point where he actually will fail. Failure is a realistic situation in life and even a child ought not be completely protected from its wrath. Children ought to be encouraged, as previously said, to solve problems. The fact that it is a problem, however, suggests that immediate solutions are not forthcoming and that the student may have to work on it for quite a while before he eventually succeeds in solving it satisfactorily. These failures ought not be frequent, nor ought they arise because of the child's actual inability to solve

323

the problem. It is the teacher's task to encourage the child in an attitude of nothing ventured, nothing gained. It is the teacher's responsibility to guide the child in such a way that he will not become discouraged but rather will try again until a solution to his problem has been reached, or until he willingly decides that he has invested enough time and seeks advice as to how to bring the problem to a satisfactory conclusion.

The final role of the elementary school to be considered here is that it is responsible for fostering some type of social organization. Although Sartre has considerable difficulty with the idea, and Kierkegaard would have some reservations, it appears that the existentialists would favor the classroom which has developed an esprit de corps, or a community feeling, rather than remaining a group of isolated children, or even worse, some type of mob. Thus, the existentialists again would agree with Dewey: the elementary classroom, at least, should be a miniature community. Children should be urged to work together and to learn how to share experiences with each other. Kierkegaard, Buber and Jaspers would strip the situation of any real need for competition. Communication between the children would be emphasized so that they could find out how they are being interpreted by each other and so that they can receive encouragement and help as they solve problems of mutual interest. In addition, the teacher would take pains to show the child how the group is influenced by the action of one or more children. Under no circumstances should the group be used as a leverage to encourage the child to cooperate or to conform. Furthermore, the children must be made to feel individually responsible for what the group does, and they should never be given the idea that the group is superior to themselves as individuals, or that the group absolves them from being responsible for what they have done in cooperation with the group.

The Educational Program for Youth

The existentialist concept of youth corresponds to an age range from ten to thirteen. Everything which applies to the education

324

of children also applies to the education of youth. However, youth are capable of tremendous insight into man's affairs, and as a result often become worried about problems which are beyond their comprehension. The teacher must be alert for signs of this type of problem. Buber thinks that youth involves a period of transition during which the person leaves his carefree childhood and begins to assume the responsibilities of adulthood. Kierkegaard is not as extreme as Buber for he states that youth is a period which involves one in song and dance, and one is still blissfully unaware of the oncoming seriousness of adult life. The existentialists are not interested in precipitating a tragic awareness in the youth's life, but if it comes teachers must be prepared to bolster him so that he will not be overwhelmed with dread of the future. The problem for the educational authorities is simply that the youth still is highly dependent on others, and is hardly capable of sustaining action to effectively combat any crisis which he may become aware of and, indeed, possibly have experience with. It is the task of the teacher to help encourage the youth who is unable to meet the problems of his day to accept the fact that he is immature, but at the same time to encourage him to put himself into the position to learn what might be done about the problem. This is an appropriate time for the child to undertake a comprehensive study of the lives of great men and how these men sought to meet their problems. Mythology would also be explored during this period. The fundamental skills would have already been expanded into a program paralleling the liberal arts. Language arts, social sudies and science would be increasingly stressed. The fine arts also would play a more important part in the curriculum, for as the person matures, his interest in aesthetics becomes more real.

The Educational Program for Adolescence

If everything has developed according to the expectation of existentialists, adolescence will be a turbulent stage. The educational atmosphere previously discussed is still applicable to the adolescent period. The main difference between the education of the child and the education of the adolescent will be in the area of commitment and concern. The child is spontaneously interested in learning. He enjoys his experiences at school. He wants to master the fundamental skills. He is, however, innocent of any realization of the problems of the age. The adolescent, on the other hand, is no longer blissfully unaware of how the future beckons him and of the crises which he faces. The adolescent is capable of committing himself to the educational program which realistically prepares him maximumly for mature responsibility. The crisis awareness has not been forced on him by educators, nor have educators sought to prevent him from realizing the turbulence which awaits him. The education is not focused on the making of a future adult in the sense that the teachers have decided that this is what the adolescent must prepare for. The adolescent himself is aware of the problems at hand. His preparation for tomorrow is a problem which confronts him in the now. Therefore the curriculum for adolescents is still problem-centered and student-centered in at least a limited sense. Currently, the educational authorities are increasing the learning pace, not because they are conspiring against the teenager but because the teenager is demanding more.

By high school the process of transmitting the culture is fully underway as well as the introduction of the young person to the political system of his nation. The curriculum is basically one which involves the seven liberal arts. Considerable emphasis is placed on a historical understanding of what has transpired to produce the problems of the current hour. All learning is related to the needs of the current hour, and the teenager is expected to understand what is being taught rather than merely being encouraged to memorize a mass of data. The emphasis is on social reconstruction. The material of yesteryear is constantly being set against the needs of the moment, and the positive applications of its teaching are being extracted. The student continues to broaden his ability in the language arts. He develops his debating skills as well as his rhetoric. Much attention is paid to semantics and the meaning of the words the student uses. The teachers are constantly encouraging him to try out his ideas in conversation with his peer group as well as with his teachers. Science education is being advanced, for the importance of science in the modern world is a fact with which the young person knows he must deal. A knowledge of science is encouraged if for no other reason than the fact that the technological age may aid man to overcome some of the dilemmas of the age. Philosophy is introduced to the teenager so that he can find a frame of reference, as did the existentialists themselves during their turbulent period. The philosophy however is of a personal mode, rather than abstract speculation. The existentialists are practical people to the degree that they argue that needs which are closest to man must be taken care of first. Somewhere between the teenage period and adulthood the person must be introduced to a knowledge of a vocation. After examining the writings of the existentialists there is little doubt that they would favor a comprehensive program of real vocational education beginning in high school and extending throughout the formative adult years. How much vocational education would depend on the nature of the child, his goals and his ambitions as well as his talents. Excellent vocational guidance services must be offered so that the adolescent will be prepared to assume vocational responsibility upon completion of his education, but care must be taken that the teenager does not take more technical courses than what he needs to develop a knowledge of vocational skills and to develop an actual vocational skill. The existentialists are far more interested in a program of humanities in education than offering an extensive vocational education.

What is most important in the education of the adolescent is the fact that the teacher will be charged with the responsibility of studying each student to learn his strengths and his weaknesses, so that he may bolster him during times of crises. It is necessary for the teacher at this time to hasten the process of penetrating the irregularities in the thinking of the adolescent for the purpose of encouraging him to know himself fully. If the teacher finds the teenager clinging to a juvenile stage he will attempt to stimulate him to assume responsibility for himself.

With science education comes the increasing possibility that the adolescent will retreat into a world of reflection and doubt.

It is important that the teacher discourage the adolescent's developing an attitude of doubt and of his developing only an intellectual evaluation of the situation. Constantly the teacher will encourage him to evaluate his situation subjectively and always will the teacher encourage him to be involved in the situation. The teacher will argue as strongly as possible against any attempt on the part of the teenager to rationalize his behavior by a concept of cause-effect or to excuse himself on the grounds that he is yielding to social pressure. Under no circumstances will the teacher condone the student's premature closures. The teacher will constantly encourage the adolescent to accept ambiguities, where such are really present, or to use an existential term of Marcel's, the mysteries of life.

Finally, the teacher will steadfastly press the adolescent to assume full responsibility for what he is doing. He will be encouraged to evaluate situations, and then encouraged to come to decisions, and finally to actualize the decisions in concrete action.

The Educational Program for Adults

The existentialists agree with Harry Stack Sullivan that there are very few mature adults, or to use the existential term, authentic individuals. Almost everyone has become tarnished by his education and other aspects of his social situation. Most people are not assuming responsibility for themselves but are trying to shift their responsibility to other agencies. Still others act thoughtlessly in the hope that they may excuse their behavior by stating that they were not thinking. Another group of people reduce their action to bare minimum living in the effort to avoid any crises whatsoever which will call for a decision. The primary aim of adult education, therefore, will be to bring a crisis into the life of the learner. The bad faith of the adult must be unmasked as meaningless and powerless to improve his situation. The adult must be exposed to the reality that there is nothing in the universe that is dependable but his own choice, and even that is in question. The ultimate situation of the adult — death —

will be brought squarely to his attention with the haunting question as to what he is going to do about it.

In philosophical courses the adult will be pushed to the limit of his intellectual endurance. He may be searching for some intellectual security, but the existential teacher will urge him into an awareness that there is no absolute knowledge. The religious man may try to reflect on how he would have aided Christ, but the existentialist educator will mercilessly demand that the individual live his faith, risk himself in missionary activity right now, and cease reflecting on the past. If this has no effect, the existentialist would shake his belief that there is a God at all.

Underlying the pressure that the existentialists would place on the adult is the basic assumption that the adult is at all ages educable. The existentialists take it for granted that authenticity is present in the personality, and that if the encrusted self is sufficiently pounded, the authentic personality will eventually emerge.

However, the existentialist will not attempt to give the adult the answers which he seeks once he has become confused. The teachers will make the adult student feel insecure but to give him direction is exactly what they would decline to do. The existentialist would attempt to clarify the adult's thinking by the Socratic approach, but the conclusions the latter comes to as a result of his education must be his own.

Some might object to the above proposals by cynically observing that no one would attend an existential class if they knew they were to be exposed to such a terrifying experience. The existentialists are aware of this and apparently are willing to compromise the issue. They realize that before the individual can be shaken his attention must first be secured. Thus, the courses which would be offered to the adults would be quite suitable to their interests and needs. There would definitely be an adult-centered curriculum. However the teachers of the various courses would constantly be pressuring the student to become more aware of his situation and would constantly be encouraging the student to assume more and more responsibility for himself. It would be the task of each existential teacher, no matter what the course would be, to stimulate in the student a desire to know himself more fully.

The curriculum will be the basic humanities courses plus whatever vocational courses might be needed to enable an individual to improve himself should he choose to become more than what he already is. The curriculum will heavily favor, if enough demand can be stimulated, philosophy and a study of human nature through a study of the great books. The adult will be encouraged to study what man has sought to do, what man is capable of doing, and what shipwreck accompanies much of man's activities. The humanistic curriculum is important to existentialists because "... its peculiar source is not a great philosophy but an attitude toward tradition and learning, an attitude of openness and human freedom, without which our Western life would be impossible."[8]

The Qualifications of a Teacher

The existentialists are quite aware that an educational program is only as good as the teachers, although if there are only inferior teachers available then the humanist curriculum will guard against too many errors. Of first importance is the personality of the teacher. The existentialists demand that he be fully involved in the teaching situation. They would not tolerate individuals whose minds or interests are distracted and who are not completely engaged in the given moment. The teacher is going to have to be conscious fully of the educational process and perceptive of what is going on in the classroom; he must not merely present his material and hear a recital of the lesson. He must listen to his students with a "third ear" so as to be able to foster effectively in them a sense of worth, a feeling of self-acceptance and a feeling that someone is concerned about them. A loving personality on the part of the teacher can do wonders in precipitating an awareness on the part of the child that he is worthy of concern. The child learns of himself through the eyes of his teacher. It is important that the child sees in those eyes respect, confidence and trust. It is the teacher who is responsible for structuring his classroom situation so that it is dependable, relaxed, trustworthy and one which fosters a positive affective tone. It is the teacher who determines whether the child will feel the need to continue chipping off his real self to form an idealized self so as to defend himself against the aggression of the teacher. Under no circumstances should the teacher be inclined towards melancholia, for this attitude penetrates the being of the child and discourages and demoralizes him before he even begins the learning process.

The teacher must be capable of great responsibility. In the first place, the teacher must accept responsibility for his being a teacher. The existentialists would favor no one in the teaching profession who has not chosen to be in the profession at the time of teaching. No one ought to feel that he is compelled by financial reasons, social pressure, or the fact that this is all he can do, to become a teacher. The teacher, in the second place, must realize that he assumes more than normal responsibility for influencing the development of the child. It is acknowledged by the existentialists that whatever one does influences other people. However, one who teaches influences a definite group of people in a definite, more structured way. In the former case an individual influences others as a by-product of what he is choosing to do for himself; in the latter case, the teacher chooses to influence directly the growth and development of ideas, hopes and aspirations in other people. Finally, the teacher must assume responsibility for whatever he is endeavoring to accomplish in the class-room situation. He should never suggest that he is merely carrying out administrative instructions, school board regulations, or is fulfilling the wish of any other person. He may choose to carry out the directives, directives that he himself does not agree with, but when he chooses to do so, he assumes responsibility for the choice and the choice becomes his. The teacher provides an example to the children of the art of handling responsibility. Should the teacher pass responsibility to another person, the children learn that they too may duck responsibility. In that the teacher may have to assume responsibility for an edict of which he does not approve but which does not appear to him to be evil enough to force his resignation, he may find himself a lonely figure as he administers the responsibility.

A teacher must know how to guide and lead the child into the ever enriching subject matter he desires to expose the child to. Not only must the teacher be in command of the subject matter which he chooses to present to the child, he must also know how to stimulate the child's interest and how to make the child realize that mastery of the subject is of vital importance to him. It is, of course, assumed that the teacher will teach only that which he believes is of significance to the student. After the student has learned to trust the teacher he soon learns to feel that whatever the teacher chooses to teach him must be important for his welfare. The existentialists are much more prone to encourage the teacher to be a guide than a leader. They prefer that he be a catalytic agent whose function is to speed the student's learning process, or a mid-wife who helps the student bring to birth new ideas. The teacher will have to prove his expertness in subject areas by withstanding the critical examinations of a motivated class of students. He must revel in their desire to be critical of what he teaches, and he is encouraged when they penetrate his inconsistencies by either rational logic or subjective insight.

It is important for the teacher to have the desire to know his students as fully as possible. The more a teacher knows his students the more capable he will be of tailoring the instructional method to meet their needs and abilities. The more the teacher knows about the students the more he is able to penetrate their irrationalities, and to expose to them their bad faith. The more the teacher knows about his students the more he can understand them. The more he can understand the students the more confidence he can place in their behavior. The more confidence the students feel the more mature their responses to the educational situation will be.

Finally, the teacher must not be in the profession to secure a rubber stamping of his own opinions. He is not teaching merely to hear himself argue his position, or to encourage students to parrot what he says. Not only does he not want disciples, he constantly exposes any student who would be dependent on his thought rather than develop his own individual initiative.

Recommendations

Most of the recommendations which arise from this study are suggested in the two charts which are found in chapter five. Most of the two hundred ninety-five statements could be rephrased into definite recommendations which would have valuable bearing on either the individual's development or on the educational system which might foster the growth of the authentic individual. For the sake of brevity, only the most important recommendations will be suggested in this section.

1. It is recommended that no attempt be made to side-step the crisis of the age by methods which would tranquillize man or would give him some panacea for the problems of the age which would permit him to avoid realizing that he is personally responsible for his situation and that what the future is to hold, he himself is shaping by his current decisions.

2. The existentialists would make every effort to recommend that each person begins an endeavor to know himself, to know himself in his situation and then to assume personal responsibility for what he will make of his situation. Every effort should be made to foster in man a sense of personal responsibility for everything that he does and an awareness that he is free to influence his situation by choices which are his alone to make.

3. Every effort must be made on the part of people who influence children to insure that their childhood period is as care-free as possible and that they have an opportunity to enjoy themselves. Every effort must be made to relieve the child of adultlike worries and responsibilities. If at all possible the child should be spared an awareness of the tragic elements in life which prevail in the world.

4. Educational authorities should make every effort to meet

the needs of the child which are going unmet in his own home. Adequate medical and dental programs should be provided as well as school lunch programs so as to guarantee, to the degree possible, that the child will not suffer the pains of hunger or be ill unnecessarily.

5. It is recommended that the school provide for every child an environment in which he will feel psychologically secure. Under no circumstances should a child be allowed to meet failures in his school work which will eventually precipitate discouragement.

6. It is further recommended that the educational authorities structure the educational experience so that while the child is at school he will experience a miniature community. Every effort should be made to aid the child develop valuable interpersonal relations with other children in an atmosphere of trust and confidence.

7. Existentialists recommend that the child's own desire to learn be capitalized on. This is a protest against an attitude found among teachers who sometimes feel that the child resists the learning process or that he wants to do nothing but play. The existential stress is that the child is impelled to learn and is eager to study more about the situation in which he finds himself.

8. Every effort should be made to relate the child's learning experiences to his everyday life. Existentialists do not favor teaching a subject merely for the sake of teaching it. Wherever possible the teaching method should encourage the child to solve problems. One primary purpose of education, to the existentialists, is to foster the child's ability to solve problems.

In the elementary grades an emphasis should be put on the fundamental processes. Also there should be a considerable emphasis on semantics. In the junior high school curriculum, as well as the high school curriculum, students should study the lives of great men. Through biographical studies, existentialists hope that the young person who is in a period of crisis might find renewed hope as he studies a person who has successfully withstood similar crises. In high school curriculums the existentialists would recommend the inclusion of philosophy courses. These courses ought not be designed to teach the history of philosophy, but rather should be designed to encourage the adolescent to philosophize.

9. The educational curriculum should provide ample opportunity for the student to learn a craft, or at least to prepare himself vocationally for the responsibilities of life.

10. Perhaps the most important recommendations the existentialists might make in the area of education would concern the personality of the teacher. The existentialists would strongly recommend that no person be employed as a teacher who at the time of employment has not definitely chosen the profession. A person ought not be hired who feels that he just happened to be interested in teaching, that the career was the only vocation he was academically prepared for or that his interest in teaching merely reflected a parental wish. Every effort should be made to employ only those teachers who have warm personalities and who are basically optimistic about the capabilities of the child. It has already been recommended that educational authorities permit themselves an opportunity to develop faith in the child and in the child's ability to cope with situations which are not extremely difficult.

11. It is important that every effort be made to give a thorough education to the prospective teacher. The existentialists recommend that no one be permitted to teach who is not an expert in his field. The existentialists would especially be interested in giving the teacher a firm background in the humanities and would insist that the teacher preparation program include an emphasis on developing a philosophical frame of reference. The teacher preparation program should also include extensive course work in human growth and development as well as courses designed to make the teacher aware of as many methods of teaching as possible.

In terms of teaching methodology, the existentialists would

recommend employing only those people who are interested in the child, who would assume personal responsibility for what the child learns, and who are prepared to be as flexible in teaching as might be conducive to good learning.

12. Finally teachers for junior high school should be screened very carefully for these teachers must be exceptionally alert to the problems of which junior high students are just becoming aware. The teacher must be prepared to penetrate every irregularity which appears in the child's thinking.

Suggestions for Further Study

An effort has been undertaken to indicate specifically what educational implications are inherent in the writings of existentialists. No statement was put forward claiming that the educational implications suggested herein are exclusively the domain of existentialism. How many of the two hundred ninety-five statements summarized in the fifth chapter would be acceptable to the creative writers of other philosophical disciplines? Studies might be undertaken to compare these statements, especially those to which all four of the existentialists gave their assent, to several writers within a school of thought, such as personalism, or to individual writers such as John Dewey.

The second suggestion for education is an outgrowth of the material found in the second chapter. In the latter chapter it became obvious that there is considerable room for disagreement not only about the value of existentialism but also about the nature of the movement itself. One might therefore take the statements of chapter five and create a questionnaire to be sent to a sample of educational philosophers asking them to check from a list of different philosophies (existentialism, logical positivism, thomism, etc.) which philosophy would accept the statement and which would reject the statement. This technique would provide evidence pertaining to whether the viewpoint was exclusively the domain of existentialism or whether the viewpoints are commonly shared.

Finally a study might be undertaken to see to what degree teachers, or prospective teachers, would agree to each of the statements made about the authentic man and about the educational endeavor to learn if there is a difference between superior and inferior teachers, experienced and inexperienced teachers, or any other significant factor which might be related to the degree to which these statements are acceptable.

FOOTNOTES AND REFERENCES

TO CHAPTER I

1. Henry Kissinger, *Nuclear Weapons and Foreign Policy* (New York: Harper and Brothers, 1957) p. 3.
2. Dr. Joseph Schlom, *Vortuka* (New York: Henry Holt and Company, 1954).
3. Gordon Allport, *The Nature of Personality*, Selected papers (Cambridge: Addison-Wesley Press, 1950), 146.
   "Take for example 'Citizen Sam' who moves and has his being in the great activity wheel of New York City. Let us say that he spends his hours of unconsciousness somewhere in the badlands of the Bronx. He wakens to grab the morning milk left at the door by an agent of a vast dairy and distributing system whose corporate maneuvers, so vital to his health, never consciously concern him until there is a strike of dairy workers. . . . At the factory he becomes a cog for the day in a set of systems far beyond his ken. To him (as to everybody else) the company he works for is an abstraction; . . . Unknown to himself he is headed next week for the surplus labor market. . . . At noontime the corporate monstrosity, Horn and Hardart swallows him up, as much as he swallows one of its automatic pies. After more activity in the afternoon, he seeks out a standardized day dream produced in Hollywood, to rest his tense, but not efficient mind. At the end of his day he slinks into a tavern, and unknowingly victimized by the advertising cycle, orders in rapid succession Four Roses, Three Feathers, Golden Wedding, and Seagrams which men who plan beyond tomorrow like to drink."
4. Paul Tillich, *The Courage to Be* (Boston: Little and Company, 1952). The fly cover of the book.
   "He distinguishes three main periods of anxiety in the Western World, the third of which is our own, characterizing it as the anxiety coming from the loss of the meaning of life.
   "The courage to take this inescapable anxiety upon oneself assumes three main forms: the courage to be a part of a larger

whole, the courage to stand alone, and the courage to accept
the fact that we are carried by the creative power of being in
which every creature participates."

5. David Bradley, *No Place to Hide* (Boston: Little Brown and Company, 1948).

6. Rollo May, *The Meaning of Anxiety* (New York: The Ronald Press 1950).

7. David Riesman (with the collaboration of Ruel Denney and Nathan Glazer), *The Lonely Crowd* (New Haven: Yale University Press 1950).

8. Rollo May, *Man's Search for Himself* (New York: W. W. Norton and Company, 1953).

9. John S. Brubacher, editor, *Modern Philosophies and Education* (Illinois: The National Society for the Study of Education, 1955) p. 14.

10. William O. Stanley, *Education and Social Integration* (New York Bureau of Publications, Teachers College, Columbia University, 1953) pp. 254ff.

11. loc. cit.

12. Riesman, *The Lonely Crowd*, op. cit.

13. Complete: Carl Michalson, *Christianity and the Existentialists, op cit.*, p. 77.

14. Complete: J. Glenn Gray, "Heidegger's Course: From Human existence to Nature," *op. cit.*, pp. 197-207.

15. Jean-Paul Sartre, *Existentialism*, tr. Bernard Frechtman (N. Y. Philosophical Library, 1947), p. 18.

16. *ibid.*, p. 19.

17. *ibid.*, p. 22.

18. Kneller, see *Existentialism and Education*, p. viii.

19. Wild, *The Challenge of Existentialism*, p. 57.

20. The investigator attempted to establish correspondence with Jasper and Sartre but received no replies to his letters.

21. Nelson B. Henry, editor, *Modern Philosophies and Education* (Illinois: The University of Chicago Press, 1955), p. 8.

22. George S. Counts, *The Challenge of Soviet Education* (New York The McGraw-Hill Book Company, 1957).

23. Michalson, *op. cit.*

24. John Wild, *op. cit.*

25. Walter Cerf, "A Study of Philosophy in Germany", *Journal of Philosophy*.

26. J. Glenn Gray, *op. cit.*

27. Karl Jaspers, *Tragedy is Not Enough* (Boston: The Beacon Press 1952), p. 7f.

28. F. H. Heinemann, *Existentialism and the Modern Predicament* (New

York: Harper and Brothers, 1953).

29. Joseph Gumbinger, "Existentialism and Father Abraham", *Contemporary*. Vol. 5, No. 2, Feb. 1948, p. 143f.

30. Soren Kierkegaard, *The Point of View*, tr. Walter Lowrie, (New York: Oxford University Press, 1939), p. 87.

31. E. L. Allen, *Kierkegaard, His Life and Thought* (London: 1935).

32. Soren Kierkegaard, *The Journals*, translated by Alexander Dru, (London: Oxford University Press, 1951), p. 197.

33. *ibid.*, p. 199.

34. *ibid.*, p. 453f.

35. Ronald Grimsley, *Existentialist Thought* (Cardiff: University of Wales Press, 1955), p. 3.

36. E. L. Allen, *Existentialism from Within* (New York: Macmillan, 1953), p. 99f.

37. D. J. B. Hawkins, *The Meaning of Existentialism* (London: The Aquinas Society, 1954), p. 12.

38. Karl Jaspers, *Man in the Modern Age*, tr. Eden and Cedar Paul (New York: Doubleday Anchor Books, 1957).

39. Herbert J. Muller, *The Spirit of Tragedy* (New York: Alfred A. Knopf, 1956), pp. 302-311.

40. Rollo May, *Existence* (New York: Basic Books, Inc., 1958).

41. Maurice Friedman, *Martin Buber* (Illinois: The University of Chicago Press, 1955).

42. Brubacher, *op. cit.*, p. 2f.

43. *ibid.*, p. 227.

44. *ibid.*, p. 229.

45. *ibid.*, p. 237.

46. *ibid.*, p. 238.

47. *ibid.*, p. 257.

48. Robert Ulich, *The Human Career* (New York: Harper and Brothers, 1955), pp. 29-31.

49. *ibid.* p. 226.

50. *ibid.*, p. 229.

51. *loc. cit.*

52. Merrit M. Thompson, *The Educational Philosophy of Giovanni Gentile* (California: University of Southern California Press, 1934), p. 2.

53. Helmut Kuhn, *Encounter with Nothingness* (Illinois: Henry Regnery Company, 1949), p. 12f.

54. Thompson, *op. cit.*, p. 47.

55. *ibid.*, p. 49.

56. *ibid.*, p. 51f.

57. *ibid.*, p. 59.

58. *ibid.*, p. 69.

59. *loc. cit.*

60. Kneller, *op. cit.*
61. *ibid.*, p. 141.
62. *ibid.*, p. 142.
63. *ibid.*, p. 43.
64. *ibid.* p. 141.
65. *ibid.*, pp. 57ff.
66. *ibid.*, p. 62f.
67. *ibid.*, p. 112.
68. *ibid.*, p. 129.
69. *ibid.*, p. 114f.
70. Educational Theory, from a new publication, was not listed in the Educational Index 1950-1953.
71. Theodore Brameld, *Educational Theory* (April, 1952), 80.
72. *ibid.*, p. 89.
73. *ibid.*, p. 89f.
74. *ibid.*, p. 90.
75. *loc. cit.*
76. *ibid.*, p. 90f.
77. J. B. Coates, "Existential Ethics", *Fortnightly* (Vol. 175, Jan.-June 1954), p. 339.
78. *ibid.*, p. 341.
79. L. I. Stowe, *Journal of Education* (Vol. 80, Mar. 1948), p. 121.
80. Charles Glicksberg, "The Lost Generation of College Youth", *Journal of Higher Education* (Vol. 28, May 1957), p. 264.
81. *ibid.*, p. 261.
82. *ibid.*, p. 261.
83. John White, "Anxiety, the Activity Program, and Individual Initiative", *Harvard Educational Review* (Vol. 14, No. 2, March 1944), p. 149.
84. *ibid.*, p. 158.
85. James Magmer, "Why Protestant Theologians Use Existentialism", *Catholic World* (Vol. 181, October 1955), pp. 19ff.
86. Karl Jaspers, "Re-dedication of German Scholarship," *American Scholar* (Vol. 15, No. 2, Sept. 1946).
87. Karl Jaspers, "The Axial Age of Human History", *Commentary* (V 5, No. 5) (1948), p. 431.
88. Jean-Paul Sartre, "The Situation of the Jew", *Commentary* (Vol. 5 No. 4, April 1948); "Portrait of the Inauthentic Jew" *Commentary* (Vol. 5, No. 5, May 1948); "Gentile and Jew" *Commentary* (Vol. 5 No. 6, June 1948).
89. Robert Champigny, "Translations from the Writings of Contemporary French Philosophers", *Journal of Philosophy* (Vol. 154, No. 11, May 1955), p. 342.
90. Martin Buber, "The Man of Today and the Jewish Bible" *Commen*

tary (Oct. 1948, Vol. 6, No. 4), p. 327.

91. Paul Tillich, "Martin Buber and Christian Thought" *Commentary* (Vol. 5, No. 6, June 1948), p. 515.

92. *ibid.,* p. 516.

93. *ibid.,* p. 518.

94. Maurice Friedman, "Martin Buber's Concept of Education: A New Approach to College Teaching" *Christian Scholar* (Vol. 40, June 1957), p. 110f.

95. *ibid.,* p. 110.

96. *loc. cit.*

97. *ibid.,* p. 113.

98. William Frank O'Neill "Jean Paul-Sartre's Concept of Freedom and Its Implication for American Education" (unpublished Doctor's dissertation, the U. of S. Calif., June 1958).

99. *ibid.,* p. 231.

100. *loc. cit.*

101. *ibid.,* p. 241.

102. *ibid.,* p. 243f.

103. *ibid.,* p. 228.

104. *ibid.,* p. 260f.

105. *ibid.,* p. 242.

106. *ibid.,* p. 267.

107. *loc. cit.*

108. Richard Stanley-Ford, "A Comparative Study of the Experiential Approach to Religious Education and Some Aspects of Existentialism" (unpublished doctoral thesis, The University of Southern California, 1957), p. 4f.

109. *ibid.,* p. 108f.

110. *ibid.,* p. 262.

111. *ibid.,* p. 263.

112. *ibid.,* p. 264.

113. Paul Pfeutze, "The Concept of the Social Self in the Thought of George Mead and Martin Buber", An unpublished doctoral thesis, presented to Yale University, 1951, p. 342.

114. *ibid.* p. 259.

115. *ibid.,* p. 342.

116. *ibid.,* p. 215.

FOOTNOTES AND REFERENCES
TO CHAPTER II

1. Marjorie Grene, *Dreadful Freedom* (Illinois: The University of Chicago Press, 1948), p. 1.

2. Helmut Kuhn, *Encounter with Nothingness* (Illinois: Henry Regnery Company, 1949), p. x.
3. *ibid.*, p. xf.
4. *ibid.*, p. xiif.
5. *ibid.*, p. 7.
6. *ibid.*, p. 148f.
7. Guido de Ruggiero, *Existentialism: Disintegration of Man's Soul* (New York: Social Science Publishers, 1948), p. 68.
8. *ibid.*, p. 14.
9. *ibid.*, p. 88f.
10. *ibid.*, p. 27.
11. Emmanuel Mounier, *Existential Philosophies: An Introduction* (New York: The Macmillan Company, 1949), p. 123.
12. *ibid.*, p. 127.
13. *ibid.*, p. 1.
14. *ibid.*, p. 121.
15. *ibid.*, pp. 24-50.
16. *ibid.*, p. 56.
17. D. J. B. Hawkins, *The Meaning of Existentialism* (London: The Aquinas Society of London, 1954), p. 3.
18. Mounier *op. cit.*, p. 18.
19. Jean Wahl, *A Short History of Existentialism* (New York: Philosophical Library, 1949), p. 34.
20. *ibid.*, p. 32.
21. *ibid.*, p. 1.
22. *ibid.*, p. 33.
23. Vergilius Ferm, *A History of Philosophical Systems*, p. 406.
24. *ibid.*, p. 405.
25. *ibid.*, p. 409.
26. James Collins, *The Existentialists* (Chicago: Henry Regnery Company, 1952), p. 3.
27. *ibid.*, p. 4.
28. *ibid.*, p. 189.
29. *ibid.*, p. 195.
30. *ibid.*, p. 185.
31. *ibid.*, p. 195.
32. *loc. cit.*
33. William Holden, *Four Prophets of Our Destiny* (New York: Macmillan Company, 1952), p. 147.
34. *ibid.*, p. 34.
35. *ibid.*, p. 163.
36. *ibid.*, p. 147.
37. *ibid.*, p. 30.
38. *ibid.*, p. 27f.

39. E. L. Allen, *Existentialism from Within* (New York: Macmillan Company, 1953), p. vii.
40. *ibid.*, p. 2f.
41. *ibid.*, p. 10.
42. *ibid.*, p. 15.
43. *ibid.*, p. 77.
44. J. M. Spier, *Christianity and Existentialism*, tr. David Freeman, incomplete in Bib., pp. 14ff.
45. *ibid.*, p. 103.
46. *ibid.*, p. 107.
47. *ibid.*, p. 107f.
48. ibid., p. 108.
49. *ibid.*, pp. 110-117.
50. *ibid.*, p. 127f.
51. *ibid.*, p. 130f.
52. *ibid.*, pp. 132-134.
53. Ronald Grimsley, *Existentialist Thought* (Cardiff: University of Wales Press, 1955), p. the foreword.
54. *ibid.*, p. 3.
55. *ibid.*, p. 55.
56. *ibid.*, pp. 6ff.
57. *ibid.*, p. 9f.
58. Hawkins, *op. cit.*, p. 17.
59. *ibid.*, p. 3f.
60. *ibid.*, p. 18.
61. John Wild, *The Challenge of Existentialism* (Indiana: Indiana University Press, 1955), p. 7.
62. *ibid.*, p. 57.
63. *ibid.*, p. 58.
64. *ibid.*, p. 85.
65. *ibid.*, pp. 86ff.
66. *ibid.*, p. 129.
67. *ibid.*, p. 180f.
68. *ibid.*, p. 181.
69. *ibid.*, p. 182f.
70. *ibid.*, p. 813f.
71. Carl Michalson, editor, *Christianity and the Existentialists* (New York: Charles Scribner's Sons, 1956), p. 3.
72. *ibid.*, p. 3f.
73. *ibid.*, p. 11.
74. *ibid.*, p. 12.
75. *ibid.*, p. 13.
76. *loc. cit.*
77. *ibid.*, p. 21.

78. David Roberts and Rodger Hazelton, editors, *Existentialism and Religious Belief* (New York: Oxford University Press, 1957), p. 4.
79. *loc. cit.*
80. *ibid.*, p. 5.
81. Will Herberg, *Four Existential Theologians* (N.Y.: Anchor Books, 1958), p. 3.
82. *loc. cit.*
83. *ibid.*, p. 4.
84. *ibid.*, p. 5.
85. Rollo May, Ernest Angel, Henri Ellenberger, editors, *Existence*: A *New Dimension in Psychiatry and Psychology*, (New York: Basic Books, 1958), p. 120f.
86. *ibid.*, p. 124.
87. *ibid.*, pp. 118-122.
88. *ibid.*, p. 37.
89. *ibid.*, pp. 78ff.
90. *ibid.*, p. 89.
91. George Kneller, *Existentialism and Education* (New York: Philosophical Library, 1958), p. vii.
92. *ibid.*, p. viiif.
93. *ibid.*, pp. 153-155.
94. *ibid.*, pp. 156-158.
95. *ibid.*, p. 158.

FOOTNOTES AND REFERENCES
TO CHAPTER III

PART I: Soren Kierkegaard

1. Lillian Swenson, editor, *The Faith of a Scholar* (Philadelphia: The Westminster Press, 1949), p. 8.
2. Alexander Dru, *The Journals of Soren Kierkegaard* (London: Oxford University Press, 1951), pp. xliii-xlviii.
3. Hugh Ross Mackintosh, *Types of Modern Theology* (New York: Charles Scribner's Sons, 1939), p. 218.
4. Soren Kierkegaard, *The Point of View*, tr. Walter Lowrie, (New York: Oxford University Press, 1939), p. 5f.
5. *ibid.*, p. 13f.
6. Robert Bretall, editor, *A Kierkegaard Anthology*, (New Jersey: Princeton University Press, 1948), p. 20f.
7. Reidar Thomte, *Kierkegaard's Philosophy of Religion* (New Jersey: Princeton University Press, 1948), p. 31.

8. *ibid.*, p. 28.
9. Bretall, *op. cit.*, p. 22.
10. Thomte, *op. cit.*, p. 46.
11. *loc. cit.*
12. *loc. cit.*
13. *ibid.*, p. 50.
14. Kierkegaard, *The Point of View*, p. 24.
15. Thomte, *op. cit.*, p. 55.
16. Bretall, *op. cit.*, p. 131f.
17. Soren Kierkegaard, *Purify Your Hearts*, tr. by A. S. Aldworth and W. S. Ferrie (London: C. W. Daniel Co., 1937), p. 102.
18. Soren Kierkegaard, *Works of Love*, tr. David Swenson (New Jersey: Princeton University Press, 1946), p. 16.
19. Thomte, *op. cit.*, p. 55.
20. *ibid.*, p. 90.
21. *loc. cit.*
22. Kierkegaard, *Works of Love*, p. 19.
23. Kurt Reinhardt, *The Existential Revolt* (Milwaukee: The Bruce Publishing Company, 1952), p. 42.
24. Kierkegaard, *The Point of View*, p. 124.
25. Soren Kierkegaard, *Fear and Trembling*, tr. Walter Lowrie, (New Jersey: Princeton University Press, 1941), p. 105.
26. Dru, *op. cit.*, p. 227.
27. Kierkegaard, *The Point of View*, p. 126.
28. *ibid.*, p. 116.
29. Thomte, *op. cit.*, p. 110.
30. Harold Vogt, "A Comparison of the Self and Self-Acceptance in Soren Kierkegaard and Karen Horney", (unpublished Master's thesis, The University of Southern California, Los Angeles, August 1952), p. 157.
31. From Carl R. Rogers, "The Significance of the Self-regarding Attitudes and Perception," in *Readings in the Psychology of Adjustment*, Leon Gorlow and Walter Kathovsky, editors (New York: McGraw-Hill Book Company, 1959), p. 195.
32. Bretall, *op. cit.*, p. 284.
33. Donald Snygg and Arthur Combs, *Individual Behavior* (New York: Harper and Brothers, 1949), p. 58.
34. Karen Horney, *Neurosis and Human Growth*, (New York: W. W. Norton and Company, 1950), p. 35.
35. Soren Kierkegaard, *Repetition*, tr. by Walter Lowrie (New Jersey: Princeton University Press, 1946), p. 48.
36. Kierkegaard, *Works of Love*, p. 19.
37. T. H. Croxall, *Kierkegaard Studies* (London: Lutterworth Press, 1948), p. 102.

38. Kierkegaard, *Purify Your Hearts,* p. 163.
39. Kierkegaard, *Fear and Trembling,* p. 115.
40. Croxall, *op. cit.,* p. 102.
41. Kierkegaard, *Works of Love,* p. 295.
42. *ibid.,* p. 12.
43. *loc. cit.*
44. Kierkegaard, *Purify Your Hearts,* p. 74.
45. Mackintosh, *op. cit.,* p. 23.
46. Kierkegaard, *The Present Age,* p. 108f.
47. Kierkegaard accepts the idea that one is a Christian if he is convinced that Jesus is the Christ, the Son of the Living God. How the person translates the conviction into action will determine the extent to which he is an "Individual".
48. Croxall, *op. cit.,* p. 139.
49. *ibid.,* p. 84.
50. Soren Kierkegaard, *Thoughts on Crucial Situations in Human Life,* tr. David Swenson (Minneapolis: Augsburg Publishing House, 1941), p. 33.
51. Kierkegaard, *Works of Love,* p. 110.
52. Carl Rogers, "Persons or Science? A Philosophical Question" (an unpublished lecture given to a seminar class in 1948), p. 2.
53. Kierkegaard, *Purify Your Hearts,* p. 32.
54. Harry Stack Sullivan, *The Psychiatric Interview* (New York: W. W. Norton and Company, 1954), p. 139f.
55. Kierkegaard, *Thoughts on Crucial Situations in Human Life,* p. 86.
56. *ibid.,* p. 94.
57. Soren Kierkegaard, *Concept of Dread,* tr. Walter Lowrie, (New Jersey: Princeton University Press, 1946), p. 139.
58. *ibid.,* p. 37f.
59. Bretall, *op. cit.,* p. 22.
60. Croxall, *op. cit.,* p. 88.
61. Patrick Mullahy, *Contributions of Harry Stack Sullivan,* (New York: Hermitage House, 1952), pp. 25ff.
62. Croxall, *op. cit.,* p. 89.
63. Kierkegaard, *The Present Age,* p. 54.
64. Kierkegaard, *Thoughts on Crucial Situations in Human Life,* p. 23.
65. Kierkegaard, *The Present Age,* p. 146.
66. Kierkegaard, *Purify Your Hearts,* p. 102.
67. *ibid.,* p. 113.
68. Kierkegaard, *The Present Age,* p. 36.
69. Thomte, *op. cit.,* p. 161.
70. *ibid.,* p. 110.
71. Croxall, *op. cit.,* p. 61.
72. *ibid.,* p. 61f.

73. Kierkegaard, *The Present Age*, p. 143.
74. Rollo May, *Man's Search for Himself* (New York: W. W. Norton and Company, 1953), p. 26.
75. Kierkegaard, *The Point of View*, p. 114.
76. Kierkegaard, *The Present Age*, p. 40.
77. *ibid.*, p. 28.
78. Bretall, *op. cit.*, p. 81.
79. Soren Kierkegaard, *For Self-Examination and Judge for Yourself* tr. Walter Lowrie (New Jersey: Princeton University Press, 1944), on the preface page.
80. Kierkegaard, *The Present Age*, p. 114.
81. Kierkegaard, *The Works of Love*, p. 43.
82. J. L. Moreno, *Who Shall Survive?* (New York: Beacon House, 1953), p. xx.
83. Kierkegaard, *Works of Love*, p. 71.
84. Kierkegaard, *The Point of View*, p. 48.
85. Kierkegaard, *Works of Love*, p. 176.
86. *loc. cit.*
87. Croxall, *op. cit.*, p. 139.
88. Kierkegaard, *Concept of Dread*, p. 5.
89. Kierkegaard, *Works of Love*, p. 11.
90. Carl Rogers, in a personal letter sent August 4, 1953.

PART II: Martin Buber

91. Martin Buber, *Between Man and Man*, tr. Ronald Smith (Boston: Beacon Press, 1947), p. 181.
92. Martin Buber, an unpublished letter written Dec. 26, 1952.
93. Buber, *Between Man and Man*, p. 136f.
94. *ibid.*, p. 14.
95. Martin Buber, *Two Types of Faith*, tr. Norman Goldhawk (London: Routledge and Kegan Paul Ltd., 1951), p. 64.
96. Martin Buber, *The Prophetic Faith*, tr. Carlyle Witton-Davies, (New York: The Macmillan Company, 1949), p. 135.
97. *loc. cit.*
98. *ibid.*, p. 1.
99. Buber, *Between Man and Man*, p. 5.
100. Martin Buber, *Pointing the Way*, tr. Maurice Friedman (New York: Harper and Brothers, 1957), pp. 7, 200.
101. Buber, *Two Types of Faith*, p. 12.
102. *ibid.*, p. 15.
103. Buber, *Between Man and Man*, p. 115.
104. *ibid.*, p. 131.

105. *ibid.*, p. 126.
106. Martin Buber, *I and Thou*, tr. Ronald Smith (Edinburgh: T. and T. Clark, 1937), p. 37f.
107. Buber, *Pointing the Way*, p. 27.
108. *ibid.*, p. 109.
109. *ibid.*, p. 221.
110. *ibid.*, p. 222.
111. Buber, *Two Types of Faith*, p. 75.
112. Buber, *Pointing the Way*, pp. 222ff.
113. *The Prophetic Faith*, p. 104.
114. Martin Buber, *Right and Wrong*, tr. Ronald Smith (London: SCM Press LTD., 1952), p. 15.
115. Buber, *Pointing the Way*, p. 181.
116. Buber, *The Prophetic Faith*, p. 1.
117. Buber, *Right and Wrong*, p. 7.
118. Buber, *I and Thou*, p. 43f.
119. Buber, *Between Man and Man*, p. 157.
120. *ibid.*, p. 6.
121. Buber, *Right and Wrong*, p. 13.
122. Buber, *Pointing the Way*, p. 214.
123. *ibid.*, p. 70.
124. *ibid.*, p. 148.
125. Buber, *Right and Wrong*, p. 16.
126. Martin Buber, *Eclipse of God* (New York: Harper and Brothers, 1952), p. 13.
127. Buber, *The Prophetic Faith*, p. 151.
128. *ibid.*, p. 56.
129. Buber, *Between Man and Man*, p. 110f.
130. Buber, *The Prophetic Faith*, p. 55.
131. Buber, *Point of View*, p. 111.
132. Buber, *Between Man and Man*, p. 44.
133. Buber, *Pointing the Way*, p. 121.
134. Buber, *Eclipse of God*, p. 137.
135. Buber, *The Prophetic Faith*, p. 55.
136. *ibid.*, p. 137.
137. Buber, *I and Thou*, p. 82.
138. Buber, *Eclipse of God*, p. 166.
139. Buber, *I and Thou*, p. 10.
140. *ibid.*, p. 11.
141. *ibid.*, p. 25.
142. *ibid.*, p. 28.
143. *ibid.*, p. 82.
144. Buber, *The Prophetic Faith*, p. 195.
145. Buber, *Pointing the Way*, p. 28.

146. Buber, *Eclipse of God*, p. 34.
147. *ibid.*, p. 26.
148. *ibid.*, p. 28.
149. *ibid.*, p. 30.
150. Buber, *I and Thou*, p. 37.
151. *ibid.*, p. 46.
152. Buber, *Eclipse of God*, p. 116.
153. Buber, *I and Thou*, p. 3.
154. Buber, *The Prophetic Faith*, p. 90.
155. *ibid.*, p 92.
156. *ibid.*, p. 104.
157. Buber, *Eclipse of God*, p. 50.
158. Martin Buber, *At the Turning* (New York: Farrar, Straus and Young, 1952), p. 12.
159. Buber, *Eclipse of God*, p. 44.
160. Buber, *Two Types of Faith*, p. 46.
161. *ibid.*, p. 48f.
162. *ibid.*, p. 8.
163. *ibid.*, p. 63.
164. *ibid.*, p. 64.
165. Buber, *Right and Wrong*, p. 31.
166. Buber, *Between Man and Man*, p. 144.
167. Buber, *At the Turning*, p. 14f.
168. Buber, *The Prophetic Faith*, p. 200.
169. Buber, *Between Man and Man*, p. 115.
170. Buber, *Pointing the Way*, p. 12.
171. Buber, *I and Thou*, p. 54.
172. Buber, *Between Man and Man*, p. 182.
173. Buber, *Pointing the Way*, p. 12.
174. *ibid.*, p. 185.
175. Buber, *Pointing the Way*, p. 205.
176. Buber, *Two Types of Faith*, p. 6.
177. Buber, *Eclipse of God*, p. 49.
178. Buber, *The Prophetic Faith*, p. 104.
179. Buber, *Two Types of Faith*, p. 93.
180. Buber, *The Prophetic Faith*, p. 41.
181. Buber, *At the Turning*, p. 14.
182. Buber, *Pointing the Way*, p. 217.
183. Buber, *I and Thou*, p. 49.
184. Buber, *Two Types of Faith*, p. 3.
185. Buber, *Pointing the Way*, pp. 222 and 224.
186. *ibid.*, p. 221.
187. *ibid.*, p. 222.
188. Buber, *Eclipse of God*, p. 125.

189. Buber, *Right and Wrong*, p. 51.
190. Buber, *At the Turning*, p. 43f.
191. Buber, *Two Types of Faith*, p. 72f.
192. Buber, *Pointing the Way*, p. 147.
193. Buber, *Two Types of Faith*, p. 10.
194. Buber, *Between Man and Man*, p. 92.
195. Buber, *Pointing the Way*, p. 205.
196. *ibid.*, p. 83.
197. Buber, *Two Types of Faith*, p. 75.
198. Buber, *Pointing the Way*, pp. 5,7, and 110.
199. Buber, *Two Types of Faith*, p. 11.
200. Buber, *At the Turning*, p. 53.
201. *ibid.*, p. 56.
202. Buber, *I and Thou*, p. 104.
203. Buber, *Eclipse of God*, p. 50.
204. *ibid.*, p. 40.
205. *ibid.*, p. 13.
206. Buber, *I and Thou*, p. 51.
207. *ibid.*, p. 57.
208. Buber, *Two Types of Faith*, p. 8.
209. Buber, *Between Man and Man*, p. 124f.
210. Buber, *Eclipse of God*, p. 11.
211. Buber, *The Prophetic Faith*, p. 74.
212. Buber, *Two Types of Faith*, p. 38f.
213. Buber, *Between Man and Man*, p. 141.
214. Buber, *Two Types of Faith*, p. 35.
215. Buber, *At the Turning*, p. 51.
216. Buber, *Pointing the Way*, p. 37.
217. Buber, *The Prophetic Faith*, p. 154.
218. Buber, *At the Turning*, p. 12.
219. Buber, *The Prophetic Faith*, p. 92.
220. *ibid.*, p. 52.
221. Buber, *At the Turning*, p. 59f.
222. Buber, *Eclipse of God*, p. 23.
223. Buber, *Two Types of Faith*, p. 132.
224. Buber, *The Prophetic Faith*, p. 2.
225. *ibid.*, p. 64.
226. *ibid.*, p. 230.
227. *loc. cit.*
228. *ibid.*, p. 104.
229. Buber, *Pointing the Way*, p. 200.

PART III: Jean-Paul Sartre

230. Jean-Paul Sartre, *Being and Nothingness*, tr. Hazel Barnes (New

York: Philosophical Library, 1956), p. xlii.

231. Jean-Paul Sartre, *Existentialism,* tr. Bernard Frechtman (New York: Philosophical Library, 1947), p. 15.
232. *loc. cit.*
233. *ibid.,* p. 18.
234. *ibid.,* p. 15.
235. *ibid.,* p. 19.
236. *ibid.,* p. 20.
237. *loc. cit.*
238. The concept "bad faith" is defined on page 177.
239. Sartre, *Existentialism,* p. 20.
240. *ibid.,* p. 22.
241. *ibid.,* p. 24f.
242. *ibid.,* p. 26f.
243. *ibid.,* p. 12.
244. *ibid.,* p. 11.
245. Sartre, *Being and Nothingness,* p. 37f.
246. *ibid.,* p. 31.
247. *ibid.,* p. 32.
248. *ibid.,* p. 25.
249 *ibid.,* p. 28.
250. *ibid.,* p. 29.
251. *ibid.,* p. 34f.
252. *ibid.,* p. 36.
253. *ibid.,* p. 37.
254. *ibid.,* p. 39.
255. Sartre, *Existentialism,* p. 14.
256. *ibid.,* p. 31f.
257. *ibid.,* p. 31.
258. *ibid.,* p. 32.
259. Sartre, *Being and Nothingness,* p. 40.
260. *ibid.,* p. 51f.
261. *ibid.,* p. 67.
262. *ibid.,* p. 68.
263. *ibid.,* p. 538.
264. *ibid.,* p. 540f.
265. *ibid.,* p. 541.
266. *ibid.,* p. 545.
267. *ibid.,* p. 532.
268. Sartre, *Existentialism,* p. 42.
269. Sartre, *Being and Nothingness,* p. 218.
270. *ibid.,* p. 229.
271. *ibid.,* p. 222.
272. Patrick Mullahy, editor, *The Contributions of Harry Stack Sullivan* (New York: Hermitage House, 1952), p. 37.

273. Sartre, *Existentialism*, p. 45.
274. Sartre, *Being and Nothingness*, p. 227.
275. *ibid.*, p. 228.
276. *ibid.*, p. 403.
277. *ibid.*, p. 390.
278. *ibid.*, p. 260.
279. *ibid.*, p. 262.
280. *ibid.*, p. 273f.
281. *ibid.*, p. 288.
282. *ibid.*, p. 289.
283. *ibid.*, p. 290.
284. Sartre, *Existentialism*, p. 45f.
285. Sartre, *Being and Nothingness*, p. 482.
286. *ibid.*, p. 483.
287. *ibid.*, p. 488f.
288. *ibid.*, p. 490.
289. *ibid.*, p. 491.
290. *ibid.*, p. 489.
291. *ibid.*, p. 492.
292. *ibid.*, p. 495.
293. *ibid.*, p. 496.
294. *ibid.*, p. 500f.
295. *ibid.*, p. 496.
296. *ibid.*, p. 502.
297. *ibid.*, p. 503.
298. *ibid.*, p. 437.
299. *ibid.*, p. 437f.
300. *ibid.*, p. 440.
301. *ibid.*, p. 449.
302. *ibid.*, p. 309.
303. *ibid.*, p. 74.
304. *ibid.*, p. 453.
305. *ibid.*, p. 464f.
306. *ibid.*, p. 556.
307. *ibid.*, p. 481f.
308. *ibid.*, p. 8.
309. Sartre, *Existentialism*, p. 12.
PART IV: Karl Jaspers
310. Karl Jaspers, *Way to Wisdom*, tr. Ralph Manheim (New Haven: Yale University Press, 1954), p. 103.
311. Karl Jaspers, *Man in the Modern Age*, tr. Eden and Cedar Paul (New York: Doubleday Anchor Books, 1957), p. 83.
312. *ibid.*, p. 84.
313. *ibid.*, p. 19.

314. *ibid.*, p. 11.
315. *ibid.*, p. 21.
316. *ibid.*, p. 46.
317. *ibid.*, p. 58.
318. *ibid.*, p. 85.
319. *ibid.*, p. 68.
320. *ibid.*, p. 3.
321. *ibid.*, p. 15.
322. *ibid.*, p. 2.
323. *ibid.*, p. 1.
324. Karl Jaspers, *Reason and Anti-Reason in Our Time*, tr. Stanley Godman (New Haven: Yale University Press), p. 26.
325. Jaspers, *Way to Wisdom*, p. 66.
326. Jaspers, *Reason and Anti-Reason*, p. 26.
327. Jaspers, *Man in the Modern World*, p. 1.
328. *ibid.*, p. 22f.
329. *ibid.*, p. 158.
330. Jaspers, *Way to Wisdom*, p. 121.
331. *ibid.*, p. 120f.
332. Jaspers, *Man in the Modern World*, p. 194.
333. *ibid.*, p. 107.
334. *ibid.*, p. 10.
335. Karl Jaspers, *Tragedy is not Enough*, tr. Harald Reiche, Harry Moore, and Karl Deutsch (Boston: The Beacon Press, 1952), p. 94.
336. Jaspers, *Way to Wisdom*, p. 141.
337. Jaspers, *Man in the Modern Age*, p. 140.
338. *ibid.*, p. 151.
339. Karl Jaspers, *Way to Wisdom*, p. 41.
340. *ibid.*, p. 13.
341. *ibid.*, p. 118.
342. *ibid.*, p. 127.
343. *ibid.*, p. 88.
344. Jaspers, *Man in the Modern Age*, p. 162.
345. *ibid.*, p. 154.
346. *ibid.*, p. 14.
347. Jaspers, *Way to Wisdom*, p. 129f.
348. Jaspers, *Reason and Anti-Reason in Our Time*, p. 78.
349. Jaspers, *Man in the Modern Age*, p. 118.
350. *ibid.*, p. 221.
351. Jaspers, *Way to Wisdom*, p. 66.
352. Jaspers, *Man in the Modern Age*, p. 225.
353. *ibid.*, p. 4.
354. *ibid.*, p. 34.
355. *ibid.*, p. 34.

356. Jaspers, *Way to Wisdom*, p. 46.
357. Jaspers, *Man in the Modern World*, p. 51.
358. *ibid.*, p. 206.
359. *ibid.*, p. 221.
360. *ibid.*, p. 222.
361. *ibid.*, p. 224.
362. *ibid.*, p. 222.
363. *loc. cit.*
364. *ibid.*, p. 109.
365. *ibid.*, p. 10.
866. *ibid.*, p. 215.
367. *ibid.*, p. 23.
368. *ibid.*, p. 3.
369. *ibid.*, p. 29.
370. Jaspers, *Way to Wisdom*, p. 56.
371. Jaspers, *Man in the Modern World*, p. 24.
372. Jaspers, *Way to Wisdom*, p. 61.
373. *ibid.*, p. 56.
374. *ibid.*, p. 64.
375. *ibid.*, p. 172.
376. *ibid.*, p. 118.
377. *ibid.*, p. 68.
378. Jaspers, *Tragedy is not Enough*, p. 85.
379. Jaspers, *Way to Wisdom*, p. 59.
380. *ibid.*, p. 58.
381. Jaspers, *Man in the Modern Age*, p. 4.
382. Jaspers, *Reason and Anti-Reason in Our Time*, p. 50.
383. *ibid.*, p. 83.
384. *ibid.*, p. 53.
385. Jaspers, *Way to Wisdom*, p. 61.
386. *ibid.*, p. 110.
387. Jaspers, *Tragedy is not Enough*, p. 77.
388. Jaspers, *Way to Wisdom*, p. 114.
389. Jaspers, *Man in the Modern Age*, p. 195.
390. *ibid.*, p. 24.
391. Jaspers, *Tragedy is not Enough*, p. 55.
392. *ibid.*, p. 53f.
393. *ibid.*, p. 53.
394. Jaspers, *Man in the Modern Age*, p. 81.
395. *ibid.*, p. 123.
396. *ibid.*, p. 156.
397. Jaspers, *Way to Wisdom*, p. 123f.
398. Jaspers, *Reason and Anti-Reason in Our Time*, p. 69.
399. Jaspers, *Way to Wisdom*, p. 121.

400. *ibid.*, p. 170.
401. Jaspers, *Man in the Modern Age*, p. 74.
402. *ibid.*, p. 24.
403. *ibid.*, p. 94.
404. *loc. cit.*
405. Jaspers, *Way to Wisdom*, p. 51.
406. *ibid.*, p. 61.
407. *ibid.*, p. 55.
408. *ibid.*, p. 52.
409. *ibid.*, p. 65.
410. *ibid.*, p. 83.
411. *loc. cit.*
412. Jaspers, *Man in the Modern Age*, p. 201.
413. *ibid.*, p. 177.
414. *ibid.*, p. 139.
415. *ibid.*, pp. 186ff.
416. *ibid.*, p. 56.
417. *ibid.*, p. 49.
418. Jaspers, *Way to Wisdom*, p. 130.
419. Jaspers, *Tragedy is not Enough*, p. 56.
420. Jaspers, *Man in the Modern Age*, p. 161.
421. *ibid.*, p. 30.
422. *ibid.*, p. 180.
423. *ibid.*, p. 202.
424. *ibid.*, p. 216.
425. *ibid.*, p. 143.
426. *ibid.*, p. 82.
427. *ibid.*, p. 204.
428. *ibid.*, p. 200f.
429. Jaspers, *Reason and Anti-Reason in Our Time*, p. 36.
430. Jaspers, *Way to Wisdom*, p. 35.
431. *ibid.*, p. 33.
432. *ibid.*, p. 47.
433. *ibid.*, p. 22.
434. *ibid.*, p. 48.
435. *ibid.*, p. 50f.
436. *loc. cit.*
437. *ibid.*, p. 67.
438. *ibid.*, p. 70.
439. *ibid.*, p. 68.
440. *ibid.*, p. 67.
441. *ibid.*, p. 45.
442. *loc. cit.*
443. Jaspers, *Man in the Modern Age*, p. 20.

444. Jaspers, *Tragedy is not Enough*, p. 25.
445. Jaspers, *Way to Wisdom*, p. 117.
446. *ibid.*, pp. 82, 85.
447. *ibid.*, p. 39.
448. *ibid.*, p. 50.
449. *loc. cit.*
450. *ibid.*, p. 98.
451. Jaspers, *Man in the Modern Age*, p. 40.
452. *ibid.*, p. 39.
453. *ibid.*, p. 107.
454. *ibid.*, p. 114.
455. *ibid.*, p. 39.
456. *ibid.*, p. 33.
457. *ibid.*, p. 51.
458. *ibid.*, p. 41.
459. *ibid.*, p. 77.
460. Jaspers, *Way to Wisdom*, p. 68.
461. *ibid.*, p. 171.
462. *ibid.*, p. 115.
463. *ibid.*, p. 114.
464. Jaspers, *Tragedy is not Enough*, p. 87.
465. Jaspers, *Way to Wisdom*, p. 124.
466. *ibid.*, p. 27.
467. *ibid.*, p. 124.
468. Jaspers, *Man in the Modern Age*, p. 214.
469. Jaspers, *Way to Wisdom*, p. 62.
470. Jaspers, *Man in the Modern Age*, p. 198.
471. *ibid.*, p. 197.
472. Jaspers, *Way to Wisdom*, p. 116.
473. Jaspers, *Man in the Modern Age*, p. 203.
474. *ibid.*, p. 210.
475. *ibid.*, p. 63.
476. *ibid.*, p. 47.
477. *ibid.*, p. 63.
478. *ibid.*, p. 48.
479. *ibid.*, p. 28.
480. *ibid.*, p. 52.
481. *loc. cit.*
482. *ibid.*, p. 59f.
483. Jaspers, *Tragedy is not Enough*, p. 95.
484. Jaspers, *Way to Wisdom*, p. 20.
485. *loc. cit.*
486. Jaspers, *Man in the Modern Age*, p. 27.
487. *ibid.*, p. 23.

488. *ibid.*, p. 1.
489. Jaspers, *Tragedy is not Enough*, p. 72.
490. *ibid.*, p. 78.
491. Jaspers, *Way to Wisdom*, p. 23.
492. Jaspers, *Tragedy is not Enough*, p. 55f.
493. Jaspers, *Man in the Modern Age*, p. 23f.
494. Jaspers, *Tragedy is not Enough*, p. 74.
495. *loc. cit.*
496. *ibid.*, p. 76.
497. *ibid.*, p. 99.
498. *ibid.*, p. 33.
499. *ibid.*, p. 36.
500. *ibid.*, p. 29f.
501. *ibid.*, p. 56.
502. Jaspers, *Way to Wisdom*, p. 22.
503. Jaspers, *Reason and Anti-Reason in Our Time*, p. 52.

FOOTNOTES AND REFERENCES
TO CHAPTER IV

PART I: Soren Kierkegaard

1. Alexander Dru, *The Journals of Soren Kierkegaard* (New York: Oxford University Press, 1938), p. 237.
2. *ibid.*, p. 150.
3. *ibid.*, p. 279.
4. *ibid.*, p. 108.
5. Soren Kierkegaard, *The Point of View*, tr. Walter Lowrie (New York: Oxford University Press, 1939), p. 76.
6. Dru, *op. cit.*, p. 314.
7. Johannes Hohlenberg, *Soren Kierkegaard*, tr. T. H. Croxall (New York: Pantheon Books Inc., 1945), p. 29.
8. Dru, *op. cit.*, p. 24f.
9. Kierkegaard, *The Point of View*, p. 76.
10. Dru, *op. cit.*, p. 565.
11. *ibid.*, p. 392.
12. *ibid.*, p. 297.
13. Kierkegaard, *The Point of View*, p. 77.
14. David Swenson, *Something About Kierkegaard*, editor Lillian Swenson (Minneapolis: Augsburg Publishing House, 1945), p. 5.
15. Dru, *op. cit.*, p. 144f.
16. Swenson, *op. cit.*, p. 5.

17. Conrad Bonifazi, *Christendom Attacked* (London: Rockliff Ltd., 1953), p. 62.
18. Swenson, *op. cit.*, p. 42.
19. Hohlenberg, *op. cit.*, p. 29.
20. Soren Kierkegaard, *Concept of Dread*, tr. Walter Lowrie (New Jersey: Princeton University Press, 1946), p. 34.
21. *loc. cit.*
22. Robert Bretall, *Kierkegaard Anthology* (New Jersey: Princeton University Press, 1947), p. 22.
23. Kierkegaard, *Concept of Dread*, p. 34.
24. Dru, *op. cit.*, p. 88.
25. *ibid.*, p. 40.
26. Soren Kierkegaard, *Sickness unto Death*, tr. Walter Lowrie (New Jersey: Princeton University Press, 1951), p. 13.
27. Kierkegaard, *Concept of Dread*, p. 112.
28. Kierkegaard, *Either-Or — A Fragment of Life*, tr. David and Lillian Swenson (New Jersey: Princeton University Press, 1944), p. 282.
29. Kierkegaard, *Either-Or*, tr. Walter Lowrie (New Jersey: Princeton University Press, 1944), p. 61.
30. *loc. cit.*
31. *ibid.*, p. 62.
32. Kierkegaard, *The Present Age*, tr. Walter Lowrie (London: Oxford University Press, 1940), p. 17f.
33. *loc. cit.*
34. Kierkegaard, *Concept of Dread*, p. 112f.
35. Kierkegaard, *Either-Or*, p. 64.
36. *ibid.*, p. 61.
37. *ibid.*, p. 60f.
38. Kierkegaard, *Stages on Life's Way*, tr. Walter Lowrie (New Jersey: Princeton University Press, 1940), p. 138.
39. Kierkegaard, *Fear and Trembling*, tr. Robert Payne (London: Oxford University Press, 1939), p. 6.
40. Kierkegaard, *Either-Or*, p. 223f.
41. Erik Erikson, *Childhood and Society* (New York: W. W. Norton and Company, 1950),
42. Dru, *op. cit.*, p. 279.
43. Erikson, *op. cit.*, p. 226f.
44. *ibid.*, p. 314.
45. *loc. cit.*
46. Soren Kierkegaard, *Thoughts on Crucial Situations in Human Life* tr. David Swenson (Minneapolis, Augsburg Publishing House, 1941), p. 174.
47. Kierkegaard, *Sickness Unto Death*, p. 93.
48. Swenson, *Something About Kierkegaard*, p. 6.

49. Kierkegaard, *Thoughts on Crucial Situations in Human Life*, p. 37.
50. Johannes Hohlenberg, *Soren Kierkegaard* (New York: Pantheon Books, 1954), p. 29.
51. *ibid.*, p. 30.
52. *loc. cit.*
53. Kierkegaard, *The Present Age*, p. 6.
54. Bretall, *op. cit.*, p. 1.
55. Kierkegaard, *Either-Or — A Fragment of Life*, p. 26.
56. Lillian Swenson, editor, *The Faith of a Scholar* (Philadelphia: The Westminster Press, 1949), p. 8.
57. Holgar Begtrup, Hans Lund, Peter Manniche, *The Folk High-Schools of Denmark and the Development of a Farming Community* (London: Oxford University Press, 1929), p. 39.
58. Hal Koch, *Grundtvig* (Ohio: The Antioch Press, 1952), p. 136.
59. *ibid.*, p. 137.
60. *ibid.*, p. 141
61. Dru, *op. cit.*, p. 429.
62. *loc. cit.*
63. A. H. Moehlman, editor, *Comparative Education* (New York: The Dryden Press), p. 345.
64. Begtrup, *op. cit.*, p. 94.
65. Dru, *op. cit.*, p. 285.
66. Reidar Thomte, *Kierkegaard's Philosophy of Religion* (New Jersey, Princeton University Press, 1948), p. 84.
67. Dru, *op. cit.*, p. 363.
68. *ibid.*, p. 371.
69. Bretall, *op. cit.*, p. 14.
70. Martin Heidegger, *An Introduction to Metaphysics* (New Haven: Yale University Press, 1959), p. 206.
71. Bonifazi, *op. cit.*, p. 62.
72. Kierkegaard, *Concept of Dread*, p. 142.
73. Dru, *op. cit.*, p. 374f.
74. Kierkegaard, *Either-Or*, p. 224.
75. Kierkegaard, *The Present Age*, p. 60.
76. Swenson, *op. cit.*, p. 119.
77. Soren Kierkegaard, *Training in Christianity*, tr. Walter Lowrie (New Jersey: Princeton University Press, 1947), p. 131.
78. Thomte, *op. cit.*, p. 131.
79. *ibid.*, p. 201.
80. *ibid.*, p. 202.
81. Dru, *op. cit.*, 325.
82. Soren Kierkegaard, *Philosophical Fragments or A Fragment of Philosophy*, tr. David Swenson (New Jersey: Princeton University Press, 1936), p. 9.

83. Thomte, *op. cit.*, p. 201.
84. *loc. cit.*
85. Kierkegaard, *The Present Age*, p. 19.
86. *ibid.*, p. 18.
87. *ibid.*, p. 19.

PART II: Martin Buber

88. Martin Buber, *Between Man and Man*, tr. Ronald Smith (Boston: The Beacon Press, 1947), 175.
89. Martin Buber, *I and Thou*, tr. Ronald Smith (Edinburgh: T. & T. Clark, 1950), p. 25.
90. Patrick Mullahy, *The Contributions of Harry Stack Sullivan* (New York: Hermitage House, 1952), p. 27f.
91. Martin Buber, *Two Types of Faith*, tr. Norman Goldhawk (London: Routledge & Kegan LTD., 1951), p. 158.
92. Martin Buber, *The Eclipse of God* (New York: Harper & Brothers, 1952), p. 61.
93. Martin Buber, *Right and Wrong*, tr. Ronald Smith (London: SCM Press LTD., 1952), p. 45.
94. Buber, *Between Man and Man*, p. 196.
95. *ibid.*, p. 83.
96. *loc. cit.*
97. *ibid.*, p. 83.
98. Martin Buber, *Pointing the Way*, Maurice Friedman (New York: Harper & Brothers, 1957), p. 177.
99. Buber, *Between Man and Man*, p. 106.
100. *ibid.*, p. 115.
101. *loc. cit.*
102. Buber, *Pointing the Way*, p. 98 and p. 181.
103. Martin Buber, *The Prophetic Faith*, tr. Carlyle Witton-Davies (New York: The Macmillan Company, 1949), p. 1.
104. Buber, *Pointing the Way*, p. 14.
105. Buber, *The Eclipse of God*, p. 129.
106. Buber, *Pointing the Way*, p. 101.
107. *ibid.*, p. 104.
108. Martin Buber, *At the Turning* (New York: Farrar, Straus, and Young, 1952), p. 29.
109. Buber, *Between Man and Man*, p. 203.
110. Buber, *Eclipse of God*, p. 12.
111. Buber, *Pointing the Way*, p. 9.
112. *ibid.*, p. 20.
113. *ibid.*, p. 17.
114. *ibid.*, p. 104.

115. *ibid.*, p. 716.
116. *ibid.*, p. 179.
117. *ibid.*, p. 176.
118. *ibid.*, p. 93.
119. Buber, *Two Types of Faith*, p. 65.
120. *ibid.*, p. 32.
121. Buber, *I and Thou*, p. 15.
122. Buber, *Two Types of Faith*, p. 115.
123. *ibid.*, p. 96.
124. *ibid.*, p. 95.
125. Buber, *Pointing the Way*, p. 33.
126. *ibid.*, p. 208.
127. *ibid.*, p. 180.
128. *ibid.*, p. 29.
129. Buber, *Two Types of Faith*, p. 19.

PART III: Jean-Paul Sartre

130. Jean-Paul Sartre, *Existentialism*, tr. Bernard Frechtman (New York: Philosophical Library, 1947), p. 18.
131. *ibid.*, p. 11.
132. Jean-Paul Sartre, *Being and Nothingness*, tr. Hazel Barnes (New York: Philosophical Library, 1956), p. 491.
133. Sartre, *Existentialism*, p. 15.
134. Sartre, *Being and Nothingness*, p. 222.
135. *ibid.*, p. 289.
136. *ibid.*, p. 612.
137. *ibid.*, p. 256.
138. *ibid.*, p. 260f.
139. *ibid.*, p. 364.
140. *ibid.*, p. 288.
141. *ibid.*, p. 353.
142. *ibid.*, p. 8.
143. *ibid.*, p. 273.
144. *ibid.*, p. 60.
145. *ibid.*, p. 429.
146. *ibid.*, p. 381.
147. *ibid.*, p. 40.
148. *ibid.*, p. 409.
149. *ibid.*, p. 553.
150. *ibid.*, p. 556.
151. Sartre, *Existentialism*, p. 52f.
152. Sartre, *Being and Nothingness*, p. 422.
153. *ibid.*, p. 521.

154. *ibid.*, p. 559.
155. *ibid.*, p. 572.
156. *ibid.*, p. 575.
157. *ibid.*, p. 510.
158. *ibid.*, p. 450.
159. *ibid.*, p. 114.
160. *ibid.*, p. 481.
161. Sartre, *Existentialism*, p. 37.
162. Sartre, *Being and Nothingness*, p. 481.
163. *ibid.*, p. 373.
164. *ibid.*, p. 372.
165. *ibid.*, p. 517.
166. *ibid.*, p. 196.
167. *loc. cit.*
168. *ibid.*, p. 612.
169. *ibid.*, p. 308.
170. *ibid.*, p. 179f.
171. *ibid.*, p. 578.
172. *ibid.*, p. 577.
173. *ibid.*, pp. 578ff.
174. *ibid.*, p. 165.
175. D. O. Hebb, *The Organiz.tion of Behavior* (New York: John Wiley & Sons, 1949), p. 228f.
176. Sartre, *Existentialism*, p. 59.

PART IV: Karl Jaspers

177. Karl Jaspers, *Way to Wisdom*, tr. Ralph Manheim (New Haven: Yale University Press, 1954), p. 10.
178. *ibid.*, p. 9.
179. *loc.* cit.
180. Karl Jaspers, *Man in the Modern Age*, tr. Eden and Cedar Paul (New York: Doubleday Anchor Books, 1951), p. 121.
181. *ibid.*, p. 124.
182. Jaspers, *Way to Wisdom*, p. 16.
183. *ibid.*, p. 140.
184. Jaspers, *Man in the Modern Age*, p. 221f.
185. Jaspers, *Way to Wisdom*, p. 96.
186. Karl Jaspers, *Reason and Anti-Reason in Our Time*, tr. Stanley Godman (New Haven: Yale University Press), p. 61.
187. Jaspers, *Way to Wisdom*, p. 106.
188. Karl Jaspers, *Tragedy is Not Enough*, tr. Harald Reiche, Harry Moore, and Karl Deutsch (Boston: The Beacon Press, 1952), p. 77.
189. *ibid.*, p. 19.

190. *ibid.*, p. 28.
191. Jaspers, *Way to Wisdom*, p. 144.
192. *ibid.*, p. 96.
193. Jaspers, *Man in the Modern Age*, p. 29.
194. *loc. cit.*
195. Jaspers, *Way to Wisdom*, p. 74.
196. Jaspers, *Man in the Modern Age*, p. 18.
197. Jaspers, *Way to Wisdom*, p. 77f.
198. Jaspers, *Reason and Anti-Reason*, p. 28.
199. Jaspers, *Man in the Modern Age*, p. 29.
200. Jaspers, *Reason and Anti-Reason*, p. 37.
201. *ibid.*, p. 64.
202. *ibid.*, p. 63.
203. *ibid.*, p. 40.
204. *ibid.*, p. 50.
205. *ibid.*, p. 53.
206. *ibid.*, p. 63.
207. *ibid.*, p. 38.
208. *ibid.*, p. 38.
209. Jaspers, *Man in the Modern Age*, 26.
210. Jaspers, *Reason and Anti-Reason In Our Time*, p. 54.
211. *ibid.*, p. 39.
212. *ibid.*, p. 53f.
213. *ibid.*, p. 67.
214. *ibid.*, p. 38.
215. *ibid.*, p. 30f.
216. *loc. cit.*
217. Jaspers, *Man in the Modern Age*, p. 145.
218. *ibid.*, p. 73.
219. Jaspers, *Reason and Anti-Reason in Our Time*, p. 31.
220. *ibid.*, p. 29.
221. Jaspers, *Way to Wisdom*, p. 151.
222. Jaspers, *Man in the Modern World*, p. 75.
223. Jaspers, *Reason and Anti-Reason in Our Time*, p. 32.
224. Jaspers, *Man in the Modern Age*, p. 148.
225. Jaspers, *Reason and Anti-Reason in Our Time*, p. 34.
226. Jaspers, *Way to Wisdom*, p. 8.
227. *ibid.*, p. 11.
228. *ibid.*, p. 12.
229. *ibid.*, p. 9.
230. *ibid.*, p. 12f.
231. *ibid.*, p. 8.
232. *ibid.*, p. 143.
233. *ibid.*, p. 167f.

234. Jaspers, *Man in the Modern Age,* p. 124.
235. Jaspers, *Tragedy is Not Enough,* p. 24.
236. Jaspers, *Way to Wisdom,* pp. 100ff.
237. Jaspers, *Man in the Modern Age,* p. 4.
238. *ibid.,* p. 168f.
239. *ibid.,* p. 163.
240. Jaspers, *Tragedy Is Not Enough,* p. 26.
241. *loc. cit.*
242. Merritt Thompson, *The Education Philosophy of Giovanni Gentile* (California: University of Southern California Press, 1934), p. 86f.
243. Jaspers, *Man in the Modern Age,* p. 137.
244. *ibid.,* pp. 24, 40, and 64f.
245. *ibid.,* p. 68.
246. *ibid.,* p. 70.
247. *ibid.,* p. 223.
248. *ibid.,* p. 174.
249. *ibid.,* p. 196.
250. *ibid.,* p. 90.
251. *ibid.,* p. 65.
252. *ibid.,* p. 195.
253. Jaspers, *Reason and Anti-Reason in Our Time,* p. 57.
254. Jaspers, *Man in the Modern Age,* p. 121.
255. *ibid.,* p. 2.
256. Jaspers, *Way to Wisdom,* p. 163.
257. Jaspers, *Man in the Modern Age,* p. 149.
258. *ibid.,* p. 86.
259. *ibid.,* p. 114.
260. *ibid.,* p. 115.
261. *ibid.,* p. 116.
262. *loc. cit.*
263. *loc. cit.*
264. *loc. cit.*
265. Jaspers, *Reason and Anti-Reason in Our Time,* p. 29.

FOOTNOTES AND REFERENCES
TO CHAPTER V

1. Guido de Ruggiero, *Existentialism: Disintegration of Man's Soul* (New York: Social Science Publishers, 1948), p. 27.
2. John Dewey, *The Child and the Curriculum* (Illinois: University of Chicago Press, 1956), p. 4.

FOOTNOTES AND REFERENCES
TO CHAPTER VI

1. Martin Heidegger, *An Introduction to Metaphysics* (New Haven: Yale University Press, 1959), p. 12.
2. Paul Tillich, *The Courage to Be* (New Haven: Yale University Press, 1952), pp. 32-63.
3. Rollo May, Ernest Angel, Henri Ellenberger, editors, *Existence: A New Dimension in psychiatry and psychology* (New York: Basic Books, Inc. 1958), p. 12.
4. D. J. B. Hawkins, *The Meaning of Existentialism* (London: The Aquinas Society, 1954), p. 18.
5. Carl Rogers, "Towards a Theory of Creativity" (an unpublished paper circulated to former students of his seminar courses while he was at Chicago University), date of circulation — 1955.
6. Heinz Ansbacher and Rowena Ansbacher, *The Individual Psychology of Alfred Adler* (New York: Basic Books, Inc., 1956), p. 399f.
7. John Dewey, *Democracy and Education* (New York: The Macmillan Company, 1916), p. 93.
8. Karl Jaspers, *Way to Wisdom*, tr. Ralph Manheim (New Haven: Yale University Press, 1954), p. 179.

BIBLIOGRAPHY

Allen, E. L. *Existentialism from Within*. New York: Macmillan Company, 1953.

————. *Kierkegaard, His Life and Thought*. London, 1935.

Allport, Gordon. *The Nature of Personality*. Cambridge: Addison-Wesley Press, 1950.

Ansbacher, Heinz and Rowena. *The Individual Psychology of Alfred Adler*. New York: Basic Books, Inc., 1956.

Begtrup, Holgar, and others. *The Folk High-Schools of Denmark and the Development of a Farming Community*. London: Oxford University Press, 1929.

Bradly, David. *No Place to Hide*. Boston: Little and Company, 1948.

Bretall, Robert. *A Kierkegaard Anthology*. New Jersey: Princeton University Press, 1948.

Brubacher, John, editor. *Modern Philosophies and Education*. New York: Bureau of Publications, Teachers College, Columbia University, 1953.

Buber, Martin. *At The Turning*, New York: Farrar, Straus and Young, 1952.

————. *Between Man and Man*, tr. Ronald Smith. Boston: Beacon Press, 1947.

————. *Eclipse of God*. New York: Harper and Brothers, 1952.

————. *Hasidim*. New York: The Philosophical Library, 1948.

————. *I and Thou*. Edinburg, T & T Clark, 1937.

————. *Point the Way*, tr. Maurice Friedman. New York: Harper and Brothers, 1957.

————. *Right and Wrong*, tr. Ronald Smith. London: S.C.M. Press, 1952.

————. *The Prophetic Faith*, tr. Carlyle Witton-Davies. New York: The Macmillan Company, 1949.

————. *Two Types of Faith*, tr. Norman Goldhawk. London: Routledge and Kegan Paul Ltd., 1951.

Collins, James. *The Existentialists*. Chicago: Henry Regnery Company, 1952.

Counts, George S. *The Challenge of Soviet Education*. New York: McGraw-Hill Book Company, 1965.

Croxall, T. H. *Kierkegaard Studies*. London: Lutterworth Press, 1948.

Dewey, John. *Democracy and Education*. New York: Macmillan Company, 1916.

——. *The Child and the Curriculum*. Illinois: University of Chicago Press, 1956.

Dru, Alexander. *The Journals of Soren Kierkegaard*. London: Oxford University Press, 1951.

Erikson, Erik. *Childhood and Society*. New York: W. W. Norton and Company, 1950.

Ferm, Vergilius. *A History of Philosophical Systems*. Philosophical Library.

Friedman, Maurice. *Martin Buber*. Illinois: The University of Chicago Press, 1955.

Grene, Marjorie. *Dreadful Freedom*. Illinois: University of Chicago Press, 1948.

Grimsley, Ronald. *Existential Thought*. Cardiff: University of Wales Press, 1955.

Hawkins, D. J. B. *The Meaning of Existentialism*. London: The Aquinas Society, 1954.

Hebb, D. O. *The Organization of Behavior*. New York: John Wiley and Sons, 1949.

Heidegger, Martin. *An Introduction to Metaphysics*, tr. Ralph Manheim. New Haven: Yale University Press, 1959.

Heinemann, F. H. *Existentialism and the Modern Predicament*. New York: Harper and Brothers, 1953.

Henry, Nelson, editor. *Modern Philosophies and Education*. Illinois: University of Chicago Press, 1955.

Herberg, Will. *Four Existential Theologians*. New York: Anchor Books, 1958.

Hohlenberg, Johannes. *Soren Kierkegaard*, tr. T. H. Croxall. New York: Pantheon Books, 1954.

Holden, William. *Four Prophets of Our Destiny*. New York: Macmillan Company, 1952.

Horney, Karen. *Neurosis and Human Growth*. New York: W. W. Norton and Company, 1950.

Jaspers, Karl. *Man in the Modern Age*, tr. Eden and Cedar Paul. New York: Doubleday Anchor Books, 1957.

——. *Reason and Anti-Reason in Our Time*, tr. Stanley Godman. New Haven: Yale University Press.

——. *Tragedy Is Not Enough*. Boston: The Beacon Press, 1952.

——. *Way to Wisdom*, tr. Ralph Manheim. New Haven: Yale University Press, 1954.

Kierkegaard, Soren. *Concept of Dread*. tr. Walter Lowrie. New Jersey: Princeton University Press, 1946.

369

————. *Either-Or A Fragment of Life* tr. David and Lillian Swenson. New Jersey: Princeton University Press, 1944.

————. *Fear and Trembling,* tr. Robert Payne. London: Oxford University Press, 1939.

————. *Fear and Trembling,* tr. Walter Lowrie. New Jersey: Princeton University Press, 1941.

————. *For Self-Examination and Judge for Yourself,* tr. Walter Lowrie. New Jersey: Princeton University Press, 1944.

————. *Philosophical Fragments of A Fragment of Philosophy,* tr. David Swenson. New Jersey: Princeton University Press, 1936.

————. *Purify Your Hearts,* tr. A. S. Aldworth and W. S. Ferrie. London: C. W. Daniel Company, 1937.

————. *Repetition,* tr. Walter Lowrie. New Jersey: Princeton University Press, 1946.

————. *Sickness Unto Death,* tr. Walter Lowrie. New Jersey: Princeton University Press, 1951.

————. *Stages on Life's Way,* tr. Walter Lowrie. New Jersey: Princeton University Press, 1940.

————. *The Point of View for my work as an Author,* tr. Walter Lowrie. New York: Oxford University Press, 1939.

————. *Thoughts on Crucial Situations in Human Life,* tr. David Swenson, Minneapolis: Augsburg Publishing House, 1941.

————. *Training in Christianity,* tr. Walter Lowrie. New Jersey: Princeton University Press, 1947.

————. *Works of Love,* tr. David Swenson. New Jersey: Princeton University Press, 1946.

Kissinger, Henry. *Nuclear Weapons and Foreign Policy.* New York: Harper and Brothers, 1957.

Kneller, George. *Existentialism and Education.* New York: Philosophical Library, 1958.

Koch, Hal. *Grundtvig.* Ohio: The Antioch Press, 1952.

Kuhn, Helmut. *Encounter with Nothingness.* Illinois: Regnery Company, 1949.

Mackintosh, Hugh Ross. *Types of Modern Theology.* New York: Charles Scribners' Sons, 1939.

May, Rollo, editor. *Existence.* New York: Basic Books Inc., 1958.

————. *Man's Search for Himself.* New York: W. W. Norton and Co. 1953.

————. *The Meaning of Anxiety.* New York: The Ronald Press, 1950.

Michalson, Carl, editor. *Christianity and the Existentialists.* New York: Charles Scribner's Sons, 1956.

Moehlman, A. H. *Comparative Education.* New York: The Dryden Press, 1952.

Moreno, J. L. *Who Shall Survive?* New York: Beacon House, 1953.

Mounier, Emmanuel. *Existential Philosophies: An Introduction.* New York: Macmillan Company, 1949.

Mullahy, Patrick. *Contributions of Harry Stack Sulliv..n.* New York: Hermitage House, 1952.

Muller, Herbert. *The Spirit of Tragedy.* New York: Alfred Knopf, 1956.

Reinhardt, Kurt. *The Existential Revolt.* Milwaukee: The Bruce Publishing Company, 1952.

Riesman, David, and others. *The Lonely Crowd.* New Haven: W. W. Norton and Company, 1950.

Rogers, Carl. "The Significance of Self-regarding attitudes and perceptions." Leon Gorlow and Walter Katkowsky, editors, *Readings in the Psychology of Adjustment.* New York: McGraw-Hill Book Company, 1959.

Ruggiero, Guido de. *Existentialism: Disintegration of Man's Soul.* New York: Social Science Publishers, 1948.

Sartre, Jean-Paul. *Being and Nothingness,* tr. Hazel Barnes, New York: Philosophical Library, 1956.

———. *Existentialism,* tr. Bernard Frechtman. New York: Philosophical Library. 1947.

Schlom, Joseph. *Vortuka.* New York: Henry Holt and Company, 1954.

Snygg, Donald, and Arthur Combs, *Individual Behavior.* New York: Harper and Brothers, 1949.

Spier, J. M. *Christianity and Existentialism,* tr. David Freeman.

Sullivan, Harry Stack. *The Psychiatric Interview.* New York: W. W. Norton and Company, 1954.

Swenson, David. *Something About Kierkegaard.* Minneapolis: Augsburg Publishing House, 1945.

Swenson, Lillian, editor. *The Faith of a Scholar.* Philadelphia: The Westminster Press, 1949.

Thompson, Merritt M. *The Educational Philosophy of Giovanni Gentile.* California: The University of Southern California Press, 1934.

Thomte, Reidar. *Kierkegaard's Philosophy of Religion.* New Jersey: Princeton University Press, 1948.

Tillich, Paul. *The Courage to Be.* Boston: Little and Company, 1952.

Ulich, Robert. *The Human Career.* New York: Harper and Brothers, 1955.

Wahl, Jean. *A Short History of Existentialism.* New York: Philosophical Library, 1949.

Wild, John. *The Challenge of Existentialism.* Indiana: University of Indiana Press, 1955.

371

PERIODICALS

Brameld, Theodore. *Educational Theory,* Vol. II, No. 2 (April, 1952), 80.

Buber, Martin. "The Man of Today and the Jewish Bible", *Commentary.* Vol. 6, No. 4, October 1948, pp. 327-333.

Cerf, Walter. "A Study of Philosophy in Germany", *Journal of Philosophy* Vol. 54, No. 5, Feb. 1957, pp. 127-130.

Champigny, Robert. "Translations from the Writings of Contemporary French Philosophers", *Journal of Philosophy,* Vol. 154, No. 11, May 1955, pp. 313-353.

Coates, J. B. "Existential Ethics", *Fortnightly* Vol. 175, January to June, 1954, pp. 338-344.

Friedman, Maurice. "Martin Buber's Concept of education: A New Approach to College Teaching", *The Christian Scholar,* Vol. XL, No. 2, June 1957.

————. "Martin Buber's 'Theology' and Religious Education", *Religious Education,* New York: The Religious Education Association, Vol. LIV, January-February 1959, pp. 5-17.

Glicksberg, Charles. "The Lost Generation of College Youth", *Journal of Higher Education,* Vol. 28, May 1957.

Gray, J. Glenn. "Heidegger's Course: From Human Existence to Nature", *The Journal of Philosophy,* Vol. 54, No. 8, April 11, 1975, pp. 197-207.

Gumbinger, Joseph. "Existentialism and Father Abraham", *Contemporary,* Vol. 5, No. 2, Feb. 1948, pp. 143-148.

Jaspers, Karl. "Rededication of German Scholarship", *American Scholar,* Vol. 15, No. 2, September 1946, pp. 180-188.

————. "The Axial Age of Human History", *Commentary,* Vol. 5, No. 5 (1948), pp. 430-435.

Magner, James. "Why Protestant Theologians use Existentialism", *Catholic World,* Vol. 181, October 1955.

Sartre, Jean-Paul. "The Situation of the Jew", *Commentary* Vol. 5, No. 4, April 1948, pp. 306-316.

————. "Portrait of the Inauthentic Jew", *Commentary* Vol. 5, No. 5, May 1948.

————. "Gentile and Jew", *Commentary,* Vol. 5, No. 6, June 1948.

Stowe, L. I. *The Journal of Education,* Vol. 80, March 1948.

Tillich, Paul. "Martin Buber and Christian Thought", *Commentary,* Vol. 5, No. 6, June 1948. pp. 515-521.

White, John. "Anxiety, the Activity Program, and Individual Initiative", *Harvard Educational Review,* Vol. 14, No. 2, March 1944, pp. 149-159.

UNPUBLISHED PAPERS

Ford, Richard. "A Comparative Study of the Experimental Approach to Religious Education and Some Aspects of Existentialism", (an unpublished Doctor's thesis, The University of Southern California, 1957).

Friedman, Maurice. "Martin Buber: Mystic, Existentialist, Social Prophet, A Study in the Redemption from Evil" (an unpublished doctor's thesis, The University of Chicago, 1950).

O'Neil, William Frank. "Jean-Paul Sartre's Concept of Freedom and its Implications for American Education", (an unpublished doctor's thesis, The University of Southern California, June 1958).

Pfeutze, Paul. "The Concept of the Social Self in the Thought of George Mead and Martin Buber," (An unpublished doctor's thesis, Yale University, 1951).

Rogers, Carl. "Towards a Theory of Creativity", an unpublished paper, circulated to former students, University of Chicago, (c1953).

Vogt, Harold. "A Comparison of the Self and Self-acceptance in Soren Kierkegaard and Karen Horney", (an unpublished master's thesis, the University of Southern California, August 1952).

INDEX